SOCIAL MEDIA FREAKS

SOCIAL MEDIA FREAKS

Digital Identity in the Network Society

DUSTIN KIDD

Westview Press was founded in 1975 in Boulder, Colorado, by notable publisher and intellectual Fred Praeger. Westview Press continues to publish scholarly titles and high-quality undergraduate- and graduate-level textbooks in core social science disciplines. With books developed, written, and edited with the needs of serious nonfiction readers, professors, and students in mind, Westview Press honors its long history of publishing books that matter.

Published by Westview Press, an imprint of Perseus Books, LLC,
a subsidiary of Hachette Book Group, Inc.
2465 Central Avenue
Boulder, CO 80301
www.westviewpress.com

Westview Press books are available at special discounts for bulk purchases in the United States by corporations, institutions, and other organizations. For more information, please contact the Special Markets Department at Perseus Books, 2300 Chestnut Street, Suite 200, Philadelphia, PA 19103, or call (800) 810-4145, ext. 5000, or e-mail special.markets@perseusbooks.com.

Designed by Trish Wilkinson
Set in 10.5-point Minion Pro

Library of Congress Cataloging-in-Publication Data

Names: Kidd, Dustin, author.
Title: Social media freaks : digital identity in the network society / Dustin Kidd.
Description: Boulder : Westview Press, 2017.
Identifiers: LCCN 2016044830| ISBN 978-0-8133-5066-0 (paperback) | ISBN 978-0-8133-5067-7 (ebook)
Subjects: LCSH: Social media. | Identity (Psychology) and mass media | Social participation. | BISAC: SOCIAL SCIENCE / Media Studies. | SOCIAL SCIENCE / Popular Culture. | SOCIAL SCIENCE / Social Classes.
Classification: LCC HM742 .K53 2017 | DDC 302.23/1—dc23 LC record available at https://lccn.loc.gov/2016044830

10 9 8 7 6 5 4 3 2 1

CONTENTS

Acknowledgments *vii*
Preface *ix*

1. Social Media, Art, and the Network Society 1

2. The Social Structure of Social Media 31

3. Leave Britney Alone: Sexuality Perspectives on Social Media 69

4. Disabling a Meme: Disability Perspectives on Social Media 97

5. GamerGate: Gender Perspectives on Social Media 121

6. Occupy Wall Street: Class Perspectives on Social Media 145

7. Black Lives Matter: Racial Perspectives on Social Media 169

8. Social Media Toolbox 193

9. Conclusion: A Social Media Revolution? 219

Appendix: Digital Media Literacy *231*
Glossary *233*
References *241*
Index *257*

ACKNOWLEDGMENTS

This book is dedicated to the students at Temple University who have traveled with me on my social media adventure, particularly the students in my undergraduate course The Sociology of Popular Culture. My students inspire me with their creativity, critical thinking, and problem solving. They have taught me over the years to enter each new learning opportunity with a spirit of play.

The book is also dedicated to the readers of *Pop Culture Freaks*, who have engaged with me on a wide range of social media platforms and given me new ideas and new questions for my research.

My social media journey received a powerful jump-start from the folks at ChatterBlast, who helped me craft a valuable social media strategy that I continue to use years later. Their creativity, expertise, and friendship are deeply appreciated. I also thank Eric Crawford for once again producing gorgeous works of art to accompany the chapters.

Deep gratitude to two graduate students, Amanda Turner and Keith McIntosh, who coauthored publications with me that were part of the journey of this research.

This is my second book with Westview Press, and I continue to feel grateful for the collaborative spirit I find there. Particular thanks to James Sherman, Catherine Craddock, and Grace Fujimoto.

Finally, I thank the many social media freaks who inspire me with their artistry and activism.

Additional resources, as well as links to my own social media platforms, can be found at www.dustinkidd.net and www.westviewpress.com/socialmediafreaks.

PREFACE

What is the relationship between social media and social inequality? This is the question that drives this book. Since the advent of social networking platforms, we have heard a great deal about how social media is changing how we live, learn, do business, and relate to one another. But is this change for the good? And if social media is achieving something positive, who exactly is benefiting, and who is being left out?

This book focuses on people who are marginalized by existing social inequalities, but especially those who embrace this experience as a source of identity, empowerment, and connection to others. I use the word "freaks" to describe those folks. Freaks might seem like a rude or controversial word to use, but I am following the lead of popular culture, in which artists have been telling us to let our freak flags fly high and to get our freak on.

Freaky things are happening in social media. People are connecting to like-minded others across the globe to practice social activism and create social movements. In social media, the core of this experience is rooted in creative expression: making images, memes, videos, music, and powerful texts that offer a new way to imagine the world, including imagining a world without social inequality.

But in using social media as a tool, these artists and activists are contending with the massive corporations that are behind our major social media platforms. Those corporations are run by a small handful of executives and board members who are overwhelmingly male, white, cisgender, American, heterosexual, nondisabled, and wealthy. In other words, social media is controlled by a handful of corporations whose leadership reflects the height of privilege.

This book is a field guide for scholars who are studying social media with a focus on identity, inequality, and social movements. It offers a broad survey of the literature on social media from across the social sciences and even the humanities, but centering on sociology. It also introduces readers to a range of theoretical perspectives and research methods—which I highlight through sidebars titled "Methodological Moments"—that can guide us in our study of social media.

In chapter 1 I offer a set of theoretical tools for understanding the relationship between social media and social inequality, drawing on concepts from classical sociology, cultural sociology, the sociology of identities (including gender, race, sexuality, disability, and class), and media studies. In chapter 2 I focus on the history and structure of the social media industry. I draw from my own posting history to construct a history of social media. I look at the issue of power in the industry through an analysis of the leadership teams and boards of the major social media companies.

Chapters 3 through 7 examine a series of case studies that explore how various social activists and social movements have engaged social media. In chapter 3 I start with queer social media celebrities and focus on the story of Chris Crocker, famous as the leave-Britney-alone guy who had a YouTube meltdown when he felt Britney Spears was being maligned in the media. In chapter 4 I examine disability activism in social media, focusing on a unique moment when the actor George Takei posted a meme on Facebook that many interpreted as mocking disability. Chapter 5 examines the case of GamerGate, a gender-centered controversy in the world of video games that played out across social media channels including Twitter, YouTube, 4chan, 8chan, and many others. By GamerGate's end, at least three women had gone into hiding in response to vicious threats on social media, but no charges had been filed.

Chapter 6 turns to the social movement Occupy Wall Street, one of the first major social movements in the United States to embrace social media as a core movement tool. I examine how social media relates to other tools used by Occupy, particularly the central tool of occupying public space. Chapter 7 turns to the more recent social movement Black Lives Matter, another movement that blends online political coordination with the occupation of public spaces. While many, including one of its founders, view Occupy as a failure, Black Lives Matter seems to be having a more lasting influence on public discourse.

Chapter 8 is a very different kind of chapter. Presuming some readers find social media to be a compelling tool for the pursuit of social change, it offers a toolkit for that practice. Drawing on my own work in social media, I provide a series of best practices for sharing creative content on social media and engaging a range of audiences.

In chapter 9 I conclude with the difficult philosophical question of whether social media can really live up to its hype and whether it will ever be truly revolutionary. To preview, my answer is no, but I provide the caveat that a restructuring of who controls social media technology might lead to more positive possibilities for social movements.

I love social media. I post often on a wide range of platforms. My social media projects have helped me to embrace an identity as an artist, even as they also help me advance my career as a scholar. I love the possibilities that social media has created for artists and activists, but I hope to see those possibilities one day become a reality of social transformation.

1

Social Media, Art, and the Network Society

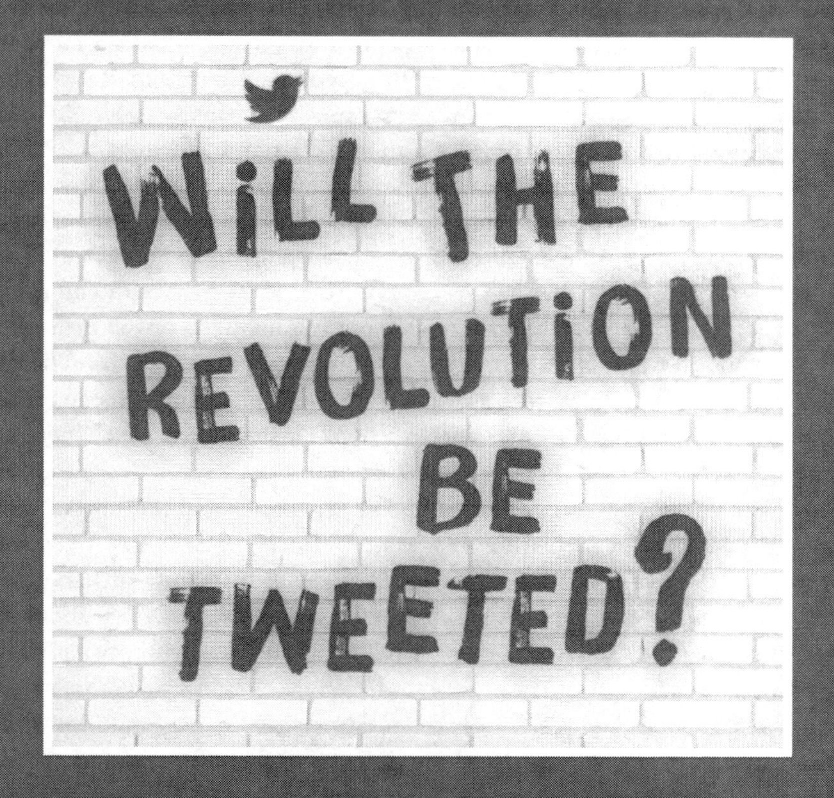

An alarm on my phone wakes me up. I reach for the phone to silence the alarm, but doing so puts the whole world in my hands. Instead of going back to sleep, I open my phone and begin tapping through apps. I always check Facebook first. The number in the red circle under notifications makes me anxious. I click through each notification to see who has liked or commented on my posts. I also have three friend requests. One I confirm, one I delete, and one I decide to let sit for a few days while I think about it. Closing Facebook, I open Snapchat. Most of the stories on Snapchat I simply click past, but I slow down when I get to my favorite Snapchatter, Chelsea Handler. Between her improvised rapping and her adorable dogs, I can't get enough of her snaps. I break to play a game on my phone for a few minutes, usually a round of an escape-the-room game. I scroll through my timehop and pick out a photo from this day three years ago that I decide to share on Facebook. Once the photo starts getting likes and comments, I'll end up having to open Facebook again. For now, I turn to Twitter. This is a more involved app-check, as I have three Twitter accounts. I check to see who has added me on each one, as well as the responses to my latest tweets. The last Twitter account I check is my work account. This awakens my work brain, and I realize I should check my e-mail. Twenty messages since I set my phone aside at midnight. Most are spam, which I open and delete. Another message from the struggling social media platform Ello, urging me to log back on. I am amazed at how many colleagues have sent messages at four in the morning. I answer the ones that just need a quick reply and leave the rest in my in-box to be answered when I get to my desk. I tap through Pinterest, Tumblr, and Blogger, though the only traction I get from those platforms happens when I post links to them on Twitter and Facebook. Instagram is next. There are fourteen likes of various photos, almost all of my cat. I scroll down the feed and click the little heart on photos I like of my friends and their pets. I note some good posts from celebrities like Matt McGorry (*How to Get Away with Murder*) and Tracee Ellis Ross (*Black-ish*). Closing Instagram, my thoughts turn to the news, so I open the Huffington Post app. I read a story about the lack of diversity in Hollywood that I think I should share with my audience, so I click the share button and post it to Facebook. I read a few more stories and realize I should get back to Facebook to check my new notifications. I click through to see who has liked my timehop and HuffPost shares. Then I start scrolling the newsfeed. Several items seem relevant to my work, so I click the option to save them. I will use the saved list later in the week when I am scheduling daily Twitter, Facebook, and LinkedIn posts using Hootsuite. Finally, I check LinkedIn and accept a connection invitation from a colleague. It's now at least an hour since my alarm went off. I move to the kitchen, where I plug my phone into my speakers and open a Spotify playlist so I have some music to listen to while I make my coffee and breakfast.

I'm such a **freak.*** A social media freak. But many people reading this will identify with my morning routine. The combination of social media and smartphones has changed the way that we interact with technology, each other, work, and the world. Social media has turned us into freaks by infiltrating our lives and making us addicted to mediated communication. But we are not passive dupes of the social media **hegemony**. Many of us have embraced the new possibilities presented by social media, and we have created opportunities for connection and change that exceed the vision of those who built this technology.

In my previous book, *Pop Culture Freaks*, I argued that popular culture turns all of us into freaks by telling us that we are never good enough. We are too fat or too skinny, too old or too young, too rich or too poor, too brown or too pale, too masculine or too feminine. Popular culture presents us with an image of beauty that has been touched up, Photoshopped, and surgically enhanced. We can never attain that level of beauty. But the industries of popular culture promise us that if we keep buying what they are pedaling, we might get there one day.

Rather than feel shame for being freaks, many of us—the consumers of popular culture—have embraced our freak sides and flown our freak flags. The R&B artist Janelle Monae asks, "Am I a freak for dancing around? Am I a freak for getting down?" in a song called "Q.U.E.E.N.," which seems to equate being a freak with being a queen, in a wonderful rhetorical inversion. In an interview, Monae explains the Q.U.E.E.N. acronym as Queer Untouchable Emigrant Excommunicated Negroid (Benjamin 2013). The artists of popular culture have defied their corporate overlords and called for us to wear our freak flags as a badge of honor.

Social media is the new kid on the pop culture block, and it too makes us feel like freaks. We are worn down with daily messages critiquing in painstaking detail our bodies, our homes, our careers, our families, and our romantic lives. But in the case of social media, those hurtful negative messages are coming from both the entertainment industry *and* our peers, and that just makes them hurt even more.

However, social media is also a tool that we can use to push back against these negative messages. It can give us a voice and a chance to participate in ways that are missing in other forms of popular culture like television or

---

* Terms in boldface are defined in the glossary.

radio. Many social media users are seizing the megaphone provided by these platforms and using it to create new stories about what it means to be human that disrupt old stereotypes and challenge the many dimensions of social inequality.

Bullying, harassment, surveillance, and stalking are just a few of the terrible things that can happen to people who use social media, and they happen most to those who have the least power: women, racial minorities, disabled persons, sexual minorities, trans people, and the poor. Yet for all of the harm that can happen on social media, marginalized and minority groups continue to embrace it. Why is that?

In this book I use a series of case studies to examine the ways that various groups in society experience oppression and harassment in social media and the ways they use social media to push back against that oppression. I propose a new lens for understanding the value of social media in the lives of those who are marginalized and oppressed or who feel they do not conform to the norms of mainstream society. I attempt to shift the discourse around social media from being a discussion about media and communication to a discussion about **art**. This shift allows us to examine the creative aspects of social media making and not just the productive aspects. It also gives us a better way to understand how social media has become sacred in the lives of many young people and adults.

ART VERSUS MEDIA

In order to claim that social media should be understood as art, not *just* as media or communication, I need to clarify what it is that I mean by art and what it is that I think is lost when we refer to social media as media or communication and not as art.

Obviously, all art involves media, whether canvas, camera, choreography, or any of a number of widely recognized art forms. However, we do not treat all types of media as art. What distinguishes artistic media from nonartistic media? Option one is quality. In some cases, quality is a useful way of understanding how the word "art" is deployed. Great examples of film or music and other genres are said to be elevated to the status of art. But many people would also agree that a great deal of "bad art" is nonetheless art. A bad painting is still seen as art simply because it is a painting, and paintings are a recognized genre of art. A second option for explaining the distinction between art and nonart is to say that art refers to a set of genres or media formats. Paintings, photographs, and ballet are all art. Pop music, newspaper articles, and line dancing are nonart. This approach highlights a legitimate arbitrariness in the distinction of art, but it doesn't tell us what the social value is of treating some things as art and others as nonart. A third option is to suggest that art distinguishes sacred objects from mundane ones. The things we call art often end up in museums that have the grandeur of temples. When an object shows up in these sacred spaces, we are more confident in recognizing it as art. However, while a great deal of art has been sacralized, there is also certainly a wealth of mundane and even profane art from across the centuries. Andy Warhol made this strikingly clear with his famous works inspired by everyday objects such as Campbell's soup cans and Brillo boxes. Robert Mapplethorpe took the point even further with his controversial photographs of kinky gay sexual interactions. After Warhol and Mapplethorpe, and so many others who have pushed the boundaries of art, we cannot make the argument that art is simply a matter of distinguishing sacred objects from mundane and profane ones.

I would like to suggest a very different way of understanding what art means and to offer an approach that makes it easier to think of social media as art. I argue that "art" refers to the creative dimension of all human action. I reject the approach that says humans make a lot of media and only designate some of it as art. Instead, I argue that humans make a lot of art, but then reduce a great deal of that art to *just* media. Instead of asking why some things are counted as art, I ask why more things are not. Trained, disciplined creativity goes into the design of all the objects that humans make—from food to architecture—and into all the ritual processes in which humans engage—from sports to fashion—yet we only allow a fraction of those objects and actions to count as art.

In line with the sociologist of art Janet Wolff (1984), I argue that one consequence of industrial capitalism is that the productive and creative dimensions of human activity were divided from each other. Most humans, the mass of laborers, were alienated from the creative dimensions of their labor, which took on a wholly productive value, making profits for the factory or corporation. Creativity then became the monopoly of an artistic elite, blessed by an intellectual elite of art critics, curators, and historians. As a consequence, most people today do not feel they have the right to call their creative work "art."

If this is the case, if my argument is correct, then the shift from an industrial age to a network society (or information age) may present the opportunity for a new formulation of the role of art in social life. But before moving on, I still need to address the question of just what I mean by art. It is this: *Art refers to disciplined, creative work that may be performed by both artistic professionals and outsiders or amateurs. Art is distinguished not by its sacredness, but rather by a sense of the integrity of the process.* This is a deliberately broad approach to art that is meant to recognize that the creative work performed by canonized artists is the same kind of creative work that all humans perform daily.

FREAKS AND MISFITS

Social media is a form of art, but in this book I am not interested in all artists. I am focusing here on the artistry of people whom I refer to as freaks. For me, this term encompasses a wide range of social media users. It includes the queer social media celebrities who are using it to offer new ways of thinking about sexuality and gender, as well as new ways to express their creativity. It includes the activist leaders of Occupy Wall Street and Black Lives Matter, who have demonstrated that images and poetry are just as important to social movements as protests and policy. It includes the gamers who colluded on Reddit and other platforms to launch the GamerGate controversy, as well as the women game developers who used Twitter and blogs to fight back. When I call these people freaks, I am not using the term as a slur. I am referencing both the ways that society has marginalized them and the ways that they have found empowerment through embracing their identities.

My use of the term "freak" derives in part from the work of the early sociologist Georg Simmel. Simmel's discussion of the **stranger** in his 1908 essay introduces us to a sociological type (Simmel 2010). The stranger is the social outsider who lives within the social unit, a traveling merchant who decides to stay. The stranger never becomes a part of the social unit, but is always an outsider within. As Simmel says: "The stranger is an element of the group itself, not unlike the poor and sundry 'inner enemies'—an element whose membership within the group involves both being outside it and confronting it" (2010, 303). The stranger serves a particular social role in reminding the other members of the social unit of the completeness of their membership. If the stranger is the outsider within, then the bulk of the other members of society are the insiders within.

But notice a little extra phrase in Simmel's prose; he refers to the "poor and sundry 'inner enemies'." Who are they? They are not strangers. They are not outsiders who visit and decide to stay. They are members of society who were pushed—not out of society, but to its margins. They are insiders pushed to the side.

For years, my reading of Simmel's "The Stranger" led me to think of minority groups and marginalized groups as variations of the stranger type. But Simmel is very specific. The stranger is one who comes from elsewhere, visits, and decides to stay. His social role is spatial in nature: "The distance within this relation indicates that one who is close by is remote, but his strangeness indicates that one who is remote is near" (2010, 302). In other words, our attempts to find a trope to understand how and why members of society are pushed to the margins will have to look elsewhere besides the stranger. Simmel at least gives us a lead in his phrase about poor and sundry inner enemies.

So I propose the trope of the freak as the lens for understanding these marginalized insiders. "Freak" is an ascribed condition, in that social institutions deem certain types of bodies and behaviors to be abnormal. No one is inherently a freak—we simply are who we are—but cultural forces deem some to be freaks. But freak is also an achievement, in that many marginalized people choose to embrace precisely that which makes them different as a source of pride and empowerment and as a tool for organization. To return to the Janelle Monae song referenced previously, embracing our freak is a way of finding our inner queens and kings.

The term "freak" is from the language of the sideshow, in which marginalized bodies—many of which would now be deemed disabled—were pushed out of the mainstream of society and forced to work in the circus. These freaks are wonderfully and fearfully portrayed in Tod Browning's 1932 film *Freaks*. Many modern disability communities continue to embrace the word "freak" as a term of empowerment, along with reclaiming other words like "cripple" (or just "crip"). Other marginalized groups have also invested in reclaiming derogatory language, from feminist embraces of "bitch," to lesbian, gay, bisexual, transgender, and queer (LGBTQ) uses of "queer," to the widely debated N-word. "Freak" also references decades of youth culture and the idea of "letting your freak flag fly."

In sociology, the term has been used in various ways, but perhaps most notably by Joshua Gamson in *Freaks Talk Back* (1998), his study of daytime talk shows. Explaining why he loves the "trash" of these shows, he says: "I identify with the misfits, monsters, trash, and perverts. . . . If you are lesbian, bisexual, gay, or transgendered, watching daytime TV talk shows is pretty spooky. . . . Almost everywhere else in media culture you are either unwelcome, written by someone else, or heavily edited. On television talk shows, you are more than welcome" (2010, 4). In Gamson's analysis, the TV talk shows of the 1990s were a platform for acknowledging, debating, and dissecting the lives of freaks and misfits. His focus is largely on sexual misfits, but class, gender, and race also play significant roles in his analysis.

Those shows persist today, and they continue to offer a space for freaks to talk back to society and media. But technological developments have also created a new set of participatory media outlets, peppered across the Internet and social media. Freaks are no longer just invited guests. Now they are hosts of their own channels, found on YouTube, Tumblr, Twitter, Reddit, and 4chan. They are honing their social media craft, training their voices, and building massive audiences. In their hands, social media technologies are not just communication tools, but also artistic tools, as they craft powerful messages couched in narrative and entertainment delivered to responsive audiences.

FROM INDUSTRIAL CAPITALISM TO INFORMATIONAL CAPITALISM

Before I turn to an examination of how freaks are using social media as an artistic medium, I want to say more about the economic and social changes that ground this development, as they impact both technological progress and artistic change. Of the stranger, Simmel says that his appearance can be understood in terms of economic history because the stranger has most often been the trader. The freak also can be understood in economic terms. To paraphrase Simmel, in the history of economic activity, the freak makes her appearance everywhere as a niche market. No economic era has ever relied so heavily on dividing consumers into niche groups.

The last several decades have been marked by transformations in the labor force and the rise of computerization. These changes are typically referred to as the dawn of the information age, a new stage of global capitalism that functionally replaces the industrial age (even as industrial capitalism continues to persist). Here, I rely primarily on the work of Manuel Castells in his three-volume set *The Information Age: Economy, Society, and Culture*, which has provided the dominant theoretical account of the information age, or what Castells calls the **network society**. "This new social structure is associated with the emergence of a new mode of development, informationalism, historically shaped by the restructuring of the capitalist mode of production towards the end of the twentieth century" (Castells 1996, 14). According to Castells, the transformation from industrial capitalism to informational capitalism has been characterized by flexible production models; increasingly horizontal systems (replacing corporate hierarchies); and most important, a growing reliance on networks by both individuals and firms.

Capitalist production is increasingly marked by corporate cooperation rather than corporate competition. We see this across fields, but media provides an excellent example. Seemingly competing corporate entities are increasingly linked through co-ownership of major properties (like the ownership of the CW network by both CBS and Warner Brothers), cooperation on major endeavors (such as the collaboration of NBC, Fox, and ABC on the platform Hulu), and contractual relationships that are mutually beneficial (as when television shows made by one network's studio are then aired on another network). The reliance on networks characterizes not only corporate production, but also individual labor force participation. A growing number of workers function as consultants or contractors and rely on professional networks to produce new income-producing contractual relationships.

Castells has a great deal to say about how identity functions in the network society. The second volume of his opus, *The Power of Identity*, is devoted to the topic. Castells begins by distinguishing three types of identity. **Legitimizing identity** refers to the identity systems of dominant groups, which ultimately function to justify their power. To be clear, legitimizing identity is not simply the identities of the dominant groups themselves, but rather the totality of the identity systems to which they subscribe, which are reproduced by the institutions they control. **Resistance identity** refers to the countermodels of identity subscribed to by oppressed or marginalized groups. **Project identity** refers to new identity systems introduced by social actors who are seeking social transformation. The three formations of identity might best be seen through the lens of Hegel's notion of thesis, antithesis, and synthesis. I am focused on the ways that individual actors use social media as a tool in resistance and project identities that seek to both assert artistic individuality and transform the way that society understands and responds to various marginalized collective identities.

Project identities are best understood as social movements. Castells has taken great interest in the prospects for social movements in the age of the network society, expressing hope that these movements may prevail in an era of flattened hierarchies and expansive networks. Occupy Wall Street is perhaps the best known example of these flattened social movements, in which the cause became a household name and yet no specific leader owned the spotlight.

Castells has essentially nothing to say about how art functions in the network society. However, I think it is useful to extrapolate from Castells a theory of the social role of art. Industrial capitalism alienated the workers from the fruits of their labors and even from themselves, even as it reduced their existence to their roles in economic production. The workers, which is to say the masses of individuals, were further alienated from their creative characters as creativity became the monopoly of an institutionalized artistic elite. Art became upper class in a middle-class society, intellectual in an anti-intellectual society, feminine in a masculinist society, and counterproductive in a society consumed by production.

In a network society, is there now the potential for these divisions to diminish? In the production of information, is there now an opportunity to recognize the creative dimension of all human work? In a world of horizontal production, might the worker no longer produce in a state of alienation?

I think the answers to these questions remain to be seen. But I do think that there are many who are working to find positive answers to these questions, and I think they are at least seizing opportunities created by new relations of production that are appearing now in the information age.

More specifically, I think there are many who are now engaging social media as an artistic tool, and they are no longer waiting to be recognized as artists by traditional arts institutions. They are not preoccupied with traditional art worlds. They are using technology and networks to achieve their artistic goals and rejecting the conception of art that restricts it to the domain of a formal elite. And they are succeeding because social media allows them to find and reach their audiences without relying on traditional artistic gatekeepers such as museums, galleries, or critics.

The role that social media may now be playing in undermining the alienation caused by industrial capitalism was anticipated in many ways by an early visionary of computerization and the information age, Theodor H. Nelson. Nelson published the double book *Computer Lib/Dream Machines* in 1974 and a revised edition in 1987. *Computer Lib* opened from one cover of the book, while *Dream Machines* opened from the other. These twin books examine the liberatory potential of computers. "Lib" stands for liberation, as in its comparable use in "women's lib." The subtitle is "You Can and Must Understand Computers Now." The books were initially written and self-published as tracts and have been compared to Thomas Paine's *Common Sense*. They are meant to not only explain computers to a lay audience, but also motivate that audience to demand that computers be made accessible in design. This was a call for personal computers before they existed. Nelson called for a revolution that was both technical and cultural, as indicated in this opening passage from *Computer Lib*:

> You hear more and more about computers, but to most people it's just one big blur. The people who *know* about computers often seem unwilling to explain things or answer your questions. . . . The chasm between laymen and computer people widens fast and dangerously. (Nelson 1987, 4)

What Nelson is describing is yet another form of alienation in the era of industrial capitalism: alienation from technology. The idea that technology may seem like the domain of a technical elite may appear logical, and yet today most of us use elaborate technology quite frequently, and most professionals are expected to possess some level of technological expertise, typically involving computer programs, the Internet, and social media. Nelson insisted that his readers assert their right and their capacity to understand computers. He saw computers as more analogous to "show biz and writing" (1987, DM3*) than to science and said of the development of this new creative tool that "we must create our brave new worlds with art, zest, intelligence, and the highest possible ideals" (1987, DM3). Nelson clearly anticipated that computers were introducing a new era in human history, and he even called it "a revolution in the way information is handled . . . come from some sort of merging of electronic screen presentation and audio-visual technology with branching, interactive computer systems" (1987, DM74). *Computer Lib/Dream Machines* is chock-full of suggestions for the emerging design of computer technologies, with a heavy emphasis on hypertext and the use of visual iconography to generate a mass computer literacy. Ultimately, Nelson called

* Page references with the initials DM refer to the *Dream Machines* side of this double book, as the pages start from 1 at both covers. Page numbers without initials are from the *Computer Lib* side of the book.

for computers to be a tool in the hands of artists and changemakers rather than scientists and technical professionals.

PROMISES OR PITFALLS

The possible impacts of social media are numerous and include a lot of good and a lot bad. At the positive end, social media is a useful tool that helps us accomplish social and occupational tasks more efficiently. At the negative end, we have bullying, surveillance, and the loss of privacy. Social media, like the Internet before it, makes big promises of community: more connections and interconnections and a greater capacity to activate our networks. But opinions on how well this promise has been delivered are strongly divided. In the next few pages I examine the social science literature on the promises and pitfalls of social media.

Bullying and Drama

Does social media create a heightened level of drama and contention in our lives? Education scholar Kathleen Allen (2014) presents a case study of a dramatic event involving a fifteen-year-old girl and her mother. "**Drama** is defined as a series of interactions characterized by overreaction, exaggeration, excessive emotionality, prolongation, inclusion of extraneous individuals, inflated importance, and temporary relevance" (2). In the case study, one teenage girl named Vanessa found herself in two such "drama" events. The first resulted from tweets between two groups of girls. When Vanessa wanted to back off of the Twitter exchange, one of her friends became angry with her, and she found herself distanced from her entire friend group. Eventually her friends apologized and welcomed her back. Soon after, she and her friends experienced more drama when they became angry that one girl's ex had been unfaithful during their relationship. They decided to share their feelings, not about the boy who cheated but about the girl he cheated with, by sending a series of tweets. Their classmates began responding to the tweets and sending mean or angry tweets back. They quickly deleted their Twitter accounts, but the drama continued on Facebook. It even extended offline, particularly when some of the girls received messages in the mail attached to printouts of their tweets. Allen observes, "[M]ediated communication has been woven, almost seamlessly into the lives and interactions of these girls" (2014, 15).

Social media gave a broad public audience to a private conflict. Allen discusses the roles that "**stirring the pot**"—resurrecting the drama after it has started to simmer—and "**baiting**"—pressing participants' buttons in hopes of ramping up the drama—play in the development of a dramatic event.

Surveillance

Communications scholar Daniel Trottier (2012) views social media through a lens of surveillance studies and outlines four main types of surveillance that occur using social media: interpersonal, institutional, market, and police. **Interpersonal surveillance** includes stalking as the most extreme example but can take lighter forms as well. Two friends discussing a third acquaintance might use social media to see what their friend has been up to. Estranged lovers often do the same, sometimes for nefarious purposes and sometimes just to fulfill some curiosity. **Institutional surveillance** takes many forms, but the most common is for organizations to keep tabs on their employees. People have lost their jobs over content posted on social media, whether that content is a critique of the employer or simply proof that a sick day was taken inappropriately. **Market surveillance** primarily involves keeping track of what we buy or search for, then delivering targeted ads to us. We have all had that experience of doing a simple Google search for something, only to immediately notice related ads appearing on Facebook and other websites that we frequent. Finally, **police surveillance** is performed by state forces to detect criminal or otherwise targeted activity, with a focus on circumventing that activity and/or apprehending the person targeted. In recent years police surveillance has been exposed at multiple levels by citizen activists like Edward Snowden, Chelsea Manning, and Anonymous. Surveillance by citizens constitutes a fifth type of surveillance not covered by Trottier. In addition to surveilling each other and being surveilled by corporations and states, we can also surveil the powerful using the tools of social media.

Communications scholar Jan Fernback (2013) studies communities of **sousveillance**, or surveillance from below. These are Facebook communities that use Facebook to study and report on its own tactics of surveillance: its strategies for collecting and utilizing seemingly private information from its members. Fernback finds that these groups can actually impact the corporate surveillant and persuade it to adjust, however incrementally, its practices of surveillance.

Media scholar and Microsoft researcher danah boyd (2011) reminds us that many social media users sign up specifically so that they can be seen, which is a way of saying that they sign up to be surveilled. They also sign up for social media in hopes of doing some surveillance themselves. She argues that social media makes all its users into both voyeurs (watchers/surveillants) and flaneurs (the watched/the surveilled). But signing up to watch and be watched does not mean we sign up to give up our own agency. "What is at stake in any conversation about privacy or surveillance is not simply power but agency. When and to what degree can individuals assert agency over a situation?" (2011, 507). boyd's ethnographic work provides examples of social media users engaging in various strategies to control what their audiences see and how they interpret what they see. She gives the example of Carmen, who posted song lyrics that would signal to her friends that she was having a rough day while also being largely inscrutable to her mother. For boyd, surveillance studies need to keep in mind our embeddedness in networks. "People aren't simply individuals or in groups; they are members of social networks, connected by information, time, and space, and they must navigate life as a series of relationships" (boyd 2011, 507). Protecting ourselves from surveillance is less about hiding all information from all eyes and more about knowing who the surveillants are and managing the kind of information they can access.

Jan Fernback (2007a) analyzed the community sections of four retail websites—Amazon, Hanes, Weight Watchers, and eBay—over an eight-month period to examine what she calls the "myth of empowerment" implied by the Internet: the sense that we can use these technologies to have a greater voice and more agency. She finds that the structure of these online retail communities invites users to volunteer a wealth of personal information, seemingly as entrée into the community. She also notes a curious relationship between stated privacy policies and the terms of the community, whereby participation effectively minimizes the consumer's right to privacy. Fernback argues that most consumers are unaware of how much privacy they are giving up when they participate in online communities. She argues that "online retailers capitalize on prevailing notions of empowerment through interactivity while increasing the use of online communication technologies to serve their own commercial ends as opposed to their customers' communicative needs" (2007a, 312). For Fernback, community itself is a potential commodity "that can be cultivated, mined, or sold like other capital commodities" (2007a, 316). She concludes: "We must realize that an unfettered marketplace does not mean that companies can intrude on our fundamental rights to privacy by exploiting our fundamental social institutions for monetary gain" (2007a, 326–327).

Agency

Communications scholar Angela Cirucci (2013) argues that scholars should study social media as a kind of video game. She identifies four themes in video game scholarship that should provide fruitful analysis when applied to social media. First, she argues that social media platforms function like mirrors that reflect back to users their own identities in ways that likely impact their identity formation and the perception of their identities. Second, social media is flooded with representational stereotypes of a sort that has been thoroughly studied in video games research but not so much in social media research. Third, social media creates a kind of immersion, much like video games, wherein users invest large amounts of time either participating in social media or thinking about it, and it increasingly frames how they experience other aspects of life. Fourth, social media creates opportunities for studying how definitions of life categories (friend, connection, like, etc.) are changing and under constant negotiation. Cirucci is simply speculating and making some suggestions for further research, but her themes suggest that social media provides a valuable course of action for its users, perhaps giving them a sense of **agency**. In a world where we feel we have little control, social media provides a way to respond and to act.

In their relatively early analysis of how and why people were using Twitter, communications scholars Java and colleagues (2007) found that the chief uses were (1) daily chatter about routines, (2) conversations (@ replies), (3) sharing information and URLs, and (4) sharing news. They divided Twitter users into three overlapping categories: (1) information sources, (2) friends, and (3) information seekers. These empirical data confirm some of Cirucci's suspicions. Social media is an immersive environment in which millions of posts and interactions can slowly create some shifts in our beliefs and assumptions, or at least lead us to believe that such shifts are possible. We post news items in hopes of both informing our network and nudging some of our connections toward thinking and acting differently. This sense of agency is not unique to social media, but social media is one more tool by which we can achieve some level of agency.

Community

Sociologist Sherry Turkle (2011) examines two major strands in technological development that are impacting social life: robotics and the social web. The social web is transforming our ways of connecting to each other by making those connections increasingly impersonal and mediated by technology. We connect to our friends, family, and colleagues via online networks rather than in-person meetings. This leaves us with a need for bodily companionship that is increasingly fulfilled by robots—from robotic pets to give us comfort to robotic sexual partners to get us off. The end result is indicated by the title of the book itself, *Alone Together*. We are ultimately left alone in our homes with just our technology for company, while we remain deeply engrained in social networks that exist almost entirely online. The book reads as a jeremiad, longing for a return to the days when we wrote letters and connected in person. It references a wealth of social science experiments and ethnographic research, but ultimately uses these to provide only anecdotes and illustrations. There is very little reference to any conclusions drawn from the decades of social psychological research conducted at the Massachusetts Institute of Technology investigating the sociability of robots and the impact of computer-mediated social interactions. Despite this lack of conclusions, Turkle is deeply concerned by the patterns she sees emerging. "Technology has corrupted us; robots will heal our wounds. We come full circle. Robots, which enchant us into increasingly intense relationships with the inanimate, are here proposed as a cure for our too intense immersion in digital connectivity. Robots . . . will pull us back toward the physical real and thus each other" (2011, 147). Turkle believes we are at a key moment when an intervention is needed to rescue us, which is to say, Turkle still has hope:

> I believe we have reached a point of inflection, where we can see the costs and start to take action. We will begin with very simple things. Some will seem like just reclaiming good manners. . . . [I]t is time to look again toward the virtues of solitude, deliberateness, and living full in the moment. (2011, 296)

In another study, Jan Fernback (2007b) examines the promise of online communities through a mix of online and in-person interviews with people who participate in them. She finds that most are ambivalent about the level and kind of community they find online. Online communities have some value to them, but it always seems to be a mixed blessing. She also finds that her interviewees have heavily internalized a stereotype of online community participants as computer geeks with no social lives, and they mostly seem to want to distance themselves from that stereotype. Using **symbolic interactionism**, Fernback argues that participants in online communities enact varying types of community, depending on the kinds of meanings that they have associated with the concept. She argues against allowing community to be the dominant metaphor through which we conceive of social interactions online. She suggests shifting the focus from the togetherness of communities to the formation of actual relational commitments.

SOCIAL MEDIA AND SOCIAL MOVEMENTS

Does social media help or hinder social movements? Can the technology of social networking help activists achieve their goals? If so, is it just one of many tools they may use, or is the technology so powerful that the right use will actually tip the scales in favor of the social movement?*

The possibilities and pitfalls that social media creates for individuals are well documented (Chayko 2014; Trottier 2012; boyd 2014; Fernback 2007b; Hargittai and Litt 2011; Fuchs 2011), but a robust and empirically driven conversation about the value of social media for social movements is only starting to emerge now, after years of hyperbolic claims. The basic question that guides most of the scholarly research on the relationship between social media and social movements is this: Can social media create the tipping point that leads to a movement's success? Those who make claims about this central question divide into camps of optimism, pessimism, and ambivalence. Optimistic approaches argue either that the revolution *can* be tweeted or that it already *has* been. These writers and scholars show great faith in the revolutionary power of social media. Pessimistic approaches argue either that social media is incapable of ushering in a social revolution or even that social media hinders positive social change. Ambivalent approaches weigh the evidence on balance and recognize that change is both difficult and possible. However,

* Much of this section is derived from my contributions to an article that I coauthored with Keith McIntosh (Kidd and McIntosh 2016).

social media is an unfolding terrain in terms of both the technology it relies on and the ways that citizens, corporations, and states make use of it.

On June 13, 2009, journalist and blogger Andrew Sullivan made a bold declaration in his blog for the *Atlantic*: "The Revolution Will Be Twittered." Technically, he should have said "The revolution will be tweeted," but it's the substance of the claim I want to examine.

Sullivan was writing near the start of the Iranian presidential election protests of 2009. On June 12 of that year, following the announcement that Mahmoud Ahmadinejad had won a second term as president of Iran despite strong indications from polls that voters had turned against him, Iranians in Tehran took to their roofs and began chanting "Allah O Akbar!" as a sign of solidarity against the election results. This was not a spontaneous or uncoordinated action. A supporter of opposition candidate Mir-Hossein Mousavi had sent a tweet announcing: "ALL internet & mobile networks are cut. We ask everyone in Tehran to go onto their rooftops and shout ALAHO AKBAR in protest #IranElection." Note the use of the hashtag as an important mechanism for tacking an individual tweet onto a larger conversation. To Sullivan, the fact that a simple tweet could channel such coordinated action seemed to be a strong sign that social media, and the millennial generation that embraces it so faithfully, would indeed topple authoritarian regimes.

Of course it did not work. Ahmadinejad claimed election victory and enjoyed a full second term that ended in 2013. So Sullivan's claim that a June 12 tweet signaled a revolution was premature and overstated. But certainly something of significance came about on that night as a tweet sent Iranians to their rooftops. Coordinated social action was taking place. Disillusioned Iranians may not have claimed power, but they surely claimed the agency not just to act, but to act *together*.

Andrew Sullivan's declaration that the revolution would be tweeted places him, or at least that opinion piece, squarely in the camp of techno-optimist. Techno-optimism is one end of a continuum of positions on the social power of the Internet and social media. That continuum looks something like the following graphic.

GRAPHIC 1.1

Techno-optimism ⟵ Techno-ambivalence ⟶ Techno-pessimism

Debates about the social power and revolutionary potential of technology date back at least to the printing press. I won't try to summarize the whole history of those debates here, but rather focus on the current era of the debate, specifically on the social and networking aspects of new media technologies.

TECHNO-OPTIMISM

One of the strongest statements in favor of the power of social media for social movements is found in Manuel Castells's *Networks of Outrage and Hope: Social Movements in the Internet Age* (2012). For Castells, the use of Twitter and Facebook as tools for political upheaval serves as confirmation of theoretical principles that he presented in his earlier works, *The Information Age: Economy, Society, and Culture* (1996, 1997, 1998) and *Communication Power* (2009). Castells argues that as the information age develops, the real power is now in the hands of programmers and switchers (those who make connections). He is referring to both technology professionals and those who metaphorically act as programmers and switchers for social institutions and social movements. Castells's theory of the network society in *The Information Age* predates the advent of social media but also predicts it. In a society based on information and networking, social media is the logical form of communication. However, even Castells insists on the need for real-world connection and collaboration for social movements, particularly in the form of what he calls "occupied space," referring to the squares and parks in which protesters gather, organize, and take action. Nevertheless, Castells is an optimist about the transformational power that social movements have when cyber activism leads to and complements street activism. Castells connects the dots among a series of social movements that occurred roughly between 2008 and 2011: Iceland's Kitchenware revolution; Tunisia's Jasmine revolution, Egypt's Tahrir Square protests, and actions in many other countries as part of the Arab Spring; the Spanish Indignados movement (also known as *acampanadas*); and Occupy Wall Street and related actions in many cities that comprised the Occupy movement. Later protests claimed to be inspired by earlier ones and also claimed to learn from their most successful techniques. Castells argues that these movements share a set of characteristics that help to explain their success. He says they have a kind of **multimodal networking**, which encompasses online and offline networks. They consistently choose to occupy urban space, but in a way that is deeply connected to cyberspatial networking. He calls the connection between urban space and cyberspace a space of autonomy. He claims that these new social movements spontaneously generate in moments of indignation and spread virally, both online and off. Perhaps most important, Castells says that these new network society social movements are leaderless because of both the distrust that the movements have for power and the ways that network society has flattened organizational hierarchies.

In their analysis of the revolutions in Tunisia and Egypt, Lotan and colleagues (2011) examine **information flows** on Twitter—tweets and retweets that pass on information from initial source posters—during the Tunisian and Egyptian uprisings that were part of the Arab Spring. They examine the role of different types of information actors, including media organizations, journalists, bloggers, and activists. "In both datasets [Egypt and Tunisia], journalists and activists serve primarily as key information sources, while bloggers and activists are more likely to retweet content and, thus, serve as key information routers" (2011, 1390). They find that individuals (including journalists and bloggers) are more successful in seeding information—starting a flow—than are organizations, perhaps because individuals are more trusted than the organizations they work for. But they also found important differences in the information flows of Egypt and Tunisia, suggesting that culture and context also shape the pattern of these flows. Their main conclusion is that social media really has transformed journalism into a conversation among different types of actors, and that activists and bloggers are significant producers of information, in addition to journalists.

Sociologist and communications professor Philip N. Howard (2015) takes a decidedly cyber-utopian stance, hopeful that the "**Internet of things**" will usher in a new world-historical period of stability that he calls the *pax technica*, referencing comparable eras like the *pax Romana* and the *pax Britannica*. Howard recognizes, with other scholars, that social media and other technologies allow for greater surveillance, but he believes this tool will work in service to citizens and level the playing field against state and corporate powers. Howard acknowledges that the technology may in fact be harnessed for less democratic possibilities, but his prediction is that it will actually foster peace and stability. "The internet of things could be the most effective mass surveillance infrastructure we've ever built. It is also a final chance to purposefully integrate new devices into institutional arrangements we might all like" (2015, xv). Howard calls this new period an "empire of connected things"

(2015, 1). He argues that social media offers three important tools during periods of upheaval: (1) allowing us to check on our loved ones, (2) giving us a space to deliberate and take positions, and (3) letting us document social and political events. Regarding the political use of social media, Howard argues:

> Politics used to be what happened whenever one person or organization tried to represent another person or organization. Devices will be doing much of that representative work in the years ahead, and social scientists need to stay relevant by expanding their tool kits and amending their analytical frames. From now on, politics is what happens when your devices represent you in the pax technica. (2015, 257)

Comparing how various states have handled the rise of the information age, Howard argues that the states that have most invested in information infrastructures have had the most prosperity, although he acknowledges China as a special case that has built its own infrastructure that it can more easily monitor and censor.

Clay Shirky's *Here Comes Everybody: The Power of Organizing Without Organizations* (2008) is one of the strongest proponents of the power and potential of the Internet and social media. Shirky is most excited about the power of new technology to foster speedy assembly around causes and concerns. He argues that the key issue is not the technology itself, but the change in human behavior the technology enables. Using a mixture of sociology and psychology, Shirky claims that humans avoid collective action because of the fear that others will freeload off their altruism. But that fear of action shifts when the speed, costs, and risks are reduced and when there are trustworthy safeguards in place that govern the actions of others and reduce the risk of freeloading. Shirky describes collective action as the top rung of a three-rung ladder of group activity, with each successive rung harder to reach than the last. The rungs, in order, are "sharing, cooperation, and collective action" (2008, 49). Social media effectively brings the rungs closer and makes the ladder easier to climb. Shirky opens with a story about a woman and her friend who used technology to find her lost phone and then to shame the thief, who refused to return it. They attracted supporters, media attention, and Internet sleuths as their cause went viral. Eventually the phone was returned and the young woman who stole it was arrested, all thanks to social media. That kind of success story would not have been possible prior to the advent of social media. But again, it isn't simply the power of the tools but rather the change in human social behavior that has taught us to believe that we can act and make a difference.

Proponents of social media often claim that it can change the world. In their book *The Dragonfly Effect*, Jennifer Aaker and Andy Smith (2010), a social psychologist at Stanford Business School and marketing consultant, respectively, argue that social media offers a powerful set of tools that can help users—especially businesses—effect social change. Their book is full of anecdotes from the business world, as well as a mix of data from both marketing and social psychology—what we might call decision neuroscience or the science of how people decide how they will spend their money and buy products—but it also reads like a motivational self-help text. Aaker and Smith present what they call the dragonfly model, based on the fact that dragonflies are able to fly in any direction through the coordinated action of four wings. In their model, the four wings of social action through social media are focus, grabbing attention, engagement, and taking action.

TECHNO-PESSIMISM

Malcolm Gladwell, a journalist known for his emphasis on social science perspectives, reviewed *The Dragonfly Effect* for the *New Yorker* (Gladwell 2010), taking the stance that Aaker and Smith are naïve and overly optimistic. He compares social media–based social movements to the lunch counter protests of the 1960s civil rights movement. The civil rights movement succeeded because of what Gladwell calls "high-risk activism" motivated by close relationships. Groups of people who were deeply connected to each other made great sacrifices in the interest of the cause. By comparison, he calls social media activism "small change."

Another author discussed in Gladwell's review is Evgeny Morozov, whose later book *The Net Delusion: The Dark Side of Internet Freedom* (2011) argues that the world has been overwhelmed by "cyber-utopians" who ignore or exaggerate the benefits of new technology with little use of evidence and a blind eye to history. To be sure, Morozov acknowledges that the Internet, social media, and social networking can be a powerful set of tools, but he raises important questions about who makes the tools, who controls them, and who has the most access to them. Morozov tells a rich set of stories from his own travels around the world and his studies of world history to demonstrate that powerful new tools are usually most effective in the hands of authoritarian regimes. The Internet, he points out, offers excellent tools for authoritarian governments—including ones that claim to be democratic—to track, infiltrate, and undermine political movements. "Technologies that were supposed to empower the individual strengthened the dominance of giant corporations, while technologies that were supposed to boost democratic participation produced a population of couch potatoes" (2011, 276). The technologies that he is referring to range from the printing press to television, and from the Internet to social media. His conclusion: "[T]he only way to make the internet deliver on its emancipatory potential is to embrace both cyber-realism and cyber-agnosticism" (2011, 339).

Navid Hassanpour (2014) finds that media disruptions during political protests, including blackouts of social media platforms like Twitter and Facebook, can actually increase participation as people seek alternative sources of information. That doesn't mean that social media doesn't have revolutionary potential. The issue is not the lack of information, but rather the disruption of information. The more access people have to the flow of information, the more they will be disgruntled by its disruption. Christian Christensen (2011) highlights the fact that social media can be just as useful for the powerful political leaders who are being protested against as it is for the protestors themselves. He cites the use of social media policing by leaders in Iran during the protests of 2009 as an example. He concludes that we should not place too much stock in the virtues of social media.

Such cyber-realist approaches strike Gladwell as the best lens for understanding the relationship between technology and activism. Gladwell's review invokes the work of sociologist Mark Granovetter, who has demonstrated the important role that "weak ties" can play in getting a job (Granovetter 1973, 1974). Gladwell argues that the same principle does not apply to social movements, because "weak ties seldom lead to high-risk activism." In response to Aaker and Smith's claim that social media can increase motivation for activism, Gladwell says, "that's not true. Social networks are effective at increasing *participation*—by lessening the level of motivation that participation requires" (2010). In other words, social media encourages people to participate by posting and liking, not by going into the streets or sitting down at the lunch counter.

TECHNO-AMBIVALENCE

Dhiraj Murthy's book *Twitter: Social Communication in the Digital Age* (2013) also invokes the work of Granovetter but looks more favorably on the role of weak ties in social movements. Although he begins with a discussion of Occupy Wall Street, the real focus of his examination of social media's role in activism is the Arab Spring, specifically activism in Cairo, Egypt, in 2011. Murthy argues against taking too strict or too binary a position on the power of Twitter. Twitter was neither irrelevant nor did it cause the revolution. Rather, it played several practical roles:

> Twitter served three purposes for Egyptian activists: 1) a real-time information stream maintained by Egyptian citizen journalists (for Egyptian consumption); 2) a means for local information and updates to reach an international audience (including international journalists); and 3) a means to organize disparate activist groups on the ground. Perhaps its greatest impact was in the second purpose and its least in the third purpose. (2013, 112)

Although Murthy argues that Twitter played important roles in the Cairo protests, which resulted in the resignation and eventual trial of President Hosni Mubarak, he nevertheless asserts that the activity on the streets of Cairo is what truly drove the revolution, while Twitter functioned more as a useful resource.

Similarly, in a qualitative ethnographic analysis of how political movements use social media, Pablo Gerbaudo's *Tweets and the Streets: Social Media and Contemporary Activism* (2012) argues for a modest approach to the power of social media in social movements. Gerbaudo uses case studies of the Cairo uprisings, the Spanish Indignados movement, and Occupy Wall Street to examine what he calls a "choreography of collective action" (2012, 4), particularly a choreography of organizing and mobilizing. He attempts to provide a middle ground between techno-optimism and techno-pessimism. Against Castells's notion that the information age is driven by leaderless networks, Gerbaudo focuses instead on how technology can be used by leaders to choreograph action. Regarding the political movement in Egypt, he concludes: "Social media played a crucial role in the Egyptian revolution, but not an exhaustive one" (2012, 74). He also sees social media as crucial to the Spanish Indignados. However, in comparison to Egypt and Spain, he argues that the Occupy movement shows an underuse of social media for choreographic purposes, and he suggests that the failure to choreograph action may explain the comparative lack of success of Occupy.

METHOD

Throughout this book I rely on an emerging research method that has been referred to variably as **virtual ethnography** (Hine 2000), netnography (Kozinets 2010), digital ethnography (Underberg and Zorn 2013), and online ethnography (Tuncalp and Le 2014). A close reading of these and other sources shows that the scholars behind the various labels do not fully agree on what exactly the method is and how it should be practiced, but they are not in so much disagreement that the various terms can be thought of as fully separate methods. Rather, the terms and scholars constitute a conversation with multiple perspectives on this emerging method. I use the term "virtual ethnography" not because of an ideological alignment with the users of that label, but rather because it is the one that I see used most often by other scholars. Throughout the book I present short methodological moments that offer insight into some of the unique aspects of this method. Here I present a broad overview of the method and how I used it in the research for this book.

Christine Hine introduced the concept of "virtual ethnography" in her 2000 book of the same name, though she acknowledges that the book is explicitly *not* a how-to guide:

> [E]thnography is strengthened by the lack of recipes for doing it. From the first, ethnographers have resisted giving guidelines for how it should be done. . . . The methodology of an ethnography is inseparable from the contexts in which it is employed and it is an adaptive approach which thrives on reflexivity about method. (2000, 13)

Virtual ethnography is simply the utilization of ethnographic methods in the context of the Internet and social media, as well as other related digital spaces such as e-mail and text messaging. Ethnography is the disciplined practice of making observations within a quasi-bounded space. Adding the term "virtual" is not meant to suggest a contrast between "real" and "virtual" spaces for ethnographic research, but rather to connote a particular context among others. Virtual ethnography is a relatively new addition to a list that includes urban ethnography, political ethnography, prison ethnography, and others. Each ethnographic context demands attention to the unique combination of features of that context. With the Internet and social media, we have to pay particular attention to both the ways that technology structures social experiences and the ways that users construct cultural practices that shape those social experiences.

I began using the Internet in 1996, as I was finishing college. When I moved to London a year later, I embraced e-mail as a way to stay in communication with my friends and family. When I started graduate school in 1998, pursuing an MA in English, the director of the concentration in American studies required all of us to learn HTML coding, and the traditional seminar paper was replaced with a web project. It seems simplistic in retrospect, but at the time we were excited about the idea that hyperlinks allow academic projects to take on more dimensions than the linear academic paper that is simply read from start to finish. I created a project on the paintings of Thomas Eakins in which the user could zoom in on some of the paintings to see the richness of detail that is so easily missed in his work.*

As I moved from an MA in English to a PhD in sociology, I continued my interest in the Internet, working as a web developer part time to supplement my stipend as a teaching assistant. Eventually I began teaching short courses at the University of Virginia on editing software such as FrontPage, Dreamweaver, and Fireworks. Throughout graduate school I continued making websites for academic projects (for myself and for others), and I also took up blogging. I began teaching a course on popular culture in fall 2001, and that seemed like a logical place to incorporate consideration of the Internet and to discuss questions of culture and community online.

Although I dabbled in social media for many years, my consolidated focus on social media began in late 2013 as I began preparing for the release of my 2014 book *Pop Culture Freaks*. I wanted to use social media to try to reach my audience in new ways, but I wasn't quite sure how to do it or where to start. I hired a social media marketing firm called ChatterBlast to work with me on creating a social media strategy. At that time surprisingly few academics were highly active on social media for professional purposes. That has changed dramatically in the years since, but in that moment I felt like I was exploring new academic terrain. Since that time I have been an active user on Twitter, Facebook, Tumblr, Pinterest, Spotify, YouTube, and many other platforms.

I share this autobiographical information here as a foreground for my research methods in this book. Although I am not a digital native—no one is born into technology—I have been immersed in new communications

* http://xroads.virginia.edu/~hyper/incorp/eakins/eakins.html.

media for many years, and I have a strong understanding of the many different contexts within social media and the Internet. That means that I enter this research with a lot of familiarity with the context, and I am not likely to miss cultural signals along the way. But it also means that I do not have the distance that is typically pursued by social scientists. The ethnographic method does not accommodate that distance well. Ethnography is so focused on culture and the process of meaning making that it requires a high degree of intimacy with the context being studied.

I began this research immediately after the release of *Pop Culture Freaks*. I spent approximately ten hours per week, sometimes much more, examining the issues discussed in this book. The themes of each chapter were mostly in place at the start of the research, so those themes directed much of the research. This will surprise and perhaps disappoint many academic readers, but I relied on *Wikipedia* entries as a starting point for the case studies. Entries there for Occupy, Black Lives Matter, GamerGate, and other issues are heavily detailed, and the participants in those events also actively review the entries for accuracy. From *Wikipedia* I linked to a long list of sites, primarily media coverage. I reviewed websites of central organizations whenever available and searched for archived copies of earlier versions of those sites. I followed Twitter accounts for all organizations involved and for all of the names that came up in the course of the research. Every time a new name was added to the story, I searched that name on all of my social media platforms and then explored their accounts to gain a better perspective on that person's participation in these stories. The primary data for my case studies come from these social media accounts and from related websites, although the types of data vary widely from one chapter to the next.

Throughout the book I explore some of the dilemmas that arise in the course of virtual ethnography through methodological moments, which appear in several chapters. This method has allowed me to find narratives of social activism and its relationship with the tools of social media. In turn, these narratives have allowed me to examine the complicated relationship between corporate-owned media platforms and grassroots activism.

CONCLUSION

"The revolution will be tweeted" is a rhetorically forceful phrase, to borrow a concept from the media sociologist Michael Schudson (1989). The phrase invokes Gil Scott-Heron's 1970 track "The Revolution Will Not Be Televised," which took the strong stance that commercial corporate culture cannot be the source of powerful social change. Technically, that's an open research question. Can commercial corporate culture trigger social change or even a social revolution? Scott-Heron's take is that systems of inequality are inextricably linked to the capitalist mode of production in which television is embedded. Can it be any different for social media? Twitter, Facebook, Google, and most other social media platforms are the assets of large corporations run by homogeneous executives and boards. Can the products of such capitalist enterprise produce the seeds of change? The notion that the revolution can be tweeted took hold in media debates about the role of Twitter and Facebook in uprisings around the world. A 2011 book by the journalist Chris Stokel-Walker asked "*The Revolution Will Be Tweeted?*" The magazine *Foreign Policy* took an optimistic stance with a June 20, 2011, headline "The Revolution Will Be Tweeted" (Hounshell 2011). And Reuters declared triumphantly: "In 2011, The Revolution Was Tweeted" (Freeland 2011).

The best empirical evidence is that revolutionary movements today will certainly include social media, and may even need it, but will also need much more than that. Protests in the streets are no less important today than they have been for movements in the past, and it may actually be harder to get people into the streets in an age of social media. Moreover, the targets of the revolutionary movements—governments, military, police, and corporations—are also on social media and using it very effectively as a tool for surveillance.

I am interested in how social activists have adopted the tools of social media to build awareness, recruit participants, and coordinate social action. But can these tools work for more than just organizational purposes? Can an organization that uses the tools of social media actually achieve social change when those tools are the inventions of a handful of elite engineers and entrepreneurs and the property of massive corporations that are deeply interconnected and governed by small, homogeneous boards and leadership teams? Audre Lorde famously declared: "The master's tools will never dismantle the master's house" (1984, 112). Whose tools are social media? Do they belong to their inventors? The corporations? Or to the actual users who decide when and how to deploy them and what kind of meaning they can have? These are difficult questions that I cannot fully answer, but we need to continue to ask them as our world becomes ever more transformed by social media practices.

To sum up, in this book I examine freaks—individuals and groups who are both marginalized by society and who embrace their marginalized identities as a form of empowerment, what Castells calls resistance and project identities—as both artists and activists who are using the creative tools of social media to challenge and transform the world around them. Throughout the book, I return to the following questions:

1. How do artist/activists engage with the idea of art in their social and political activism?
2. How do they bring artistic practices to their use of social media?
3. What opportunities does social media offer them that they might not find with other tools?
4. How do they—and how can we—assess the effectiveness of social media as a creative tool for social and political activism?
5. How do groups within project identities negotiate the tension between being marginalized peoples and using a tool that is effectively owned and controlled by those with the most social power: economic elites who are overwhelmingly male, **cisgender**, white, nondisabled, and heterosexual?

I think each of the case studies I pursue in this book offers us insight into the different ways that marginalized groups can engage with social media. Using these questions throughout the book allows me to cultivate some insights into the relationship between social media and activism, which I summarize and analyze in the final chapter.

2

The Social Structure of Social Media

Users often think of social media as a democratizing force that makes information and expression available to all. This idea that social media is democratic is both very accurate and very misleading. Social media is incredibly democratic in comparison to other commercial forms of telling and sharing stories. Film and television are the culture industries that I grew up with, and neither is terribly democratic. Sure, you can make your own film with little more than a video camera, but the mechanisms for sharing film with a broad audience are tightly controlled by the film industry. And television is even more difficult to participate in. Just imagine trying to start up your own television series. We may have an indie genre in the film world, but indie television is more rare.*

By comparison, social media seems incredibly participatory. Social media users are makers of stories, not just consumers. They can ignite conversations with a tweet, a Pinterest board, or a YouTube video. Of course most tweets, Pinterest boards, and YouTube videos ignite almost nothing—no comments, no likes, and no reposts. But all of those dud posts are a kind of practice for the ones that matter.

However, users of social media are not the owners of social media. In terms of ownership, social media looks much like all other kinds of media. A small handful of massive corporations owns most of the social media properties. These corporations are characterized by horizontal integration, vertical integration, diagonal integration, corporate interlocks, and homophily.

Horizontal integration refers to the tendency for corporations to expand their share of the market within the field. The corporations that control social media are constantly eyeing new start-ups and purchasing them, making seemingly unrelated properties part of the same corporate family.

Vertical integration refers to the tendency for corporations to expand their share of the production and distribution process. Some corporations that predate social media have purchased social media platforms so they can use them to promote other goods that they produce. Although MySpace has changed significantly since its early days as a precursor to Facebook, when it was owned by News Corporation it provided an excellent tool for promoting Fox television and film. This was a two-way street. News Corporation also used shows like *Glee* to promote the value of MySpace.

Social media has the effect of blurring lines, so that vertical and horizontal integration processes are increasingly difficult to distinguish from one another. When Google bought YouTube, was it horizontally expanding its control of the social media field or vertically expanding its control of the

* There are creative professionals striving to make creative independent television. A great example is OpenTV, found at http://www.weareopen.tv.

information delivery process? Technically, the answer is both, but that also highlights the fact that discrete lines of industry practice are harder to discern.

Diagonal integration refers to the tendency for corporations to expand their holdings into new sectors. The media conglomerates that control the production of nearly all entertainment media—particularly the Walt Disney Company, 21st Century Fox, Comcast, Time Warner, and National Amusements (owners of the CBS Corporation and Viacom)*—all have holdings across multiple entertainment sectors, including television, film, publishing, the Internet, social media, music, and sports, among others.

Corporate interlocks are points of connection between corporations that undermine competition and instead promote interconnectedness and a sense of shared interests. In economic sociology, there is a conversation dating back at least as far as the writings of Karl Marx that asks why class groups—especially working-class groups—do not have a stronger sense of class consciousness. Perhaps surprisingly, class consciousness is actually best developed in the corporate class, that group of nonhuman persons who are driven by a profit motive. As citizens and consumers, we are often told that our buying power gives us a kind of control over corporations and that their ultimate goal is to compete against each other for our loyalty. But with fewer and fewer corporations controlling ever larger shares of the market in any given field, the need to compete has diminished, along with the purchasing power of the citizen consumer. In social media, board members of one corporation are often executives for another. There is nothing unusual about this; it is a common practice across corporations of all types. But those who are unfamiliar with the practices of corporate leadership may be surprised by how few people are running these corporations and how much these interlocks negate the notion of corporate competition.

Homophily refers to the tendency to associate with others who are like ourselves. It is often used to explain the durability of white dominance in a supposedly postracial society and of male dominance in an era of ostensible equal rights for women. Social media, like other forms of media and like many other industries, is dominated by men, whites, nondisabled people, cisgender people, straight people, and economic elites.

* Due to buyouts and mergers, the list of major media conglomerates changes with some frequency. This list is current as of 2016.

In this chapter I take a closer look at the individuals and the corporations that own social media. My findings align with the characteristics described above and give us good reason to doubt the democratic nature of social media. Throughout this book I encourage the reader to take social media seriously and to seriously consider becoming a social media maven. But in this chapter I highlight some good reasons to be cautious with social media. Audre Lorde famously said that the "master's tools will never dismantle the master's house" (1984, 112). If some of the problems of the modern world are caused by the expanding power of corporations, can those problems be challenged and alleviated using a tool that is owned by those same corporations?

THE CORPORATIONS THAT OWN SOCIAL MEDIA

Social media feels like a big concept. It seems to refer to a lengthy list of apps and Internet sites that can be used to share ideas with an audience that we carefully cultivate. In some ways, almost every phone app and almost every Internet site includes a component of social media. I can share my *Clash of Clans* victories on Facebook or tweet about my latest purchase from Amazon. I would be hard pressed to find a site that did not include at least a few social media buttons at the top. But in terms of discrete social media channels, we are actually only talking about a small handful of big players. There are plenty of small fish in the social media sea. Most will have short lives, while a small few will get eaten up by whales like Facebook, Twitter, or Google.

In the analysis that follows, I begin with the social media titans of Facebook and Twitter, as the two largest independent and publicly traded social media corporations. I examine their assets as well as the composition of their management teams and board of directors. The names of the management and board were acquired through investor reports published online and verified through additional sources. I then turned to **Google** and **Yahoo**, which are of course much bigger than social media, but are also major players in the social media realm thanks to assets like Google+, YouTube, and Blogger on the part of Google, and Flickr and Tumblr on the part of Yahoo. Google and Yahoo are also both publicly traded corporations.

Among the smaller social media platforms, **Yelp** and LinkedIn are the only independent and publicly traded companies, so I also examine their management teams and boards. Foursquare, Pinterest, Academia.edu, and ResearchGate are independent but privately owned. For these platforms, I examine only the composition of their relatively small management teams. All data are from January 2015. Before this book is published, the key players at each company will have changed to some degree, but the overall patterns of inequality will likely not change so swiftly. And many of the big names will simply move from one company to another.

Facebook

Facebook is the largest single social media corporation. It is a publicly traded company, owned by shareholders and run by a management team that is held accountable to a board of directors. The management team of Facebook is composed of five people, the most prominent of which are Mark Zuckerberg (founder, chairman, and chief executive officer) and Sheryl Sandberg (chief operating officer). The good news, right off, is that we have a woman in a prominent role at Facebook. The bad news is that she is the only woman on the five-person management team. All of the managers at Facebook are white, straight, cisgender, and nondisabled.

Table 2.1 provides a leadership diversity profile for Facebook. Information about the management and board was gleaned from Facebook's investor relations website. The characteristics of the leaders were gleaned from web searches. Gender and race are relatively easy to confirm. Trans status (trans or cisgender), disability status, and sexuality are more difficult to confirm. However, these are relatively prominent leaders about whom much has been written online and elsewhere. For my purposes, what matters is whether the leader has publicly discussed their gender identity, disability, and sexuality. This method holds true across the companies discussed in this chapter. We are fairly accustomed to counting folks by their race or gender. This kind of data is collected on a regular basis, and most individuals are accustomed to identifying these characteristics. Disability is counted less often, but it is counted by the US Census Bureau and other groups. Sexuality and transgender identity are more complicated, and my decision to make these counts might seem controversial. How can I know if someone is gay or straight, or trans or cis, just by looking them up on the Internet? In fact, I cannot know anyone's *true* identity from an Internet search, but I can learn a lot about their *public* identity: what that person's colleagues and employees and customers know about them. In that sense, I am interested in knowing how many members of the corporate leadership for these organizations are *openly and publicly* identified as gay, lesbian, bisexual, and/or transgender. Similarly, I am interested in knowing which members of these leadership teams are open about any disabilities that they may have, such that their leadership reflects a representation of the disability community.

Facebook's board of directors has nine members, including Zuckerberg and Sandberg. Sandberg is just one of two women on the board. The entire board appears to be white, cisgender, and nondisabled. One board member, Peter A. Thiel, is openly gay. Thiel was a cofounder of PayPal and served as its chief executive officer (CEO) until it was purchased by eBay.

There are many interlocks that connect Facebook's board of directors to other media companies. Jan Koum is the founder and CEO of WhatsApp, a popular instant messaging service. WhatsApp Inc. is owned by Facebook. Reed Hastings is the CEO of Netflix. Donald E. Graham is the CEO of the Washington Post Company. Susan Desmond Hellman is the CEO of the Gates Foundation. Erskine Bowles is a senior adviser at investment firm BDT Capital Partners. He was also the cochair of Barack Obama's National Commission on Fiscal Responsibility and Reform and is a former president of the University of North Carolina. Marc Andreessen was the cofounder of Netscape and is a general partner of the venture capital firm Andreessen-Horowitz. Sheryl Sandberg is on the board of directors for the Walt Disney Company and is a former board member of Starbucks.

The primary property of Facebook, Inc. is the website itself, though Facebook also owns Instagram, WhatsApp, Oculus VR (virtual reality headset

TABLE 2.1. Facebook Leadership Diversity Profile, January 2015

Management	5
Board of directors	9
Combined	12*
Percent male	83
Percent white	100
Percent straight	92
Percent cisgender	100
Percent nondisabled	100

Source: https://web.archive.org/web/20150116053001/http://investor.fb.com/directors.cfm.

*Two members of the management team are also on the board.

company), and over fifty more small technology companies.* Facebook's assets are worth over $24 billion.†

Twitter

Like Facebook, **Twitter** is also a publicly traded company owned by shareholders and run by a combination of management and board. Twitter has a ten-person management team that is very white and very male. If General Counsel Vijaya Gadde were to step down, the management team would lose its only woman and its only nonwhite member. There are no trans, disabled, or LGBTQ members of the Twitter management team, nor are there any such people on the board of directors at Twitter. Twitter's board has eight members, and only CEO Dick Costolo sits on both the board and the management team. The board, which is chaired by Twitter cofounder Jack Dorsey, is entirely white and has only one woman. Table 2.2 provides a leadership diversity profile for Twitter.

TABLE 2.2. Twitter Leadership Diversity Profile, January 2015

Management	10
Board of directors	8
Combined	17*
Percent male	88
Percent white	94
Percent straight	100
Percent cisgender	100
Percent nondisabled	100

Source: https://web.archive.org/web/20150114050732/https://about.twitter.com/company.
*One member of the management team is also on the board.

* A full list of Facebook's holdings that is updated regularly can be found at http://en.wikipedia.org/wiki/List_of_mergers_and_acquisitions_by_Facebook. An archive of this list from December 29, 2014, can be found at https://web.archive.org/web/20141229115212/http://en.wikipedia.org/wiki/List_of_mergers_and_acquisitions_by_Facebook.

† Updated information about Facebook's assets can be found at http://ycharts.com/companies/FB/assets.

Twitter has many board interlocks with other companies. Board chairman Jack Dorsey is the CEO of Square, a credit card processing company that is best known for providing devices that allow smartphones to swipe and process credit cards. Peter Fenton is also on the board at Yelp and is a partner at Benchmark Capital. Benchmark invests in Twitter, Uber, Snapchat, Instagram, Yelp, Zillow, and a number of other media properties. Peter Currie is the CEO of Currie Capital and is also the former chief financial officer (CFO) of Netscape. Peter Chernin is the head of both Chernin Entertainment and the Chernin Group. Chernin Entertainment is behind a number of films and TV shows, including the series *New Girl*. The Chernin Group owns several media and technology assets, the most well-known of which is SoundCloud. David Rosenblatt is the CEO of the high-end online shopping site 1stdibs.com. He is a former Google executive and was also the CEO of DoubleClick. Marjorie Scardino built her career in the publishing industry, as CEO of Pearson from 1997 to 2012. She is the chairman of the board at the MacArthur Foundation. Finally, Evan Williams is a former CEO of Twitter and the current CEO of Medium. Another company that he ran, Obvious, has since shut down.

Twitter found itself in the center of media controversy in 2013 when it was criticized for its lack of diversity. Although CEO Dick Costolo was publicly very defensive, he eventually appointed Marjorie Scardino to the board as a gesture toward gender diversity (Biddle 2013).

Twitter's assets are worth over $5 billion.* Twitter owns Vine and has acquired more than thirty additional media assets.†

Google

Google boasts a much larger management team and board of directors than either Facebook or Twitter. It lists twenty people on its management team,

* Updated information about Twitter's assets can be found at http://ycharts.com/companies/TWTR/assets.

† A full list of Twitter's holdings that is updated regularly can be found at http://en.wikipedia.org/wiki/List_of_mergers_and_acquisitions_by_Twitter. An archive of this list from December 21, 2014, can be found at https://web.archive.org/web/20141221045021/http://en.wikipedia.org/wiki/List_of_mergers_and_acquisitions_by_Twitter.

led by Larry Page, Eric E. Schmidt, and Sergey Brin, all three of whom also sit on the board. The management team is somewhat racially diverse, with one black team member and four Asian team members. One of the team members that I am counting as white is Omid Kordestani, who is of Iranian descent. I follow racial definitions used by the US census, which codes white as anyone of European or Middle Eastern heritage. Census definitions do not always align with broader cultural conceptions of racial categories. However, using them allows me to compare the composition of these companies to census data on the demographics of the United States. Google's management team also includes three women, all of whom are white.

Table 2.3 presents the leadership diversity profile for Google. The board does not contribute much additional diversity for the company. The eleven board members include three white women and one Asian man. All members of the management team and the board of directors are straight and cisgender. I am listing Google's CEO Larry Page as disabled due to his paralyzed vocal cords. Page minimizes public speaking and is said to have a raspy voice and breathing problems after two different illnesses, years apart, took out each of his vocal cords (Miller 2013).

TABLE 2.3. Google Leadership Diversity Profile, January 2015

Management	20
Board of directors	11
Combined	28*
Percent male	79
Percent white	79
Percent straight	100
Percent cisgender	100
Percent nondisabled	96

Source: https://web.archive.org/web/20150113095153/http://www.google.com/about/company/facts/management/.
*Three members of the management team are also on the board.

In terms of corporate interlocks, there are several at Google. L. John Doerr is a general partner at the venture capital firm Kleiner Perkins Caufield & Byers (KPCB). According to its website, KPCB is an investor in a variety of technology and media companies, including Amazon, Twitter, Uber, Square,

Google, Electronic Arts, Flipboard, Snapchat, Shazam, Spotify, and many others.* Doerr is also on the boards for Zynga and Amyris. Diane B. Green was a cofounder and former CEO of VMWare. She is also on the board of directors for Intuit and the board of trustees for MIT. John L. Hennessy is the president of Stanford University and a member of the board of directors for Cisco. Ann Mather is a former Pixar executive who holds a range of board positions, including Netflix, Shutterfly, Glu Mobile, and Solazyme. Alan R. Mulally is a former president and CEO of Ford and former executive for Boeing. Paul Otellini is a former president and CEO of Intel. K. Ram Shriram is the founding partner of venture capital company Sherpalo Ventures. Sherpalo's investments include Google, PaperlessPost, Zazzle, StumbleUpon, Pinkberry, EasyPost, and several others. Shriram is also on the board of directors for several of these companies. He is a former executive with Amazon. Shirley Tilghman is a standout among this group as a former academic. She holds a PhD in biochemistry from Temple University and was a professor at Princeton University before serving as its president from 2001 to 2013. She is also on the board of the Advantage Testing Foundation, Amherst College, the Carnegie Endowment for International Peace, the King Abdullah University of Science and Technology, and Leadership for a Diverse America. She lacks the corporate interlocks that the other board members hold.

Google's assets are valued at over $120 billion.† In the world of social media, Google operates Google+, its challenger to Facebook. It also owns video platforms YouTube and Vevo and the blogging platform Blogger, and owned the picture-sharing site Picasa before it was shut down in 2016.

Yahoo

Yahoo lists sixteen people in its executive leadership, helmed by CEO Marissa Mayer. There are five women in leadership, three of whom are white. The fifth woman, Rose Tsou, is Asian. Tsou is the only nonwhite person on the management team, and there are no nonwhite people on the board of directors. Including Mayer (who is on both the management team and the board), there are three women on the board of directors.

---

* https://web.archive.org/web/20150206001252/http://www.kpcb.com/companies.

† Updated information about Yahoo's assets can be found at http://ycharts.com/companies/GOOG/assets.

Table 2.4 presents the leadership diversity profile for Yahoo. There are no LGBTQ people, disabled people, or trans people in leadership at Yahoo.

TABLE 2.4. Yahoo Leadership Diversity Profile, January 2015	
Management	16
Board of directors	9
Combined	23*
Percent male	70
Percent white	96
Percent straight	100
Percent cisgender	100
Percent nondisabled	100

Source: https://web.archive.org/web/20141113084729/http://info.yahoo.com/management-team and https://web.archive.org/web/20141113081227/https://investor.yahoo.net/directors.cfm.
*Two members of the management team are also on the board.

Not surprisingly, there are several board interlocks at Yahoo. Maynard Webb Jr. is the sole partner of the venture capital firm Webb Investment Network (WIN), which has a large portfolio of technology investments that include IndieGogo, Koality, and Hangtime.* He has held previous positions at eBay and Gateway. Jane E. Shaw is retired from the pharmaceutical industry. She is also on the board of directors for Talima Therapeutics and AeroSurgical. H. Lee Scott is a former president and CEO of Walmart. Charles Schwab is the founder, former CEO, and current chairman of the financial services firm that bears his name. Thomas McInerney is the former CFO of InterActiveCorp (IAC), which owns Vimeo, and also the former CFO of Ticketmaster. He serves on the boards of the Home Shopping Network (HSN) and Interval Leisure Group (a spin-off of IAC). Sue James is a retired partner from Ernst & Young. She serves on the boards of both Applied Materials and Coherent. Max Levchin is the chairman and CEO of HVF Labs. HVF stands for "hard, valuable, fun," and the company focuses on developing new business ideas that are driven by big data. Levchin is also on the boards of Yelp, Kaggle, and Evernote. He is a former executive of both Google and PayPal.

*https://web.archive.org/web/20150119012720/http://winfunding.com/portfolio.

Yahoo CEO Marissa Mayer serves on the boards of both Walmart and Jawbone (makers of fitness trackers, speakers, and headsets).

Yahoo's assets are worth over $55 billion. Yahoo owns Flickr and Tumblr, but its biggest assets are Yahoo-branded products, including its mail service, search service, instant messaging service, and news service.

Yelp

Yelp is a publicly traded, independent company with five members on its leadership team and nine members of its board of directors. Table 2.5 presents a leadership diversity profile for Yelp. Yelp's management is composed entirely of white men. Yelp's board is composed of seven white men and two white women.

TABLE 2.5. Yelp Leadership Diversity Profile, January 2015	
Management	5
Board of directors	9
Combined	12*
Percent male	83
Percent white	100
Percent straight	100
Percent cisgender	100
Percent nondisabled	100

Source: http://www.yelp-ir.com/phoenix.zhtml?c=250809&p=irol-govhighlights (the site design prevents archiving).
*Two members of the management team are also on the board.

The board of directors has a number of interlocks with other companies. Fred Anderson is a former Apple CFO and a current managing director at the equity firm Elevation Partners. At Elevation, he works alongside the U2 singer Bono as part of the investment team. Elevation has investments in Facebook, Forbes, MarketShare, and Yelp. Peter Fenton is also on the board of Twitter (see above for more details). Robert Gibbs is a former White House press secretary and adviser during Barack Obama's administration. Diane Irvine has one of the broadest backgrounds on the Yelp board. She is a former executive of both Plum Creek Timber Company and Blue Nile (online jewelry sales). She is a former board member of Ticketmaster. Max Levchin is also on the board at Yahoo (see above for more details). Jeremy Levine is a partner at the venture capital firm Bessemer Venture Partners. Bessemer has investments in Skype, Yelp, LinkedIn, Pinterest, Box, and many other companies in technology, media, and other fields. Mariam Naficy is the founder and CEO of Minted, an online design retailer. Yelp CEO and cofounder Jeremy Stoppelman is a former PayPal executive. Chief operating officer (COO) Geoff Donaker and CFO Rob Krolik are former executives at eBay. Joseph R. Nachman is a former Yahoo executive.

Yelp's assets are worth more than $575 million.*

LinkedIn

LinkedIn is a publicly traded company with eight people on the management team and seven on the board of directors. Table 2.6 presents a leadership diversity profile for LinkedIn. LinkedIn's management is entirely white, with six white men and two white women. Its board includes only one woman, who is white, and one Asian male. There are no trans, LGBTQ, or disabled people in leadership at LinkedIn. LinkedIn's assets are worth nearly $4 billion.

TABLE 2.6. LinkedIn Leadership Diversity Profile, January 2015

Management	8
Board of directors	7
Combined	14*
Percent male	79
Percent white	93
Percent straight	100
Percent cisgender	100
Percent nondisabled	100

Source: https://web.archive.org/web/20150131063801/https://press.linkedin.com/about-linkedin/management and https://web.archive.org/web/20150210110754/http://investors.linkedin.com/directors.cfm.

*One member of the management team is also on the board.

LinkedIn cofounder and board chair Reid Hoffman is a former PayPal executive. He also sits on boards for Kiva, Shopkick, Wrapp, Edmodo, and Mozilla. He is a partner at venture capital firm Greylock Ventures. Greylock has

* http://ycharts.com/companies/YELP/assets.

investments in Pandora, Facebook, LinkedIn, AirBnB, DropBox, Instagram, Tumblr, and many other companies.* A. George Battle is a former executive with the company that is now Accenture (formerly Arthur Anderson and Anderson Consulting), and he also serves on the boards for FICO, Expedia, Netflix, Sungevity, and Workday. Leslie Kilgore is a former executive at Netflix and Amazon and also serves on the board of directors at Netflix. Stanley Meresman is a former executive at Technology Crossover Ventures and is also a board member at Zynga, Turn, ModCloth, and HyTrust. Michael J. Moritz is a partner at the venture capital firm Sequoia Capital. Sequoia has investments in Whisper, AirBnB, Jawbone and many other companies. Moritz is on the boards of directors of Green Dot Corporation, Sugar, Klarna AB, and 24/7 Customer. David Sze is a partner at Greylock (see above). CEO Jeff Weiner is a former Yahoo executive.

Foursquare

Foursquare is a private company. That means it is not publicly traded and has no board of directors. It is run by a team of six people, who are all white men. None of them are disabled, trans, gay, or bisexual. There is no leadership diversity profile for this platform because it is so easy to describe in a sentence. There simply is no diversity at Foursquare. Cofounder Dennis Crawley had previously founded Dodgeball, a similar service, which was purchased by Google. Jeff Glueck, the COO, was previously with Travelocity. Three other team members—Andrew Hogue, John Steinback, and Noah Weiss—were previously Google executives.† Foursquare's assets include Swarm, a spin-off of the original Foursquare app.

Pinterest

Pinterest is a private company, operated by Cold Brew Labs. It is currently run by two men, Ben Silbermann and Evan Sharp. Both are straight, cisgender, and nondisabled. Silbermann is of Asian descent, and Sharp is white. Silbermann was previously with Google, while Sharp was previously with Facebook.

---

* https://web.archive.org/web/20150319031348/http://www.greylock.com/greylock-companies/.

† https://web.archive.org/web/20150317191655/https://foursquare.com/about/team.

Academia.edu

Academia.edu is a private company run by Richard Price and Ben Lund. Both men are straight, white, cisgender, and nondisabled. Price has a doctoral degree in philosophy from Oxford. Ben Lund has a bachelor's degree in biological anthropology from Cambridge University.

ResearchGate

ResearchGate is a private company based primarily in Berlin but with additional offices in Cambridge, Massachusetts. It was founded by two physicians, Ijad Madisch and Sören Hofmayer, and a computer scientist, Horst Fickenscher. For all three of these men, a great deal of professional information, but very little personal information, can be found online. ResearchGate has so far been funded by investments of venture capital.

These last four platforms—Foursquare, Pinterest, Academia.edu, and ResearchGate—are newer and smaller fish in the social media sea and still thriving off private investment. Their futures are uncertain, although all three seem to be doing well. They may get bought up by one of the larger social media companies in the near future, or they may manage to stay independent.

UNDERSTANDING DIVERSITY

How do we judge the numbers on leadership diversity? As these companies are based in the United States, I begin by comparing the companies to the demographic diversity of the United States. Table 2.7 presents a profile of American diversity.

By any measure, the people who control social media reflect little of the diversity of the United States and even less of the diversity of the world. It is important to recognize what a small handful of people we are discussing here. Across all of the companies examined in this chapter, only 114 people are in leadership on either a management team or a board of directors. Those who hold these positions of leadership have been leaders at the intersection of technology and media for many years. The leadership of social media is a small group of people with a great deal of durability. It is not a rapidly expanding group, so there are few roles for new people—and by extension, new types of people—to seize. That means that our supposedly diverse social

TABLE 2.7. A Profile of American Diversity

Percent white	61.6
Percent black	13.3
Percent Hispanic	17.6
Percent Asian	5.6
Percent Native American	1.2
Percent female	50.8
Percent trans	.3
Percent lesbian, gay, or bisexual	3.5
Percent disabled	18.7

Sources: US Census Bureau (census.gov) and Gates (2011). Race and gender percentages are from 2015. Sexuality and trans percentages are from 2011. Disabililty percentage is from 2010.

media technology is run on an economic model that has no social diversity and little capacity to develop it.

Identifying the small size of the group controlling social media is not meant in any way to let these companies off the hook for their lack of diversity, but rather to highlight the difficulty we may face in pressing for change. The users of these services are incredibly diverse. Minority groups have embraced social media as a set of tools that can be used to connect with others, share resources, organize politically, and advocate for change. Social media is incredibly important to many minority communities, so it is disappointing to see so little representation of women, blacks, Hispanics, Asians, Native Americans, bisexuals, gays, lesbians, trans people, and disabled people at the helms of this industry.

METHODOLOGICAL MOMENT: The Internet Archive

One major hurdle to jump in practicing online ethnography is the seemingly ephemeral character of the Internet. What we see on a website today is not necessarily what visitors to that site saw five years ago, or even just yesterday. The Internet is essentially a trove of texts that is constantly being updated. Traditionally, when we want to see an old text, we go to the library. To see an old version of a website, we can visit the **Internet Archive**, which is really a new kind of library. The Internet Archive began in 1996 as an effort to capture and store the digital content that was rapidly proliferating. As described on the site: "The Internet Archive

continues

METHODOLOGICAL MOMENT: The Internet Archive *continued*

is working to prevent the Internet—a new medium with major historical significance—and other 'born-digital' materials from disappearing into the past."* The primary feature of the Internet Archive is the **Wayback Machine**, a search tool that allows users to view archived versions of websites. The user simply enters a web address into the search bar and hits enter. The search results are presented in the form of a calendar, with a range of years listed across the top and the current calendar year below. Blue circles appear on the dates when that website was archived. The user clicks on the circles to see the archived pages or clicks on alternative years at the top to see how often the site was archived in the past.

The Internet Archive only captures pages that are available to the public and that allow Internet crawlers to enter and archive the pages. Sites that restrict robot access are not allowed. For the purposes of the Internet, robots are programs that retrieve information from websites. Search engines rely on robots in much the same way that the Wayback Machine does. Sites that choose to limit the information collected by robots place those protocols in a file called robots.txt on the site. The **Robots Exclusion Standard** is a practice followed by the professionals who build and maintain these robots to ensure that the robot finds and follows the protocols provided in the robots.txt file. Typically, those pages that limit access will not be available on the Wayback Machine. For example, the Wayback Machine has archives of the home page for Facebook, but it does not archive the user profiles and posts from inside Facebook. However, public Twitter profiles are archived. The Wayback Machine is an excellent tool for examining the history and evolution of the Internet and blogs, as well as of social media platforms that are available online (as opposed to those that are strictly application based).

In addition to the Wayback Machine, the Internet Archive offers a tool called Archive-It that allows users to create an immediate archive of a particular page, store that archive on the Internet Archive's servers, and build sets of archives into collections. The Archive-It tool can be found online at https://archive.org/web/, while the archive collections are at https://archive-it.org. If you are observing a website that you fear may change soon and want to have ongoing access to the site as it appears now, Archive-It is a useful option. Some other tools for archiving pages yourself are Cached View (http://cachedview.com) and Archive.is (http://archive.is).

*https://archive.org/about/.

THE HISTORY OF SOCIAL MEDIA

I turn now to a tour through the history of our major social media platforms. To illustrate this history, I make reference to my own early posts on these platforms, since for many of the platforms that is the only way that I can still access what the user interface actually looked like. This section is a bit autobiographical, not because my own relationship with social media is interesting but precisely because it is not. My mundane interactions with social media reflect the ways that most users adopted these platforms, in clumsy fits and starts, trying to figure out just what exactly we were supposed to be doing on there.

Social Networking: Friendster, MySpace, Facebook, Google+

In 2003 I moved from my hometown in central Virginia to New York City with the plan of spending my last year on a fellowship writing my dissertation in the middle of the greatest city on Earth. I had two friends who welcomed me there, and we found a three-bedroom apartment on the Lower East Side. I was glad to have those friends, but moving into a massive city was still a lonely experience, and making friends seemed daunting when my main task was to spend a lot of time in isolation writing my dissertation.

Not knowing how to meet people for friendships and dating, I turned to the Internet and discovered a website that had started just one year earlier: **Friendster**. I signed up for Friendster and began perusing the profiles of young creative New Yorkers like me. Eventually someone contacted me and invited me to meet for coffee. She was a textile artist who collaborated in a shop that made and sold covers for phones and gadgets, with cool (dare I say "hipster?") designs. After my first Friendster date I decided to go on the offensive and start actively making new friends online. This led to a lot of coffee drinking and a few dinners, movies, and sporting events.

Friendster called itself "the new way to meet people," and its opening splash page presented this explanation of the site:

> Friendster is an online community that connects people through networks of friends for dating or making new friends.
>
> You can use Friendster to:
>
> - Meet new people to date, through your friends and their friends

- Make new friends
- Help your friends meet new people

> Create your own personal and private community, where you can interact with people who are connected to you through networks of mutual friends. It's easy and fun!*

Following a link to frequently asked questions (FAQ) we learn that "Friendster is an online social networking community."† There we have it! Those magic words: social networking. Friendster is often designated as the first social network, and by extension, the first form of social media.

Friendster had two precursors. The first is online dating, particularly the service Match.com, which began in 1995. The second precursor for Friendster consists of all those services that were designed to help high school and college classmates reunite, including the American site Classmates.com, launched in 1995, and the British site Friends Reunited, launched in 1999. In fact, we could argue that both online dating and online alumnae networking are themselves the first forms of social media. But Friendster, I argue, was the first social media that truly understood itself and sold itself as social media.

Friendster was created in 2002 in Silicon Valley by Jonathan Abrams. "We viewed ourselves as the David, not the Goliath. There were the Yahoos and the AOLs and we were this tiny, little startup" (Fiegerman 2014). A year after Friendster's launch, **MySpace** was launched; it mimicked Friendster in nearly every way.

Having just adopted Friendster, it seemed easy enough for me to join MySpace then as well. As early MySpace users will recall, Tom is everyone's friend. Thanks to Tom, we all had one friend right away when we joined MySpace. There he sat, in his profile picture, looking over his shoulder at us from his desk. A whiteboard behind him was filled with scribbles about California: beach, Pasadena, LAX. His name was Tom Anderson, and he was one of the cofounders of MySpace, along with Chris DeWolfe.

MySpace called itself "a place for friends," clearly poking at its rival Friendster. Its opening splash page listed its uses:

---

* https://web.archive.org/web/20030407170314/http://www.friendster.com/index.jsp.

† https://web.archive.org/web/20030401232753/http://www.friendster.com/info/faq.jsp.

With MySpace you can:

- Find Old Friends
- Meet New Friends
- Suggest Matches Between Friends
- Share Photos*

That last bullet is actually important because it highlights the fact that the "media" in social media is not just the Internet and related applications. It also refers to new uses for old media. Those photographs we had filling up old boxes could now find new life, once we scanned them in, as we posted them on MySpace and invited our friends to comment.

The media on MySpace quickly expanded beyond photographs to include music. The site has been credited with launching the careers of many successful musicians, including Justin Bieber, Soulja Boy, and Lily Allen.

Trouble started brewing very quickly for MySpace, when Facebook launched in 2004. Facebook was created by a group of Harvard students: Mark Zuckerberg, Eduardo Saverin, Andrew McCollum, Dustin Moskovitz, and Chris Hughes. Its origins have become the stuff of legends and lawsuits, and one major motion picture, *The Social Network* (2010).

According to my Facebook timeline, I joined in October 2007, making me a "late adopter." My first post said, "Dustin Kidd is grading papers!" I recall that prior to that time, Facebook had seemed unavailable to me, as it was restricted first to Harvard, then to Boston area schools, and then to students at schools across the country. I had graduated with my PhD from the University of Virginia just months after it started at Harvard, so I was never enrolled at a school during a period when its students could join Facebook. Facebook opened to everyone in September 2006, by which point I was a committed MySpace user. But after growing pressure from friends, I joined Facebook just after my thirty-second birthday. I told my students in my Sociology of Popular Culture seminar about my new social media venture, and I remember feeling hurt and awkward when one of my students spoke up and said that it was "creepy" when "old men" like me joined Facebook.

Facebook has changed its design significantly since its launch, and users have had to relearn how to use the site. Older versions of the site cannot be

* https://web.archive.org/web/20031004101518/http://myspace.com/.

found on the Wayback Machine at archive.org because the site does not allow automated site crawling of the kind that is required for the Internet archival process.

Predictions of Facebook's demise have appeared for years now, and they seem to be greatly exaggerated. It is the largest social networking site in the world. However, social media's future is significantly tethered to technology, so that future is difficult to predict. The replacement for Facebook may appear tomorrow or never.

MySpace hung on against competition from Facebook for years, with significant help from News Corporation, which bought MySpace in 2005. When the television show *Glee* began airing on Fox in 2009, it was careful to show its teen characters using MySpace and never Facebook—a sign of solidarity with a fellow News Corporation property.

Myspace still exists today, although they have stopped capitalizing the S. It is primarily a website for musicians and music fans that is co-owned by singer Justin Timberlake and Specific Media LLC, who bought the site from Rupert Murdoch's News Corporation in 2011.* Friendster launched a new identity in 2011 as an online social gaming service; most of its users were located in Southeast Asia. It suspended operations in 2015.

Facebook has won the market for social networking. In its 2013 annual report, it identifies its main competitors as **Google+** (Google plus) and various regional social networks around the world (Facebook 2013, 11). But Google+ only claims to have 300 million monthly active users, compared to at least 1.2 billion monthly active users on Facebook (Facebook 2013, 7). What's more, Google+ users spend far less time on the site than Facebook users do at that site. Nielsen figures reported in May 2013 indicate that on average Google+ users each spent just six minutes and forty-seven seconds on the site during the entire month of March 2013, as compared to Facebook users each spending six hours and forty-four minutes (Facebook 2013, 7). Although the same report indicates that Facebook's user engagement time was down by twenty-five minutes compared to the same month in 2012, clearly Facebook is far beyond the reach of Google+.

Google+ launched in June, 2011. An avid Google user, I entered the Google+ terrain in July 2011, posting the line "Trying to figure this shiz out." I

* https://web.archive.org/web/20150115134442/https://myspace.com/pressroom/aboutmyspace.

posted several photographs in July and August 2011, then returned in November and December to post a few links and videos, and then ignored the application entirely for 2012 and 2013. The main problem that I encountered with Google+ was Google's universal log-in system. I had created my Google+ profile using a personal Gmail (Google's e-mail application) address. But I spend most of my time using my school's e-mail address, and that e-mail is also Gmail based. So in order to get to my Google+ profile, I had to log out of my work e-mail and log in to my personal e-mail. Google is somewhat better now in how it allows navigation among multiple accounts, but this continues to be a sticking point for many users. Google+ functions less like a website and more like a space within a broader Google account. Because of this unique design, it cannot be archived and is not searchable on the Wayback Machine.

I returned to Google+ in 2014 for two reasons. First, I chose to set up a Google+ page to promote a new book (using yet another Gmail account). Second, I spent the summer of 2014 in a massive open online course (MOOC), and the learning community for that course was particularly active in Google+. But like most users, my engagement remains minimal. As of this writing, Facebook retains dominance on the social media battlefield.

boyd and Ellison offer a clear and concise definition of social networking sites (SNSs): "We define social network sites as web-based services that allow individuals to (1) construct a public or semi-public profile within a bounded system, (2) articulate a list of other users with whom they share a connection, and (3) view and traverse their list of connections and those made by others within the system" (2008, 211). Although the term SNS is primarily used to describe platforms explicitly devoted to networks, such as MySpace and Facebook, their definition applies just as well across nearly all forms of social media because platforms like YouTube, Pinterest, and Flickr also include lists of followers/friends that are visible to other users. However, social media platforms that demand anonymity, like Yik Yak or Secret (when it was still in existence) do not meet boyd and Ellison's definition of an SNS.

Microblogging: Twitter

Twitter was created in 2006 by a team of folks looking to expand the SMS (short message service) model of text into something closer to a social network. The original team included Jack Dorsey (@Jack), Evan Williams (@Evan),

Biz Stone (@Biz), and Noah Glass (@Noah).* Noah Glass was reportedly fired from the company that eventually developed, but the remaining three continue to run the business of Twitter.

Twitter is best known for its microblogging model, which limits text tweets to 140 characters. Although images, video, and links can now be included as well, in the early days of Twitter all tweets consisted of short texts. A capture of the September 30, 2006, splash page of Twitter provides this description of the service:

> Twitter is for staying in touch and keeping up with friends no matter where you are or what you're doing. For some friends you might want instant mobile updates—for others, you can just check the web. Invite your friends to Twitter and decide how connected you want to be.†

The most striking part of that description is that it cannot be tweeted—too many characters! The description was a bit trimmer nearly a year later, on August 30, 2007:

> A global community of friends and strangers answering one simple question: What are you doing? Answer on your phone, IM, or right here on the web!‡

Technically, we're still six characters over the limit. These descriptions highlight the early multiplatform character of Twitter. Users could opt to use Twitter on their computers' browsers but could also easily use it on their mobile phones. In 2014 the splash page description expanded again:

> Welcome to Twitter. Connect with your friends—and other fascinating people. Get in-the-moment updates on the things that interest you. And watch events unfold, in real time, from every angle.§

---

* The items in parentheses are the Twitter handles of these individuals. Anyone wanting to follow them or just see their tweets can search for these handles using the search window on Twitter.

† https://web.archive.org/web/20060930214639/http://twitter.com/.

‡ https://web.archive.org/web/20070830155120/http://twitter.com/.

§ https://web.archive.org/web/20140908060943/https://twitter.com/.

I joined Twitter in 2008 and sent my first tweet on December 1 of that year: "Doing can't believe Tom talked him into this." You'll notice I was having a little trouble from the get-go. The word "doing" was obviously not supposed to be there, so just ignore it. What's left is a sentence fragment that is missing a subject. I was importing a model that Facebook used at the time, in which every status update automatically started with the user's profile name. I seemed to think that tweets were the equivalent of a status update, so my first tweet was meant to read: "Dustin Kidd can't believe Tom talked him into this." I've used Twitter consistently ever since and now operate both a personal account and a professional account. I also send tweets from my department's account.

Twitter really has no peer. In some ways, it does compete with social networks, particularly the social network giant Facebook, but its value for users is very different. Twitter reports having over 271 million monthly active users, making it much smaller than Facebook, although it has over a billion registered users.* Twitter users average two hours and fifty minutes of monthly engagement each, based on 2012 data (Isaac 2012). So it is used much less than Facebook and much more than Google+.

Blogging: Blogger, WordPress, Tumblr

The practice of blogging really predates the concept of social media, but it is nevertheless an authentic form of social media in that it involves an overarching technology that is utilized to create and share media content. The word "blog" is a truncation of "weblog" and dates to the 1990s, when Americans were really just beginning to embrace the web. Many early web users began online diaries on their personal web pages or pages hosted by colleges and other organizations.

I started an online journal in the fall of 1998, using server space allotted to me as a graduate student at the University of Virginia. It was a mixture of awkward poetry and academic papers. A web capture from April 24, 2001, shows that I decorated the page with a picture of me hiking in Scotland.†

---

* https://web.archive.org/web/20150122065319/https://investor.twitterinc.com/releasedetail.cfm?ReleaseID=862505.

† https://web.archive.org/web/20010424142932/http://www.people.virginia.edu/~dk4z/.

(This highlights the fact that the Wayback Machine is a useful tool for digging up embarrassing personal items that we thought we had left behind in cyberspace.) The line between an online diary and a more generic personal website is blurry, but a blog implies a degree of regularly added content, sorted by date. When I finished graduate school in 2004, I started my own personal web page, but that site was much more static than a blog and really functioned as both an online résumé to share with others and an online desktop for my personal use (with my favorite links, tools, etc.).*

True blogs are often associated with blogging sites that help to facilitate the appearance of an online journal. Google's tool **Blogger** was one of the first of these sites. It was created in 1999 by Pyra Labs and purchased by Google in 2003. Initially, Blogger was designed as a tool that would help the user update information on an existing site, as indicated in this description from 1999:

> You make posts to your weblog (or your What's New page or any other web page you want to update frequently with chronologically sorted posts) by submitting a form on this web site, and the results immediately show up on *your* site, with *your* design.†

Once Google took it over, it quickly moved in a more social direction by allowing comments and other ways to connect within the service. But it also shifted away from externally hosted sites to a new functionality, in which Blogger actually became the location of the blog, typically under the name Blogspot. I was very much a late adopter with Blogger, but I finally gave in after abandoning my personal website in 2009. My first post followed an enthusiastic reading of Suze Orman's *The Money Book for the Young, Fabulous, and Broke* and was entitled "Credit Reports and FICO Scores."‡ Exciting stuff indeed!

Although Blogger is credited with creating the blog format and the business model for content management systems (CMS), it was quickly surpassed in popularity by **WordPress**. WordPress launched in 2003 as an offshoot of an earlier platform called B2/cafelog. A capture from June 18, 2003, reveals

*https://web.archive.org/web/20040615072921/http://www.dustinkidd.com/.

† https://web.archive.org/web/19991012022531/http://blogger.com/.

‡ http://dustinkidd.blogspot.com/2009/08/credit-reports-and-fico-scores.html.

the following description: "WordPress is a semantic personal publishing platform with a focus on aesthetics, web standards, and usability."* WordPress was developed by Matthew Mullenweg and Mike Little, but using the general public license (GPL) model, which means that the owners of WordPress are the members/contributors. Matthew Mullenweg functions as a chief contributor, and he guides the business, but WordPress is free and open source, which means that access and distribution are designed to be available to all. In 2012 WordPress boasted having over sixty million websites, but very little profit (Colao 2012). It is a very different business model from our other major technology leaders.

Blogger and WordPress have been left in the dust by **Tumblr**, the latest blog platform on the block. Tumblr claims to host over 200 million blogs.† It is leaps and bounds beyond WordPress or Blogger, but less popular with major companies. Tumblr is the blog platform for the masses. In principle, Tumblr is meant to host a different kind of blog known as a tumblelog, which is a shorter form blog. Tumblr's splash page from a January 5, 2007, capture explains the premise: "Tumblelogs are blogs with less fuss and more stuff. Tumblr is your friendly and free tool for creating tumblelogs."‡ But the reality is that WordPress and Blogger can be used for short-format blogging, and Tumblr can be used for long-format blogging. The term "tumblelogs" was eventually abandoned, as illustrated in the language from the "about" page on May 22, 2010.

> Tumblr lets you effortlessly share anything. Post text, photos, quotes, links, music, and videos, from your browser, phone, desktop, email, or wherever you happen to be. You can customize everything, from colors, to your theme's HTML.§

The platform was created in 2006 by David Karp and Marco Arment, under the auspices of Karp's company Davidville. Tumblr was purchased by Yahoo in 2013 for $1.1 billion.

I started my first Tumblr blog in June 2012. My first post was a photograph of a book that I had checked out from the library called *Filming Difference*,

* https://web.archive.org/web/20030618021947/http://wordpress.org/.

† https://web.archive.org/web/20150212102039/https://www.tumblr.com/about.

‡ https://web.archive.org/web/20070105095540/http://tumblr.com/.

§ https://web.archive.org/web/20100522002622/http://www.tumblr.com/about.

edited by Daniel Bernardi. As with much of social media, particularly Twitter, hashtags are a very important element of Tumblr because they help users find posts based on specific interests, and they also help to index posts within a site. I used the hashtags "film," "sexuality," "production," "race," and "gender" for that first post.*

Tumblr use began to increase dramatically in 2012, as indicated by an analysis using Google Trends.† This particular analysis used "Blogger," "WordPress," and "Tumblr" as search terms. Tumblr has been associated with short-form funny posts, particularly ones that utilize memes and animated gifs. It is also heavily associated with pornography. Karp has estimated that 2–4 percent of traffic on Tumblr is porn related. Whether for porn, humor, or sociological analysis, Tumblr is the prime site for blogging as of 2014.

Social Images: Flickr, Picasa, Instagram

People have been sharing photographs online almost as long as they have been online at all. Sites like Picasa and Flickr have made it easy to share your photographs and photo albums not only with your friends, but also with a broader audience. Picasa is the older of the two, dating back to 2002. It was purchased by Google in 2004 and is now part of the broad suite of programs available through Google accounts that includes Gmail, YouTube, and Google+, among others. Picasa emphasizes the integration with Google+ especially, which means that its social media dimensions are mediated by Google+.

On its website on June 10, 2004, Picasa listed the following features:

> Everything you need to enjoy your digital photos in a single software product:
>
> - Auto-transfer photos from your digital camera.
> - Organize and find pictures in seconds.
> - Edit, print, and share photos with ease.
> - Create slideshows, order prints and more!‡

---

* http://dustinkidd.tumblr.com/post/25381690242/filming-difference.

† http://www.google.com/trends/explore#q=blogger%2C%20wordpress%2C%20tumblr&cmpt=q.

‡ https://web.archive.org/web/20040610145110/http://www.lifescapeinc.com/picasa/.

Prior to the mass use of digital cameras, sharing photos online meant scanning your photographs in one at a time, which was usually a very slow process. Now, of course, phones double as digital cameras and even professional (nonphone) cameras have social options that allow the photographer to utilize a Wi-Fi signal and automatically send images to Facebook and other sites. Many users now bypass the image hosting sites altogether and send their photographs directly to their favorite social media applications.

Flickr is the largest competitor to Picasa. Flickr was created by Ludicorps in 2004 and purchased by Yahoo in 2005. It has worked especially hard at increasing its social media presence by hosting images that bloggers and other social media mavens can use to illustrate their posts. That also means that photographers can find new audiences by making their images available for these purposes. Flickr used revolutionary language to describe itself in 2004: "Flickr is a revolution in photo storage, sharing and organization, making photo management an easy, natural and collaborative process. Get comments, notes, and tags on your photos, post to any blog, share and chat live and more!"* This language, as compared to Picasa's early description, makes it clear that Flickr always emphasized the social dimension.

The most social of social media platforms for the world of images is **Instagram**. It largely functions as a phone app, although images can also be seen online. Typically, though not always, Instagram images are less formal and more candid—images taken on the fly. Instagram was created in 2010 by developers Kevin Systrom and Mike Kreiger. A capture of Instagram's web page from June 10, 2011, provides the early description of the application:

> Meet Instagram.
>
> It's a fast, beautiful and fun way to share your life with friends through a series of pictures.
>
> Snap a photo with your iPhone, choose a filter to transform the look and feel, send to Facebook, Twitter or Flickr–it's all as easy as pie. It's photo sharing, reinvented.
>
> Oh yeah, did we mention it's free?†

Notice that this description uses the phrase "share your life" rather than simply "share your photos." This notion that the media that you post

* https://web.archive.org/web/20040701020748/http://flickr.com/.

† https://web.archive.org/web/20110610075831/http://instagram.com/.

provides access not only to the documents of your life but even to your life itself is integral to the marketing of social media. Socrates famously said that "the unexamined life is not worth living." Social media applications like Instagram make our lives available for seemingly endless scrutiny. Trapped at home alone on a wintry day? Snap a selfie, and you can still connect with your friends.

Instagram was purchased by Facebook in 2012 for $1 billion. I joined Instagram in 2012. My first post was a picture of a six-pack of Kinda Blue Blueberry Wheat Beer from Boulder Brewery. Then there are a couple of pictures of food. And then my fourth post was the first of many cat pictures. If the Internet is for porn, as the musical *Avenue Q* has proclaimed, then Instagram is for pets. Especially cats.

The rise of Instagram correlates with a general decline for Flickr and Picasa.* Many users tend to think of Picasa and Flickr as photo *storage* programs, whereas Instagram marked itself early on as a photo *sharing* program. But in addition to storage and sharing, Instagram can also control your camera so that you can take photographs within the application. So instead of taking a photograph with your camera, loading it into Picasa or Flickr, and then sharing it, with Instagram taking, editing, posting, and sharing an image are all part of the same process. Google replaced Picasa with Google Photos in 2016.

Social Video: YouTube, Vevo, and Vimeo

Video may have killed the radio star, but it has created many Internet celebrities. **YouTube** is the crown jewel of Internet video. It was created in 2005 by former PayPal employees and has been owned by Google since 2006. Although anyone can access YouTube, accounts are managed as part of the larger array of Google services (along with Gmail and Google+). Early on, YouTube's self-description was fairly matter-of-fact: "YouTube is the first online community site that allows members to post and share personal videos."† Since then YouTube has adopted stronger language that highlights its centrality as a form of social media:

---

* https://www.google.com/trends/explore#q=Picasa%2C%20Flickr%2C%20Instagram&cmpt=q&tz=Etc%2FGMT%2B4.

† https://web.archive.org/web/20050428171556/http://www.youtube.com/about.php.

> YouTube allows billions of people to discover, watch and share originally-created videos. YouTube provides a forum for people to connect, inform, and inspire others across the globe and acts as a distribution platform for original content creators and advertisers large and small.*

Note the introduction of advertisers into the mix. YouTube makes money by placing ads both in front of, and on top of, videos that users post, but it also allows advertisers to post their own videos, from commercials to infomercials, and it transforms video advertisements into entertainment commodities. For example, the Super Bowl has become known as a centerpiece for new and inventive advertising. The ads that appear during the Super Bowl can almost all be found on YouTube either during or immediately following their original appearance during the game.

I was using YouTube from the beginning, but I didn't post a video until 2010. My first video was called *The Life Course of a Sociology Major*, and I made it for my sociology students at Temple University.† It was made using a now-defunct application that Google once offered whereby the user could identify a series of search terms related to a topic of interest and Google would make a short video, complete with soundtrack, that showed the results of those searches. In addition to posting and sharing videos, YouTube also allows users to create playlists of videos from other users, subscribe to other users, engage in discussion of videos, and share videos using other social media formats using either links or "embed codes."

Vevo is a separate service that partners with YouTube to provide music video content. It is a joint venture of Google (owners of YouTube), Universal Music Group, and Sony Music Entertainment (Shu 2013). The goal of Vevo is to generate advertising revenue through the controlled sharing of music videos on YouTube. Vevo videos can also be watched on the company's website, vevo.com.

Vimeo is a competitor to YouTube. It launched in 2004 and was created by Jake Lodwick and Zack Klein. Both had previously helped to create CollegeHumor.com. In 2006 InterActiveCorp (IAC) bought Vimeo from the creators and eventually removed them from the company. Vimeo is considered a more professional space to post videos, in part because the community

* https://web.archive.org/web/20140912014823/https://www.youtube.com/yt/about/.

† http://www.youtube.com/watch?v=PisWrryg1xs&list=UU_VZX7urJjuaV_JZNV4cHUg.

is smaller and in part because there are no advertisements. Users can post a limited number of videos with a free account or purchase a "plus" or "pro" account. The more exclusive nature of Vimeo means that content is shared in a more directed manner. Like YouTube, Vimeo videos can be shared via either links or embedded codes.

Short-form Video: Vine and Instagram

Twitter launched its short-form video service Vine in January 2013, having purchased the company just months earlier from its creators. Vine is an app that takes six-second videos that can then be shared directly through Vine or indirectly through Twitter and Facebook. In response to Twitter's launch of Vine, Instagram added a video option in June 2013 that allows users to create and share fifteen-second videos.

Geosocial Networking: Foursquare, Swarm, Yelp

Social media is often framed in opposition to real-world, real-time sociality, though there has always been a counterargument that social media facilitates face-to-face meeting. Geosocial networking offers the strongest example of social media generating a connection with real-world spaces. "Geosocial media" refers to any platform that allows users to register their locations in physical space and engage with those locations. The strongest example has been Foursquare, which allowed users to "check in" to their locations, share those check-ins with their connections, and offer helpful suggestions about things to do in these spaces. For example, if I were meeting a friend at a bar for some social time, I could have used Foursquare to check in to the bar, let all my friends know I was there, perhaps in hopes that they would join, and recommend my favorite beer on tap. I could even include a photograph of my beer and check my friend in with me.

I use the past tense here because Foursquare changed significantly in 2014, splitting off its check-in function to a new app called Swarm. Foursquare remains in place but now functions as a tool for finding and sharing about specific businesses. Users no longer check in; rather, they search for specific kinds of services near them, access reviews left by other users, and perhaps post reviews of their own. In that sense, Foursquare has now become a competitor to Yelp, a geosocial service that also allows users to find and review local services. All three applications make use of the GPS function of smartphones, although Yelp pairs the app with a website where users can also leave reviews.

Yelp launched in 2004. The company was founded by former PayPal employees Jeremy Stoppelman and Russel Simmons, who continue to run the company, having resisted a Google takeover bid in 2009. An October 28, 2004, screen capture of Yelp's website highlights the appeal for users:

> Reasons to use Yelp!
>
> - Find the best local businesses
>   Search and browse recommendations.
> - Ask friends for recommendations
>   Get advice from the people you trust.
> - Better then [*sic*] sending an email
>   Responses are saved and shared with friends.*

The company has since embraced much slicker marketing language: "Yelp is the best way to find great local businesses. People use Yelp to search for everything from the city's tastiest burger to the most renowned cardiologist. What will you uncover in your neighborhood?"† Yelp claims 138 million unique users per month via its website, in addition to 68 million unique users on the mobile app, as of September 2014.‡ I've used Yelp for years to find businesses, but I have only written three reviews, all in 2012. I opened an account for the sole purpose of writing a positive review of my local bicycle shop, because I was so impressed with the service. A few days later, I wrote a positive review of my gym and a scathing review of the local pawn shop. After that, I returned to passive use of Yelp, relying on others' reviews but not writing my own.

Foursquare launched in 2009. It remains privately owned, and Foursquare Labs controls both Foursquare and Swarm. Its splash page on December 23, 2009, read: "Check-in, find your friends, unlock your city. Foursquare on your phone gives you & your friends new ways of exploring your city. Earn points & unlock badges for discovering new things."§ Note the emphasis on

* https://web.archive.org/web/20041028043305/http://www.yelp.com/.

† https://web.archive.org/web/20140814234018/http://www.yelp.com/.

‡ http://www.yelp-ir.com/phoenix.zhtml?c=250809&p=irol-irhome.

§ https://web.archive.org/web/20091223234552/http://foursquare.com/.

rewards and play. Foursquare even allowed locations to have mayors: people who had checked in the most at that location. Many users became competitive in their campaigns to be mayor of their coffee shops and gyms. I joined in 2010, and my first check-in was at my apartment with the comment "home." My history reveals many check-ins at very few locations, mostly my coffee shop and my gym. I access this history now from Swarm, which inherited the check-in aspects of Foursquare when it branched off in the summer of 2014. As the services were split, all Foursquare users automatically had Swarm accounts; they just needed to download the application. Across the services, the company claims forty-five million users.* Foursquare's current marketing language on its website highlights the change in the service: "Introducing the all-new Foursquare, which learns what you like and leads you to places you'll love." Unlike Yelp, which serves as a kind of yellow pages (remember those?) for local businesses, Foursquare is more responsive to user behavior and attempts to direct users to businesses around them that might be of interest but may have escaped the user's awareness. Admittedly, some may find this attempt to read the user's mind a little discomfiting.

Although Foursquare, Swarm, and Yelp are rooted in geosocial networking, they do not hold a monopoly on it. Facebook, Instagram, and many other services now include check-ins and other aspects of geosocial networking.

Media-Based Social Media: TVTag, Goodreads

Services that allow users to discuss the media they consume are much smaller aspects of the social media universe, but they are worth a mention. TVTag and Goodreads allow users to post reviews and share them with their networks and facilitate interaction with people who have similar interests. Instead of checking in to places, users check in to movies, TV shows, and books. Goodreads launched in 2006 and was purchased by Amazon in 2013. TVTag launched as GetGlue in 2010 but closed operations in December 2014.

Curation: Pinterest

Pinterest is, in my opinion, a very unique form of social media. It can be very difficult to explain to the uninitiated, and many potential users complain that they just do not know what to do with it. But avid users like it and use it a

---

* https://web.archive.org/web/20140112133529/https://foursquare.com/about.

lot. The centerpiece of Pinterest is the "board." Users create boards around particular topics and themes by "pinning" images and videos to the board, as explained in a screen capture from February 2, 2010, the year that Pinterest launched:

> Pinterest lets you publish beautiful galleries from the things you find interesting. Pin up anything you find online—recipes to make, clothing to buy, art that inspires. . . . Pinterest is loved by fashionistas, shoppers, wedding planners, foodies, designers, and more.*

The description was shortened by late 2014 to just: "Pinterest is a place to discover ideas for all your projects and interests, hand-picked by people like you."† Pinterest was created by Ben Silbermann, Paul Sciarra, and Evan Sharp under the auspices of Cold Brew Labs. As of July 2013, Pinterest claimed seventy million users (Horwitz 2013). Users spend an average of ninety-eight minutes per month each on the site (Byrum 2013). I joined Pinterest in 2012, and my first board was titled "For the Home." Apparently I was looking for some new furniture and made a board of sofas, armchairs, and breakfast tables.

The Social Media Underworld: 4chan, Reddit, Secret

The Internet has always had its underworld, and some aspects of that underworld have adopted social media dynamics. We could almost call this "antisocial media." 4chan is an excellent example. It was started in 2003 by a fifteen-year-old named Christopher Poole. The primary purpose of 4chan is to share images and to create dialogue about those images. It was modeled on Japanese websites and originally focused on Japanese popular culture. Its catchphrase, according to an August 18, 2005, capture, was: "What you need, when you need it."‡

4chan is a board for posting images anonymously. It was the original creation point of the worldwide anonymous collective of hacktivists (hacker

* https://web.archive.org/web/20100202235045/http://pinterest.com/.

† https://web.archive.org/web/20141220121653/https://about.pinterest.com/en.

‡ https://web.archive.org/web/20050818191647/http://dp.information.com/?a_id=35&domainname=4chan.com.

activists) known as Anonymous, which has been linked to campaigns against Scientology and the Westboro Baptist Church, as well as attempts to garner greater media attention to a number of crimes (Gilbert 2014).

Reddit has some similarities to 4chan, but it focuses strictly on text posts rather than images. Reddit was created in 2006 by a group of students at the University of Virginia. It was quickly bought by Condé Nast and then became a subsidiary of its parent company, Advance Publications. However, it became independent again in 2012. Its self-description, as seen in a capture from November 25, 2006, explained that "reddit is a source for what's new and popular online. reddit learns what you like as you vote on existing links or submit your own!"* Unlike 4chan, Reddit users have to register in order to post content, typically in the form of links to pages, stories, and videos. Users can post links, comment on links posted by others, and vote links up or down, which allows them to gain more visibility and reach a larger audience. These users are called **redditors**, which highlights the role that users can play as gatekeepers who influence ideas and creative content on the Internet. If you are watching the *Today Show* and a segment opens with the phrase "now trending on social media," there is a good chance that the item came to prominence through Reddit—whether it's a video of a creative marriage proposal or a blog rant about politics. As of September 2014, Reddit was using a dictionary definition format in its self-description:

> Reddit: noun, verb
> redd·it, redd·it·ing; see redditor, subreddit
> noun: a type of online community where users vote on content
> verb: to take part in a reddit community†

Although the home page in Reddit reads as a series of posts, with up and down arrows next to them, users can also search through a wide variety of topical subreddits, or create their own. Some of these subreddits have been particularly controversial and have even been shut down, including the subreddits /r/jailbait, r/niggers, and r/beatingwomen. I attempted to find archive copies of these subreddits using the Internet Archives, but for every

* https://web.archive.org/web/20061125065658/http://www.reddit.com/?tbnl-session=9316:0E1D16DC6D639E728538B99D69582C29.

† http://www.reddit.com/about/.

capture I clicked on, I was taken to an age verification page. Clicking "yes" in answer to the question "Are you over eighteen and willing to see adult content?" only resulted in the age verification page reloading. So I was unable to get into the archives for these controversial subreddits.

Secret was an app for Android and iOS devices that was released early in 2014. It started as a tool for tech professionals to share secrets about the tech business (Lawler 2014). Secret functioned as a partner app to Facebook. Users downloaded the app and gave Facebook permission to share their contacts with Secret. Users then saw a feed of secrets shared by either a "friend" (a direct connection on Facebook) or a "friend of friend" (a second-level connection on Facebook, someone with whom the user has a mutual friend). But the people who shared the secrets were not identified. Users could comment on secrets that had been posted or simply click a heart shape to indicate liking the secret. Users could also post secrets of their own or flag secrets with inappropriate content. Secrets could be posted with background photos. Not surprisingly, the design of Secret resulted in online bullying and harassment. In Brazil a judge ordered Apple and Android to stop selling the app and to disable the app for existing users in the country (Campbell 2014). The makers of the app made the monitoring systems more sophisticated, so that secrets with actual names or pictures of people were recognized and forbidden. Secret launched with the concept that people want a forum for sharing thoughts or questions they would not post publicly. This concept has predecessors in the form of the website PostSecret* and the app/website Whisper,† but Secret added the social media element by incorporating Facebook friend lists. By sharing on Secret, users were broadcasting not to a generalized and ambiguous world, but rather directly to their own networks. The company behind the app initially stood by the product, as stated on its blog on January 30, 2014:

> From what we've seen so far, we believe that Secret is something truly special and will carve out a new way for people to connect with one another. The goal is to not build only an app, but a platform that will bring more authenticity, self-awareness and empathy to the world.‡

* http://postsecret.com/.

† http://whisper.sh/

‡ https://medium.com/secret-den/speak-freely-61a73ed561b4.

On April 29, 2015, the company shut down the app. Secret was run by David Byttow and Chrys Bader-Wechsler, both veterans of the tech world with experience on numerous apps and sites.

The Social Media Overworld: LinkedIn, Academia.edu, and ResearchGate

All social media exists on a continuum of respectability. The most popular social media platforms like Twitter and Facebook are generally seen as ambiguously respectable, at best. Reddit and 4chan are in many ways the least respectable spaces on social media. At the other extreme, we find professionally oriented platforms that are designed to garner the most respect and legitimacy by focusing on very specific kinds of professional content that is generated within very specific norms.

LinkedIn is a professional social networking site that launched in 2003.* It actually predates Facebook. It functions like an online résumé-sharing service that also allows the user to generate a network of colleagues and peers across the country. Users can upload portfolios and professional documents and post short- and long-form posts. LinkedIn claims to have over 300 million users in more than two hundred countries.† LinkedIn members use the site to build professional networks, search for job openings, and share professional insights. LinkedIn was created by former PayPal employees and board members, led by Reid Hoffman. I use it to keep track of former students, alumni from my program, peers in the field, and business professionals who might be interested in hiring my students. Unlike many other forms of social media, LinkedIn is not organized chronologically, so I cannot go back and view my earlier posts. It always functions instead as an up-to-date, interactive résumé.

Academia.edu works much like LinkedIn, but for the even narrower community of college and university professionals, particularly faculty and graduate students. Whereas LinkedIn is organized as a résumé, Academia.edu is organized like an academic curriculum vitae, focused on publications, which can be shared on the site, as well as presentations and teaching. The site was

---

* LinkedIn's design does not allow its pages to be searched by crawlers, so I was not able to access archived versions of the site.

† https://www.linkedin.com/about-us?trk=hb_ft_about.

launched in 2008 and claims on its website to have over forty-three million users as of September 2016.*

ResearchGate functions in a very similar way to Academia.edu, but with a particular focus on science, including the social sciences, rather than the broader set of academic fields. Although Academia.edu has more users, ResearchGate users are more active on the site than Academia.edu users, perhaps because ResearchGate requires users to have an e-mail address from a recognized academic institution. The site was launched in 2008 and claimed over eleven million users as of September 2016.†

SUMMARY

This chapter has offered an overview of the most used social media platforms, and several—but not all—of the lesser used platforms. Social media is a concept that refers to the ways that websites, apps, and other platforms can be organized to generate connection and build networks. As a concept, it is open to new platforms and also to adoption by existing platforms. For example, sites and services that we do not typically think of as social media have adopted aspects of this concept. Amazon lets you brag about your new purchases on Facebook. Netflix lets you see your friends' favorite movies. An exhaustive list of social media platforms is not possible, and the history of social media continues to be written every day.

I did not discuss the subject of art in this chapter. I use that lens to examine how social activists are using social media through a series of case studies that I present in the next several chapters. In this chapter I focused on outlining the parameters of power and control in the social media industry. As I stated in chapter 1, social media companies are controlled by a surprisingly small group of powerful individuals who overwhelmingly experience privilege based on their gender, race, social class, and other dimensions of identity. The activists who use social media to challenge inequality have to contend with the fact that they are using a tool that is controlled by those who benefit from inequality. That conundrum is central to the analysis in the rest of the book.

---

* https://www.academia.edu/about.

† https://www.researchgate.net/about.

3

Leave Britney Alone: Sexuality Perspectives on Social Media

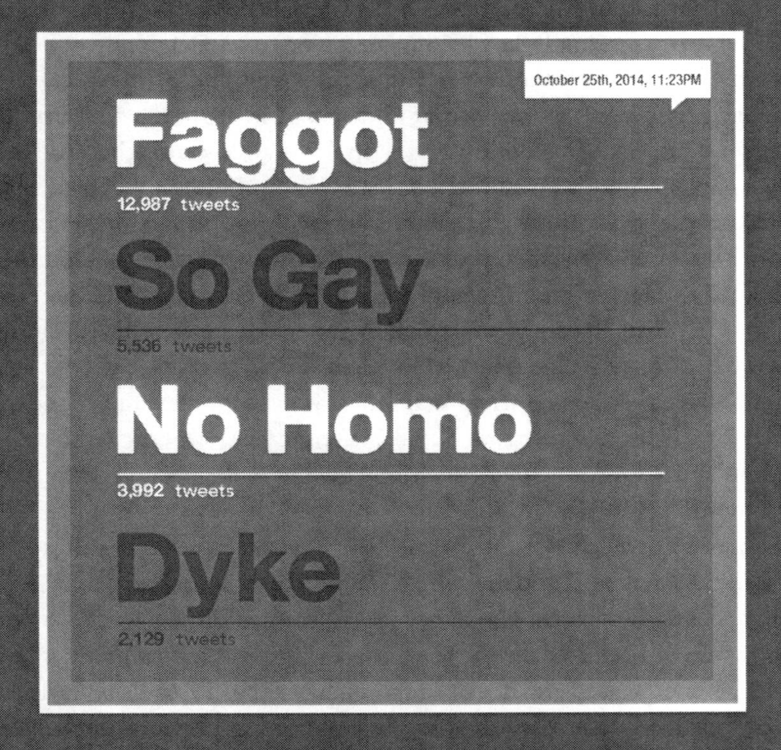

When Britney Spears took to the stage to open the *MTV Video Music Awards* (VMAs) on September 9, 2007, it wasn't a complete disaster, but mistakes were made. Britney's fans, and her record label, were hoping for a comeback moment. Britney had been struggling with a very public meltdown that can be dated as early as February 2006 (Singer 2007). The eighteen months leading up to the 2007 VMAs were filled with difficult incidents for Spears. Child welfare officers had investigated her for endangering her children, including an incident when she was photographed driving with a child on her lap (Moodie 2008). She had given a widely criticized *Dateline* interview to Matt Lauer in which she attempted to push back at the ways the paparazzi had invaded her life and endangered her children (Lauer 2006). She had posed naked and pregnant for the August 2006 cover of *Harper's Bazaar* (Brown 2011). And then her marriage ended when she filed for divorce in November 2006.

In the weeks that followed the VMAs, Spears generated controversy with a variety of antics and wild partying. A fan site called WorldofBritney.com announced it was closing in late December 2006. This was initially interpreted, primarily by gossip blogger Perez Hilton, as a sign that Britney's career was crumbling. However, the site owner hit back, insisting to the contrary: "I am simply not interested in continuing my efforts on this website because of how things have become so dysfunctional lately, and that is my choice and my choice only, and for those that cannot and will not respect that, I can only say sorry to you."* Ownership of the site eventually transferred, and the site continued as a fan community until early 2013. In February 2007, after a one-day stint in rehab, Spears went to a salon and had her head shaved, causing a new wave of concern. She returned to rehab a week later, checked out again a day after that, and then returned again for a monthlong stay that ended in late March 2007. Her divorce from Kevin Federline, with whom she shared two children and a former reality television show, was finalized in August 2007, just a month before the VMAs.

So perhaps we can forgive Britney for not being in the best head space when the show opened and the song "Gimme More" started to play.† The performance did not go well. Her dance moves seemed off, especially compared to those of her backup dancers. Her lip-synching was intermittent at best. It was a low-energy performance of a high-energy song. Tabloids unfairly called her fat, but she was not as toned as she had been in previous public performances, made all the more noticeable by her revealing clothing. If there was any hope that viewers would just forget about it, that hope was dashed when

---

* https://web.archive.org/web/20061230224743/http://www.worldofbritney.com/.

† Videos of the performance are easily found on YouTube.

the host of the VMAs, comedian Sarah Silverman, came out and spoke right after Britney's performance:

> Britney Spears everyone! Wow! She is amazing. I mean, she is twenty-five years old and she's already accomplished everything she's going to accomplish in her life. It's . . . it's mind-blowing.*

Silverman made a crude face to demonstrate the joke, before moving on to make fun of other celebrities in the audience.

The headlines the next day were all about Britney's bad performance. Not surprisingly, TMZ offered a pointed summary of the coverage: "There's barely anyone on the planet who hasn't panned Britney Spears' shockingly sucktastic MTV 'performance' of 'Gimme More'—and even Brit thought it was so crappy that she cried backstage afterwards" (TMZ Staff 2007). The criticism was relentless and seemed to indicate that Britney's long spiral down to the bottom had gone further yet. But in the desert of Britney Spears's life in 2007, there was a lone voice calling to us.

LEAVE BRITNEY ALONE

Those are the words of a die-hard Britney fan who took to YouTube the day after the VMAs to speak up for his celebrity hero. A young, effeminate kid, apparently lying on his bed and holding the camera over his face, pleads with the American public and the entertainment industry to give Britney some space and remember that she is a human. As the video begins, he is mostly angry, asking his audience to empathize with Britney Spears. He expresses concern that she might consider suicide as a result of the criticism. "If anything ever happened to Britney Spears, the world can kiss my ass goodbye. Because if anything ever happens to her, I'm jumping off the nearest fucking building. I don't care what anyone says. I love Britney!" He quickly moves from anger to sadness and tears. He starts recounting the issues that Britney has been facing as he becomes increasingly hysterical, finally erupting in the crucial line "Leave Britney alone!" which now functions as the title of the video .†

---

* Videos of Silverman's comments are easily found on YouTube.

† The video maker, Chris Crocker, has since deleted his YouTube account, but copies of the video are available on the service.

Leave Britney Alone is a great example of a **viral** video. The person who made the video—whom I discuss below—placed it on YouTube, MySpace, and Metacafe (a video-sharing site comparable to YouTube but focused on entertainment). According to Know Your Meme, it had two million views in the first two hours (Dubs 2009). News and entertainment outlets picked it up within a day and began sharing and discussing the video, expressing a range of opinions about the weeping teenager who seemed to completely lose his mind over Britney Spears. Parody videos began appearing, including one from blogger Perez Hilton. Many of the comments about *Leave Britney Alone* were filled with homophobia as well as transphobia. Viewers expressed confusion about whether the young person appearing in the video was a boy or girl, and this androgynous appearance was interpreted through both gender and sexuality lenses.

So who was this androgynous videographer who "broke the Internet" as he stepped up to defend Britney Spears? His name is Chris Crocker. In 2007, when he made the video, he was nineteen years old, having been born on December 7, 1987. Though young, he looked younger in the video, and many thought that he was a high schooler. Crocker is from Cunningham, Tennessee, and that is where he was living when he posted the video. Cunningham is a small town in Montgomery County, northwest of Nashville and close to the Kentucky border. So Chris Crocker is a gay man from rural Tennessee, far from the gayborhoods of Philadelphia, New York, and San Francisco. Much of our contemporary understanding of gay culture is focused on these urban epicenters but misses the fact that many gay people live in small towns.

As an aside, there is an interesting social media project that attempts to dismantle this association of gay people with urban centers. *I'm from Driftwood* is an online LGBTQ story archive that is dedicated to gathering the community-based narratives of queer people from all over the world, with an emphasis on the diversity of backgrounds that queer people are from and the importance of community and place in their lives.*

Chris Crocker was not a gay man living in rural isolation. He has certainly expressed frustration with the lack of gay culture in his hometown, but even in his youth he was able to use media production and the Internet as tools for building a network of support and for finding an audience for his work. In 2007 Chris Crocker was not a naïve young gay boy in a small town. He

* https://imfromdriftwood.com/.

was a sophisticated media maker with a wealth of experience. He was already an active **vlogger**—video blogger—on both YouTube and MySpace and had posted more than sixty videos. In other words, Crocker wasn't just a fan of an artist, he was and is an artist himself.

I argue that queer social media makers (1) embrace and embody a freak identity as a source of social empowerment, (2) seize control of the media tools provided by social technologies to represent themselves, and (3) utilize the network element of the informational age to build audiences and direct their social media work toward artistic identity projects.

QUEER SOCIAL MEDIA ART

I turn now from Chris Crocker to Brendan Jordan, whose entrée into the media world came via the local news. During a Las Vegas news segment in October 2014 about the opening of a new mall, Jordan stood at the front of the crowd behind the reporter. As the live shot started, Jordan seized the viewers' attention with both his vogue moves and his intense facial expressions. The video went viral, with stories on a number of online news sites, and was eventually picked up by the national television news. The original video was shot on October 11, 2014. On October 29 Jordan made a striking appearance on the *Queen Latifah Show*, where he explained the origins of the viral video. "When I saw the camera I'm like, oh my god, Brendan, this is your moment, don't mess it up. So I'm like, what shall I do? You know every time I see a spotlight like there's this mode I snap in to. My inner superstar comes out."* Jordan may seem like a lucky media sensation who wandered blindly into his fifteen minutes of fame, but he's actually indicating that he's more deliberate and more media savvy than that, and his actions in the weeks that followed proved this true.

In his interview with Queen Latifah, Jordan cited Lady Gaga as his inspiration. As anyone who pays attention to Lady Gaga's career knows, she is more than just a successful singer. Gaga has cultivated a very unique relationship with her audience. She refers to her fans as little monsters and identifies herself as the mother of monsters. She has issued a "Manifesto of Little Monsters" that appeared inside her album *The Fame Monster*. It reads:

---

* There is no official copy of the interview online, but clips may be found on YouTube.

> There's something heroic about the way my fans operate their cameras. So precisely and intricately, so proudly, and so methodically. Like Kings writing the history of their people. . . . They write the history of the kingdom, while I am something of a devoted Jester. (Lady Gaga 2009)

Gaga is identifying her fans not just as audience members, but as media makers—as both camera operators and writers. In fact, Gaga even tweeted about Brendan Jordan just days after his initial video, saying, "I know I was on vacation, but when are we going to talk about the boy who did applause choreography in the background of a news report."* The tweet was capped off with a crying emoji. She followed up with another tweet on October 16 in which she expressed her love for Brendan and called him "a real monster."

Brendan's news appearance went viral on October 11, 2014. He started his twitter account, @jordvnhaus, on October 12, tweeting at 3:54 p.m.: "Does anyone know how to work this thing? Twitter is confusing me it's harder than algebra."† He launched his YouTube channel on November 4, 2014, with a video titled *BRENDAN JORDAN-ARE YOU GAY?*‡ The video shows Brendan answering questions from his fans. The title of the video refers to one of the questions that he happened to answer with a simple smirk (putting it lightly). In the video he also made a kind of artistic statement about his developing social media projects and his growing celebrity status: "I obviously wanna be a voice for people who are coming out. Let them know that it's okay to be who you are because once you are happy with yourself—you love yourself—you just get the sense of confidence that you can do anything, you don't care what people think about you." Brendan used the video to announce his other social media platforms: Twitter, Instagram, Vine, Tumblr, and Facebook. He also spent a good portion of the video discussing his favorite clothes, naming and showing three items from American Apparel. One month later Jordan was announced as a new face of American Apparel with an exclusive modeling contract. Since that time Jordan's star has continued to rise. He's been photographed by Miley Cyrus, and he appeared in very impressive drag at RuPaul's DragCon 2015, where he was featured in an interview with the program *Boys in Tech. Boys in Tech* wanted to talk to Brendan about being just that, a boy in tech who was using social media technology to amplify his growing artistic

* https://twitter.com/ladygaga/status/522554915298627584.

† https://twitter.com/jordvnhaus/status/623352275264651264.

‡ https://www.youtube.com/watch?v=NSsdvdB4qLY.

voice.* He's had collaborations with Davey Wavey, Todrick Hall, and other gay social media stars. He's posted over thirty YouTube videos. As of 2016, Brendan has 207,000 followers on YouTube, 61,000 followers on Twitter, 503,000 followers on Instagram, and nearly 11,000 followers on Vine. Across his posts, he explores and challenges notions of gender and sexuality, while also insisting on an identity is that is multidimensional. His work certainly explores the notion of not just being a freak, but embracing a freak identity.

Brendan is just one of many major LGBTQ social media stars that I would argue are in fact social media artists. Brendan offers one of many models for how to embrace social media as an artistic medium and also an identity medium.

QUEER THEORY AND SOCIAL MEDIA

Why does social media have such a draw for LGBTQ youth when it is also such a dangerous space for them? Perhaps the danger of social media is irrelevant, given how dangerous the offline world is for LGBTQ people. Is online bullying worse than offline bullying? Perhaps. Perhaps not. But offline bullying always comes with the threat of immediate physical violence. For that reason, and maybe others, we can begin to understand the draw of social media.

Young people are inherently social. All humans are social, but no other age group has such a strong need to socialize with peers. danah boyd (2014) explores that issue in *It's Complicated: The Social Lives of Networked Teens*. Teens have always sought ways to develop social connections outside of their homes. This probably drives many parents crazy, but it is a necessary part of preparing to be adults in a society that expects young people to leave their parents' homes and forge new networks of relationships to give their lives meaning and connection. But limited access to money and cars makes socializing difficult for teens.

The need to socialize is no less important to LGBTQ teens. If their parents are hostile toward their sexuality, or simply unaware of it, these young people may be even more driven to reach for connections beyond the family. Depending on how their sexualities are received at school, they may have limited access to local offline networks for friendship and romance. This means social media actually has a lot to offer them, even with any dangers they may face online.

* https://www.youtube.com/watch?v=JVA6cEOtqx8.

Whether we focus our analysis on teens or adults, I believe that we can make use of the tools of **queer theory** to explain the relationship between sexuality and social media. Riki Wilchins (2014) provides an excellent and accessible introduction to queer theory in *Queer Theory, Gender Theory: An Instant Primer*. For Wilchins, queer theory is principally a political theory: "Queer theory is at heart about politics—things like power and identity, language and difference" (2014, 9). The politics of women's rights, gay rights, and trans rights forms the foundation of her approach to queer theory. But her examination of the issues of rights in these three sets of movements also highlights the ways that rights move some members of each group closer to the mainstream while excluding others. It is in the variety and the transmutations of each group that Wilchins finds the queerness that is most interesting to her. Wilchins is interested in gender queerness and sexual queerness across all experiences of identity; the gender play of feminist women, gays and lesbians, and trans folks; and the queerness of desire across all identities.

To continue developing her articulation of queer theory, Wilchins turns to postmodern philosophy. The rejection of meta-narratives and the postmodern embrace of multiple and conflicting local narratives is a cornerstone of queer theory, just as it is for postmodernism. In that sense, queer theory and postmodernism are connected and overlapping, but not one and the same. Wilchins draws heavily from the work of postmodern philosopher Jacques Derrida, incorporating his interrogation of language and binaries and his emphasis on the socially constructed truth claims that shape our social existence. From the philosopher Michel Foucault she draws an analysis of sex that looks at the ways the rules of sexuality have, over centuries, come to confine and restrict human life and taught us to police ourselves well before any policing from social authorities. The disciplines by which we police ourselves and each other, and the contestations of power that this policing produces, were central not only to Foucault's analysis of sex but also to his analyses of criminal justice. Finally, Wilchins turns to Judith Butler, a philosopher who is frequently hailed as a queer theorist, but who also refuses to identify as either queer or a theorist. Butler's work focuses on undermining the "realness" of categories like gender and sexuality and race, instead understanding them as performances that may help to construct reality but also constantly reveal that our concept of reality is a fiction.

It may seem odd to bring up queer theory in a chapter that is focused on a set of categories of sexuality and how those categories fare online and in social media, but there are a number of logical reasons for doing so. Queer audiences have been queering commercial culture for years, and they increasingly do so with social media. In traditional media consumption, we consume what we are given and then maybe afterward have an opportunity to play with the meaning by doing something new with it. Queer audiences have been doing this for years, and the term "queer readings" has come to refer to expressive reimagining of content gleaned from commercial culture, usually by discovering a homosexual story line that is not present in the official version. These queer readings often take the form of **slash fiction**, a form of fan fiction that creates new relationships between existing characters. The term "slash" refers to the solidus (/) between the names of the two characters. I once heard a participant in a forum on Harry Potter slash say: "In canon [the original novels by J. K. Rowling], I'm committed to Harry/Hermione but in fanon [the world of Harry Potter fan fiction], I am devoted to Harry/Draco." She was a writer of Harry/Draco slash fiction online. An excellent archive of Harry Potter slash fiction can be found at the Harry Potter FanFic Archive.* There are even sites devoted to just one specific slash pairing, such as Snarry.net, a collection of Snape/Harry slash.† Slash has subgenres, such as MPreg, which refers to stories about male pregnancy, and femslash, which refers to stories about relationships between female characters.

Increasingly, queer readings happen in social media spaces. In the YouTube search engine, type any two names from a fictional work (novel, television show, film) and then the word "slash" and almost always you will find a treasure trove of fan-generated (re)imaginings of the story. A search for "Harry Draco slash" yielded twenty-seven thousand results.‡ I certainly will not claim that all of those are queer readings, but I did confirm that the first six hundred were. Twitter is full of fan fiction tweeters, such as @fanfiction_txt, @FemSlash, and many, many others.

Queer readings and slash fiction subvert the "original" stories and undermine the artist/audience binary. They undermine grand meta-narratives and burst the bubbles of concentrated power, sending power in all directions. The modernist approach to literature says that authors tell stories to audiences,

* http://www.hpfanficarchive.com/.

† http://www.snarry.net/.

‡ https://www.youtube.com/results?search_query=harry+draco+slash. Search done on October 25, 2014.

mediated by the institutional power of publishers, giving authors and publishers the power over meaning. But queer readings restore power to audiences, making them the ultimate meaning makers. J. K. Rowling tells us one story about Harry Potter. Harry Potter fan fiction writers tell us a million more. Can we say that only one version of a fictional story is true?

Beyond the world of slash fiction and queer readings, other forms of LGBTQ engagement with social media seem ripe for queer theory analysis. Just as slash democratizes the world of fiction, social media can democratize the social world by giving greater agency to individuals who often feel constrained. It provides a kind of agency to speak and to act in a world where many people, including LGBTQ people, do not have opportunities to tell their stories. Social media is a kind of tool for the project of queering the world.

Finally, social media is the ultimate space of play. We have great freedom to play with our identities in the space of social media. Some people maintain multiple accounts on multiple platforms to reflect different aspects of their identities. Playing with gender and sexuality is actually rather common in social media. But anytime someone rewrites their profile on a social media platform, including platforms designed for dating and sex, they are engaging in a kind of queer play that reveals the performative nature of life and undermines the notion that the self is fixed.

Although many of the studies described in the sections that follow are not presented through a queer theory lens, they all highlight the ways that people play and engage in sexuality focused identity-work using the tools of social media.

METHODOLOGICAL MOMENT: Evaluating Sources

Throughout this book I cite a wide range of sources that range from books and scholarly journal articles to online news sources and social media posts. In academic scholarship, evaluating sources to identify those that are most trustworthy is an important issue. But it is also an issue that is under some transformation in the era of social media and the network society. Historically, scholars were wary of sources that could not be obtained at the library, which limited them to books, journals, reference sources, and archives of newspapers and magazines. But scholars

continues

METHODOLOGICAL MOMENT: Evaluating Sources *continued*

have changed the way we think about texts, particularly thanks to a field called **cultural studies.** Cultural studies is a scholarly paradigm developed in the 1960s and 1970s, largely within humanities disciplines like literature and history. It essentially involved taking the traditional methods of textual analysis (from historical texts to literary texts) and applying those methods to a broader range of texts. Thanks to cultural studies, scholars now recognize the validity and significance of a wide range of texts that include both **cultural objects** (television shows, films, songs, music videos, tweets, etc.) and **cultural practices** (conversations, performances, protests, eating, etc.).

In scholarship, we recognize two broad types of sources: **primary sources** and **secondary sources**. Primary sources are the original texts that are the subject of our study, and secondary sources are the texts that other scholars have produced about those primary sources. Secondary sources include scholarly books and articles, as well as documentaries.

But the combination of cultural studies and new media give us good reason to question the boundary between primary and secondary sources. If a scholar tweets an analysis of a text, are those tweets a secondary source? Or do the ideas within the tweets only become secondary sources when they are revised, submitted, and published in a more traditional form? The key issue defining a scholarly secondary source is **peer review**. A work that has been reviewed by peers—typically other scholars—is presumed to hold greater credibility than a work that has not been reviewed by peers. Scholars are encouraged to use as many peer-reviewed works as possible among their secondary sources.

But I was never going to find a definitive peer-reviewed discussion of the story behind Chris Crocker's *Leave Britney Alone* video. To piece together that story, I had to delve into the murky waters of nonscholarly, non-peer-reviewed sources that described the events of Britney's meltdown in real time. The journey from *The American Journal of Sociology* to *TMZ* is not an easy path for a scholar to take, but for those of us who study media and popular culture, it is a necessary adventure in the quest for sociological insight.

If we become too caught up in the quest for *authoritative* sources, we fail to question the issues of power that are interwoven with authority. Scholars are experts at their disciplines, but they do not have a monopoly

continues

METHODOLOGICAL MOMENT: Evaluating Sources *continued*

on knowledge about the topics they study. Moreover, positions of tenure in academia and positions of power in scholarly publishing are overwhelmingly held by straight white men, who tend to promote people like themselves, for reasons of both discrimination and homophily (discussed in chapter 2). As a result of homophily in scholarship, many important perspectives are difficult to find in peer-reviewed sources. In order to gain a broader perspective, we have to be willing to consider a wider range of perspectives and expertise. We also have to listen to the expertise of those who are working in the fields that we study.

The University of Illinois at Urbana-Champaign offers a useful list of tips for evaluating online sources that includes the following:

1. How did you find the page?
2. What is the site's domain?
3. What is the authority of the page?
4. Is the information accurate and objective?
5. Is the page current?
6. Does the page function well?*

These questions are a helpful starting point, but I would add the following questions as useful tools for evaluating both online sources and social media sources:

1. What is the purpose of the site or account? Is its goal to sell products, convey information, inspire action, express dissent, or something else?
2. Who is the audience? Is the site or account appealing to peers, customers, participants, citizens, or some other group? How much do we know about the audience demographics?
3. Where does the money come from? For individual social media accounts, there is little or no money in question, but for websites and accounts belonging to political groups, media sources, nonprofit organizations, academic institutions, and

*http://www.library.illinois.edu/ugl/howdoi/webeval.html.

continues

METHODOLOGICAL MOMENT: Evaluating Sources *continued*

corporations, we need to ask about the funding source behind the information.

4. How does any single post sit within the larger context of the information shared on this site or platform? If you find an article online, you need to evaluate more than just the article. You need to examine the home page of the site to gain an understanding of what kind of site it is. You need to read the "About" page, sometimes hidden at the bottom. For commercial sites, look for an "Investor Relations" page as well.

There is no clear line between definitive sources and poor sources. All sources sit on a continuum, and it can be difficult to evaluate exactly where they rest. We have to be willing to look at sources that sit in a murky place on that continuum, because these sources are real texts that shape the world we live in. But we also need effective strategies for making sense of this murky information.

THE STUDY OF SEXUALITY IN SOCIAL MEDIA

Greg Bowe (2010), a social researcher in Dublin, Ireland, conducted a small (eleven participants) qualitative study using interviews to examine the role that Facebook plays as a mediating force in romantic relationships. He found that individuals in relationships experience Facebook as both a tool and a problem as they navigate the course of the romance. While some of his participants felt quite positive about sharing a relationship status online ("In a relationship with . . .) or using Facebook as a way to commit a public display of affection (PDA), others experienced these moves with concern that they were expressions of jealousy and possession. Ex-partners are also a major problem on Facebook. Some participants expressed concern that their partners maintain a Facebook connection to their exes. If the connection is maintained, the ex may also appear online without warning to comment on a status. Others expressed a desire for their partners to untag their exes from photographs. Despite the problems created by Facebook, the author also notes that the social networking site is a useful tool for cementing a relationship, both for its contribution to the interpersonal dynamics of the couple and for its capacity to make declarations of love and romance public. The author notes that social media relationship statuses and other forms of online PDA function like a lower order wedding: they alert the world that the members of this couple have declared a romantic interest in each other.

When the relational tools of Facebook are taken to their extreme, it can lead to behaviors frequently described as stalking. Kasey Chaulk and Tim Jones (2011) use the term online obsessive relational intrusion (o-ORI) to describe a variety of behaviors that a Facebook user may engage in that allow people to engage with and monitor others' behavior—from tracking event attendance to "poking" people. Chaulk and Jones use an online survey to gather data about people's experiences with these behaviors on Facebook. They randomly assigned some participants to answer based on their own behaviors toward another and others to answer based on behaviors that others had directed toward them. These two groups were subdivided into groups that answered based on behaviors to/from an ex-intimate partner, a close friend, and an acquaintance. They sent the survey to 1,022 people (drawn from e-mail lists of college faculty members) and received 230 responses.

The two studies discussed above highlight the possibilities and pitfalls of focusing either on depth or on breadth. Bowe is able to capture a lot of the dynamics of navigating Facebook while in a relationship, but his ability to make claims about those dynamics is limited because he only has eleven participants, all of whom are college students in an urban environment in Ireland. Chaulk and Jones can make much broader claims, but the nature of their survey makes it difficult to understand the Facebook behaviors of their participants. For example, 47 percent of respondents admitted to looking at what events their ex-partners were attending, but we cannot know their exact intentions in this behavior. Perhaps they were checking their exes' events in order to avoid running into them at a party hosted by a mutual friend. Or perhaps they have stayed close to their ex-partner and they checked event attendance in hopes of confirming they would run into this friend, who happens to be an ex-partner.

Facebook is frequently singled out among social media as creating a problem for romantic relationships. Anthropologist Ilana Gershon (2011) found this to be the case in her interviews with seventy-two college students about their experiences with new media during periods of romantic breakup. She argues that Facebook is not conducive to romantic relationships because it trains us to be "neoliberal selves" that function as collections of assets always seeking to increase our social value. "The US version of neoliberalism requires that people should be selves that reflexively understand themselves to be metaphorically structured like an idealized US business" (2011, 873). What does that have to do with Facebook?

> My interviewees were explicit about the ways in which their Facebook profiles gave them an arena in which to perform a self that was referentially tied to who they understood themselves to be but was not an exact match. This difference between their real life selves and their Facebook selves offers them a reflexive distance between who they are "truly" and who they are as a compilation of skills and alliances. (Gershon 2011, 878)

Gershon argues that Facebook trains us to behave in particular ways, for example, looking for evidence of a loved one's claims on their Facebook wall (proof that they have ended communication with an ex, or are not flirting with others), and that her respondents found themselves disliking their new Facebook behaviors. Many of her interviewees either chose to cancel their Facebook memberships to preserve future romantic relationships or at least talked explicitly about why Facebook and romance cannot coexist.

Another issue of concern that is frequently mentioned with regard to sexuality and social media is **sexting**, the production and dissemination of text, images, and/or video of a sexual nature, often used in the context of a sexual or romantic relationship (or a desired relationship) via mobile phone, the Internet, or a social media platform. Communications scholar Amy Adele Hasinoff (2012) takes an approach to the issue of sexting that some might find surprising. She argues that sexting constitutes a form of media production that, despite a variety of possible negative consequences, can also be beneficial for youth as part of their sexual and relational development. She emphasizes that sexting as media production on the part of girls allows them to practice with communication and self-expression. It lets them explore their own sense of pleasure, in a world that frequently treats women as sources for male pleasure. The anonymous character of some forms of sexting can allow girls (and boys, particularly young people from marginalized groups) to find supportive communities and gather information in ways that might not be available to them in nonanonymous contexts. Finally, treating the *creation* of a sext as a positive form of media production allows for a recognition that abusively distributing a sext without the creator's permission is a form of harassment and abuse. Current policies and practices regarding sexting tend to treat the creation and distribution of a sext as the same process, with no special recognition for the intentions of the media producer. As a result, some law enforcement agencies have charged teens with crimes related to child pornography simply for taking a picture of themselves, while also failing to protect young people, especially girls, who have pictures of themselves distributed against their will. Hasinoff suggests that treating sexting as a form of media production will allow social policy makers to treat social media in a way that is more in line with how we regulate offline interactions.

Communications scholar David Gudelunas (2012) has studied the ways that gay men use social media, including platforms that are designed primarily as hookup sites—sites that connect people with similar sexual interests and facilitate sexual activity, often between strangers. Gudelunas distinguishes between credible and less credible social media, placing hookup sites (Manhunt, Grindr, Adam4Adam, and others) in the less credible category and mainstream social networking (Facebook, Twitter, Tumblr, etc.) in the credible category. Using focus groups with seventy-six individuals and intercept interviews with an additional sixty-five individuals, he argues that gay men turn to hookup sites in order to avoid varying levels of stigma: for their sexual orientation, for their desire to speak about sexuality, or for their specific sexual desires. Online hookup sites, he argues, function as safer forms of cruising because they allow members of stigmatized sexualities to connect within a world that otherwise renders them anonymous. Even in situations in which being gay is not really stigmatized, such as in a gay bar or gay neighborhood, open discussions of sex and of specific sexual desires nevertheless remain relatively marginalized, making the Internet a needed alternative for those seeking a sexual connection.

Gudelunas also argues that gay men use credible social media in distinctly gay ways. Many of his respondents mentioned using Facebook to verify information about a potential sexual partner they had obtained on a hookup site or to get more information and pictures than they received on the hookup site. He quotes one of his respondents explaining this:

> "It's odd, you'll see some guy on like Grindr, and then you'll see the same pic on Facebook as a friend of a friend. And, you, know, on Grindr he's talking about how he likes something insanely kinky, leather or whatever, and then you see he is a lawyer or a dentist and it's just cool." (2012, 360)

Gudelunas uses the term "sexual capital" to explain the kinds of networks that gay men develop on both credible and less credible social media. Perhaps surprisingly, he finds that sexual capital and social capital map neatly onto each other in the lives of gay men. He concludes:

> While much research on SNSs is concerned with the social capital achieved by building networks of friends, gay men indicate that one of their primary uses of SNSs is to accumulate sexual networks that are about a different kind of gratification. For gay men in this study, sexual capital is closely aligned with social capital. (2012, 360)

We need further research to explore the same questions about lesbian and bisexual use of social media and hookup sites, as well as the growing use of hookup sites like Tinder by straight people.

What about particular representations of sexual identity within social media? How is social media used to tell stories and convey messages about sex and identity? Communications scholar Amber Johnson (2013) offers a window into the complex relationship among sexuality, representations, and social media through her case study analysis of the social media sensation Antoine Dodson. Dodson shot to fame through a most improbable scenario. His sister was the victim of an attempted rape in their low-income community of Lincoln Park in Huntsville, Alabama. When the local television affiliate WAFF-48 went to investigate and tell her story, it captured a powerful interview with Dodson, including the statement: "Hide yo kids, hide you wife, and hide yo husband cuz they rapin' er'body up in here."* Video footage drawn from the newscast was posted on YouTube and quickly spread across social networks, which is why Johnson identifies the original video as "viral." Subsequently, YouTube users produced a number of parodies of the original footage, including an autotuned mix known as the "Bed Intruder Song," which is available on iTunes. In comparison to the original viral footage, Johnson calls these subsequent media forms "memes." Whereas viral content becomes unintentionally famous and takes on a life beyond that intended by the original creators, memes take original footage and inject it with new meaning that is clearly intended by the editors/remixers involved. Johnson argues that Dodson's embodiment of a black, gay, southern, and seemingly unintelligent

* Cited in Johnson (2013, 152).

identity makes him vulnerable to misappropriation and stereotypes, particularly a stereotype that she calls the "homo coon": a black male representation that is comedic, buffoonish, and insufficiently masculine. Nevertheless, Dodson also managed to capitalize on his viral fame, garnering enough income to move his family into a new home, becoming a spokesperson for a security system (known as the Bed Intruder App), raising funds for a juvenile diabetes foundation, and performing at the BET hip-hop awards.

> Dodson is exploiting the media in the same way the media exploit him. We can be critical of representations of race, class, sexuality, education level, and gender, but, in the end, Dodson used social media to create a niche for himself, protect his family, and better his life-style. (Johnson 2013, 164–165)

Johnson identifies the double-edged sword that is characteristic of social media. It allows us our fifteen minutes (or more) of fame—during which we may be able to transform our own lives or challenge society—but it also makes us susceptible to the appropriation of our identities for commercial and political purposes. We have agency as makers of culture to inject our messages into the world, but our power is limited by our inability to control how those messages are used or misused.

One group that embraces the capacity to make culture, regardless of the consequences of misappropriation, is the community of drag queens. From the Twitter accounts of Lady Bunny[*] and Mimi Imfurst[†] to the Facebook pages of Martha Graham Cracker[‡] and RuPaul,[§] from the YouTube videos of Hedda Lettuce[¶] and Sharon Needles[**] to the Instagram accounts of Shangela[††] and Tyra Sanchez,[‡‡] drag queens are launching social media campaigns that not only promote their brands but also further their interests. When Facebook attempted in 2014 to require members to use their legal names, an army

* https://twitter.com/LADYBUNNY77.

† https://twitter.com/MimiImfurst.

‡ https://www.facebook.com/MarthaGrahamCracker.

§ https://www.facebook.com/RuPaul.

¶ https://www.youtube.com/user/MissHeddaLettuce.

** https://www.youtube.com/user/SHARONNEEDLESisDEAD.

†† http://instagram.com/itsshangela.

‡‡ http://instagram.com/tyrasanchez.

of drag queens stepped up and said "no!" Drag queens, and many leaders in LGBTQ communities, began a campaign to ban Facebook and recruit consumers over to a new platform called Ello.* Facebook eventually backed off, with Chief Product Manager Chris Cox issuing a striking apology:

> I want to apologize to the affected community of drag queens, drag kings, transgender, and extensive community of our friends, neighbors, and members of the LGBTQ community for the hardship that we've put you through in dealing with your Facebook accounts over the past few weeks.†

The sudden rush to Ello quickly ebbed. Drag queens claimed credit for their community for the policy change.

Drag queens use social media to do both politics and the creative gender work they are known for. Communications scholar and media activist Bradford Nordeen (2014) has examined the ways that drag queens are embracing social media. He likens it to the kind of work that drag queens were doing in the 1980s with experimental video. "It is interesting that this vying for intimacy feels most poignantly rendered through the loquacious Twitter profile" (2014, 14). Social media allows drag queens to perform for an audience immediately, without the burden of scheduling an event. Certainly, events are an important part of the community, but for a handful at least, "Twitter becomes the major work itself" (2014, 14).

Anneliese Singh (2013), a professor of counseling and human development, found that social media plays an important role in the life of trans youth of color. She conducted in-depth interviews with thirteen trans youth of color located in the American South. Although her sample size is very small, the group that she is studying is a small portion of the population that is widely distributed across the nation. Despite a lack of breadth, she was able to achieve some depth in her interviews. All of her interviewees reported using social media and identified it as a powerful tool for their own resilience against transphobia, racism, sexism, and adultism (dominance of adults over the lives of young people). These young people talked about the importance of following role models on Twitter, discovering community on Facebook, and sharing informational resources on YouTube. Many trans youth, especially trans youth of color, do not know anyone else like them. They have

---

* http://sfist.com/2014/10/01/facebook_apparently_backing_down_fr.php.

† https://www.facebook.com/chris.cox/posts/10101301777354543.

a hard time finding trans people to inspire them or even just to encourage them. But social media gives them access to a much larger world that affords them a wealth of social support. These young people also reported difficulty accessing trans resources online at school, because sites with the term "sex" in them were usually blocked. So an attempt to improve the lives of trans youth may need to include a focus on making social media platforms available to them.

THE STUDY OF SEXUALITY WITH SOCIAL MEDIA

Social media provides a space for people to tell their stories and share their voices. For much of the history of social science, our methods have focused on finding ways to hear the perspectives and experiences of the masses. Rather than understanding politics by listening to political leaders, social science seeks to understand the habits and inclinations of the voters (and the nonvoters). Rather than understanding religion by interviewing the clergy, social science seeks to discover the values and beliefs of the laity. The leaders of social institutions matter to social science as well, but the disciplines of social science wrest away any claims that leaders might make to have a monopoly on the right to speak.

But getting to those voices of the masses proves difficult. The interviews, focus groups, and surveys that we have used to learn more about the viewpoints and practices of various groups have always been time-consuming and sometimes expensive. And they have always raised issues of the validity of our claims. How many participants are enough to capture the most important currents in public opinion? Regardless of the problems that social research methods may create, they have always been necessary to gain access to stories of the masses.

Although social media in no way undermines the value of our traditional research methods, it does add a whole new set of tools to our arsenal. Thanks to social media, the masses—or at least some of them—are telling their own stories and placing those stories in a public forum where they are readily available for analysis by social researchers.

Kenta Asakura and Shelley L. Craig (2014) use social media to study the experiences of LGBTQ people, drawing on the amazing stories that have been shared online as part of the It Gets Better Project. This campaign was started by writer and sex advice columnist Dan Savage and his partner, Terry

Miller, as a campaign to combat suicide by LGBTQ youth. The strategy is to use online videos, primarily hosted by YouTube, to let LGBTQ adults share their own stories of overcoming adversity in youth and achieving happiness as adults. It Gets Better utilizes a variety of platforms to share these messages with young people. These platforms include the following:

YouTube channel: https://www.youtube.com/user/itgetsbetterproject
website: http://www.itgetsbetter.org/
Twitter: https://twitter.com/ItGetsBetter
Tumblr blog: http://itgetsbetterproject.tumblr.com/
Facebook: https://www.facebook.com/itgetsbetterproject
Pinterest: http://www.pinterest.com/itgetsbetter/

Asakura and Craig point out that getting access to LGBTQ perspectives can be especially difficult because of the many ways in which they are a vulnerable population. As a result, queer celebrities tend to dominate the attention and discussion. "[The] IGB [It Gets Better] project has provided noncelebrity LGBTQ people with an avenue to share their stories with the public" (2014, 255).

Asakura and Craig's primary goal is to outline themes of resilience in the narratives they study. Stories of resilience provide an important counter-narrative to the dominant story of LGBTQ vulnerability. Scholar Stephen T. Russell (2005) has pressed social researchers to devote more attention to the resilience of LGBTQ people, rather than always framing them as vulnerable and weak. To study resilience in the narratives of LGBTQ people, Asakura and Craig (2014) conducted a qualitative content analysis of twenty-one videos from the Its Gets Better project. They chose to focus only on videos presented by LGBTQ people, not straight allies, who described overcoming a difficult youth. Identifying current employment as a sign of positive adaptation to adulthood, they only analyzed videos that were posted by people identifying by their place of employment. Examples include employment at Apple, Google, Etsy, and Disney.

The authors develop a typology of themes of resilience that appear across these narratives. First, the theme of *leaving hostile social environments* identifies the way that many LGBTQ people began a change toward improving their lives by leaving behind households, hometowns, and other places that had proved dangerous for them. Second, the theme of *experiencing "coming out" in meaningful ways* highlights the fact that officially announcing their sexual identity became pivotal for personal transformation. Third, the theme of *re-membering the social environments* focuses on the ways that LGBTQ people actively and purposively chose the members of their social worlds in order to create a positive and empowering context for their own flourishing. Finally, the theme of *turning challenges into opportunities and strengths* emphasizes the fact that resilience is often found precisely through the darkest moments. For many LGBTQ adults, the darkest moment was a suicide attempt or considering committing suicide. Asakura and Craig quote one storyteller as saying "if this does get better and I'm gone, then I've really screwed up" (2014, 11). That realization became a tool for overcoming the very problems that had pushed the storyteller to the brink of suicide.

A team of medical experts has used social media as an effective site for studying sexual health behaviors (Ross et al. 2013). The European MSM (men who have sex with men) Internet Survey (EMIS) was conducted in the summer of 2010 and had over 180,000 participants. It was conducted online and promoted through gay social media channels under the banner "Be part of something huge!" One publication that came out of the study focused on the issue of internalized homonegativity, as revealed through a series of survey questions, and its relationship with risky sexual behaviors such as not getting tested for HIV. The researchers found that high levels of internalized homonegativity are indeed associated with risky behaviors, which leads them to conclude that tackling HIV requires reducing the stigma surrounding homosexuality. Their study highlights the value of online surveys and of promoting surveys through social media. A similar, though much smaller, study was conducted by researchers at the University of Michigan, addressing a similar issue in the American context (Veinot et al. 2013).

A study using focus groups conducted in Australia found that many young people did not believe social media was an appropriate space for disseminating information about sexual health because sharing such information or participating in an online conversation would expose them to stigma and compromise their carefully crafted online presentations of self (Byron, Albury, and Evers 2013). However, a related study in the United States actually implemented a Facebook campaign to see how effective social media might be as a tool for preventing HIV transmission (Young 2013). The focus in this study was on retention rates in HIV prevention programs, from recruitment to later stages. The author found that participants who are heavy Internet users were twenty-five times more likely to be retained in the study through to later stages. This led him to the conclusion that online campaigns, when the participants are recruited for their heavy Internet and social media use, have the potential to yield good data because of the likelihood of high retention rates.

Maggie Werner (2014) uses social media in a very different way in her examination of responses to the repeal of the US military policy known as "Don't Ask, Don't Tell" (DADT). She uses a method called fantasy-theme analysis (FTA) to study popular discourse leading up to and since the repeal of DADT. While most studies of popular discourse tend to draw from a narrow field of voices by relying on news accounts, Werner is able to access a deeper and less accessible general discourse by tracking social media discussions on Facebook and Twitter. Her concern is that celebrations following the repeal of DADT silenced an important queer and feminist critique of US military actions around the globe. In other words, the repeal of DADT was seen as such a victory for LGBTQ equality that the community then ceased an important critique of the military. I cite the article here as another example of a creative way to conduct social analysis using the tools of social media.

SEXUALITY RESEARCH ON SOCIAL MEDIA

A number of research centers are making great use of social media to share their research with a broad audience and to provide new teaching and research tools for the scholarly community. Here, I highlight a few of those centers and discuss the ways they are using social media to develop new audiences and new levels of engagement with their work.

Institute for Sexual Minority Studies and Services (ISMSS) and the NoHomophobes Project

websites: http://www.ismss.ualberta.ca/ and http://www.nohomophobes.com/
Twitter: @UofASafeSpaces and @Nohomophobes
Facebook: https://www.facebook.com/iSMSS
YouTube: https://www.youtube.com/user/NoHomophobes

The Canadian-based ISMSS is a research center that supports grant-funded research on the lives and needs of sexual and gender minorities. It also runs a variety of programs that train and support organizations that work with sexual and gender minorities. One of its most prominent projects is NoHomophobes, a website that tracks homophobic language on Twitter. Four terms in particular are tracked—faggot, so gay, no homo, and dyke—and visitors can see counts of those terms for today, last week, and all time (dating back to July 5, 2012, when the project started). For example, as I write this at 11:23 p.m. on October 25, 2014, the counts are as follows:

Today (October 25, 2014)

- Faggot: 12,981
- So Gay: 5,536
- No Homo: 3,992
- Dyke: 2,129

Last Week (October 19–October 25, 2014)

- Faggot: 112,851
- So Gay: 43,726
- No Homo: 30,696
- Dyke: 18,979

All Time (July 5, 2012–October 25, 2014)

- Faggot: 29,550,670
- So Gay: 8,322,927
- No Homo: 8,205,458
- Dyke: 3,487,939

A social media marketing firm called Calder Bateman was contracted to build the site. The site has had millions of viewers and won numerous awards.*

The Gay and Lesbian Alliance Against Defamation (GLAAD)

website: http://www.glaad.org/
Twitter: @GLAAD

* http://www.ismss.ualberta.ca/20122013Report.

Facebook: https://www.facebook.com/GLAAD
YouTube: https://www.youtube.com/user/glaadmedia
Pinterest: http://www.pinterest.com/glaad/
Tumblr: http://instagram.com/glaad
Instagram: http://glaad.tumblr.com/
Google+: https://plus.google.com/+glaad
Flickr: https://www.flickr.com/photos/glaad

GLAAD is an advocacy organization that largely focuses on the media. It issues annual reports that are very useful for examining LGBTQ representations in the media, including the following:

- The Network Responsibility Index
- The Studio Responsibility Index
- Where We Are on TV

GLAAD is not yet turning its research attention toward social media, but it is certainly using social media to broadcast its findings and to advocate for changes in response to those findings. In 2012 Facebook became the first social media platform to win an award at the GLAAD Media Awards, taking home a special recognition award for its antibullying work.* Facebook worked with GLAAD and several other organizations to create "A Network of Support," designed to educate and promote practices that diminish bullying.†

The Kinsey Institute

websites: http://www.kinseyinstitute.org/ and http://kinseyconfidential.org/
Twitter: @kinseyinstitute and @kinseycon
Facebook: https://www.facebook.com/kinseyinstitute and https://www.facebook.com/kinseyconfidential
Google+: https://plus.google.com/+kinseyinstitute/posts
YouTube: https://www.youtube.com/user/KinseyInstitute

*http://www.glaad.org/releases/facebook-becomes-first-social-media-company-receive-glaad-media-award.

† https://www.facebook.com/note.php?note_id=161164070571050.

Thanks to the work of Alfred Kinsey, the Kinsey Institute carries the most iconic name in sexuality research. Based at Indiana University, where Alfred Kinsey first began the Institute for Sex Research, the renamed Kinsey Institute supports academic research by graduate students and faculty members across the country. The Kinsey Institute makes use of social media in many ways, but its strongest social media campaign is Kinsey Confidential, a blog-based program to promote sexual health. Participants can submit their own sexual health questions for the Kinsey experts to answer.

CONCLUSION

In 2012, a few days after President Barack Obama announced his support for same-sex marriage, one leader in the world of marketing and technology declared that: "the inherent qualities of social media make the passage of same-sex marriage and equal rights for LGBTQ individuals and families inevitable" (Hoffman 2012). The author, John Hoffman, was then a director of new markets at ZeroDivide, a California-based nonprofit that delivers technology support to community organizations. Hoffman argued that social media makes gay marriage inevitable because "[s]ocial media is about storytelling, and so is the movement toward LGBTQ equality." As he explains, from the political leadership of Harvey Milk to the powerful narratives of the It Gets Better Project, gay politics has focused on the power of stories to disrupt assumptions, undermine stereotypes, and conjure empathy. Social media platforms like Facebook give us more information about more of the people in our lives than we have had access to before, which means many people discover through Facebook that they have partial or even extensive networks of gay friends and family members.

Whatever vulnerabilities social media creates for gay people may be no more than the vulnerabilities they face offline, where the real problems facing LGBTQ communities are violence, homelessness, and poverty, especially for queer youth and queer people of color. In the face of these issues, queer activists are taking to social media to build networks, share information, and tell their stories. Social scientists need to pay attention to this queer experience with social media to better understand both technology and sexuality. Moreover, the technology of social media can transform the ways that we gather data about the world and direct our findings toward policy, advocacy, and social change.

Chris Crocker and Brendan Jordan are just two of a huge host of queer social media artists who are embracing social media as a tool for challenging assumptions and transforming society. Other queer social media artists include Todrick Hall, Davey Wavey, Lohanthony, and Drew Droege. The artistic disciplines they employ include comedy, fashion, music, and drama. But for most of these artists, social media itself is a central discipline. They invest high levels of time, money, and creativity in their social media creations. And they are all very prolific artists, churning out hundreds and even thousands of images, videos, and texts (from tweets to essays).

The examples discussed in this chapter constitute what Manuel Castells would call a resistance identity because they are pressing back against the limiting effects of the legitimizing identity of heterosexuality and heteronormativity. I do not put them in the category of project identity because they are not pressing for the level of social transformation that we see in other cases. I discuss Occupy Wall Street and Black Lives Matter later as examples of project identity.

For both the individual artists like Crocker and Jordan and the creative organizations like It Gets Better and NoHomophobes, the use of social media for creating new narratives of sexuality and identity is crucial to their acts of resistance. And they do this despite the dangers of bullying and harassment. The dangers of social media may be precisely why these artists are utilizing it. Through social media, creative work can be shared with lightning speed. This makes social media a surprisingly effective tool for undermining assumptions and changing minds.

4

Disabling a Meme: Disability Perspectives on Social Media

Picture it.* The setting is either a liquor store or the liquor section of the grocery store. We see the many colorful glass bottles of various liquors on the shelf. A customer in denim shorts and print blouse is reaching for something on the top shelf. Nothing extraordinary, right? But this is an image with text across the top and bottom in all caps:

*Alternatively, go online and search for "George Takei disability meme."

[top]: THERE HAS BEEN A MIRACLE

[bottom]: IN THE ALCOHOL ISLE [*sic*]

A miracle? Why so? Because the woman is standing in front of a wheelchair that she was presumably seated in just moments before.

This is an image that circulated on social media in 2014. Mockery in social media happens every day. Sometimes it targets specific behaviors—that pic you snap at the gym of someone sitting on a bench staring at a phone rather than working out—and sometimes it targets specific groups. Here, a seemingly disabled person is being targeted, perhaps as an affront to anyone who fakes a disability in exchange for social benefits, perhaps as an attack on all people with disabilities.

The image gained a spotlight when the actor George Takei posted it on Facebook, adding his own caption: "She was filled with the holy . . . spirits." Although at first the image received the usual likes, shares, and inane comments, a backlash quickly developed that was led by activists and influencers in the disability community.

THAT'S SO TAKEI

George Takei is most famous for his role as Hikaru Sulu on the original television series *Star Trek*, as well as the many *Star Trek* films, up until the recent reboot. As a young child, he spent time in two Japanese internment camps during World War II, first in Arkansas and then in his native California. This period in his life was the inspiration for his award-winning 2012 play *Allegiance*, which debuted on Broadway in 2015. In 2005 he first shared with the media the fact that he is gay, although he had already been with his partner Brad for eighteen years and was certainly not living in the closet. Since that time, he has become one of the most outspoken celebrity activists for LGBTQ rights.

In 2011 Takei embraced the role of activist when Tennessee state legislators introduced a bill to ban teachers from using the words "gay" and "homosexual" at school. It became known as the "Don't Say Gay" law. Among other things, the law would have made it nearly impossible for LGBTQ students to discuss their sexual identities with their teachers. The proposed law raised concerns for LGBTQ leaders about possible impacts on kids. What would happen if, for instance, a student was bullied for being gay? How would teachers talk to the bullies under such a language ban? How would they console the bullied student? George Takei decided to draw attention to the proposed law by partnering with MoveOn.org to make a video called *Dude, That's So Takei!*[*] In the video Takei offers his name as a gay signifier that can stand in place of the word "gay" under the proposed ban:

> I'm here to tell Tennessee, and LGBT youth, and teachers who would be affected by this law, that I am here for you. In fact, I am lending my name to the cause. Anytime you need to say the word "gay," you can simply say "Takei!"

He then presents an array of merchandise featuring the phrase "It's okay to be Takei," available online, with proceeds going to an unnamed charity.

The Don't Say Gay law never passed, despite being advanced several times by State senator Stacey Campfield before he lost reelection in 2014 (Terkel 2014). As the law faded from the limelight, George Takei's star began to shine brightly again. He had become the new face of equality and had discovered his own power in social media. He had been active on Twitter already and in early 2011 launched his Facebook account, which is liked by just under ten million users as of mid-2016. He posts several times throughout the day, sharing the work only with his husband Brad and an intern (Knapp 2012). He's also active on YouTube[†] and Tumblr[‡] and runs a blog called *That Blog Is So Takei*,[§] but Facebook is the platform on which he is most active. His Facebook page is largely driven by a mix of humor, positivity, and progressive politics.

Given the positive and progressive focus of Takei's work on Facebook, it was surprising when he posted the disability/miracle **meme** on August 2, 2014. Disappointed fans and disability activists began responding immediately, calling on the actor to remove the image and issue an apology. At first he insisted that the humorous intent and the multiple possible interpretations rendered the image safe and the issues fair game, stating: "If I had to 'take down' everything that some section of the universe found offensive, this

---

* http://front.moveon.org/dude-thats-so-takei-b.

† https://www.youtube.com/user/allegiancebway

‡ http://georgetakei.tumblr.com.

§ http://georgetakei.com/that-blog-is-so-takei/.

would be a lonely and barren page indeed."* But he changed course eleven days later and issued a lengthy apology. Summarizing the meme and his quip about it, he writes:

> I've just come back from an extended trip to England, and I came home to a large number of fan emails concerning a meme I shared more than a week ago. In that meme, a woman in a wheelchair was standing up to reach for a bottle of liquor in the store, and the caption said something about a miracle in the alcohol aisle. To this I added a quip about her being touched by the holy spirits.
>
> I did not expect the level of offense this meme caused. I had naturally just thought of those movies where the evangelical preacher miraculously cures someone who was disabled. What I'd never really considered before so many fans wrote in is how that portrayal of disabled persons is filled with ignorance and prejudice—two things I never want to promote, even inadvertently.

What Takei is contending with here is the issue of voice. His social media projects, particularly Facebook, reflect a unique voice that emphasizes a mixture of humor and progressive politics. Politically, Takei has been a champion of equal opportunity. In posting a meme that ridiculed a person with a disability, he essentially violated his own voice.

He continues:

> The fact that I was surprised by the response the wheelchair meme received indicates that I do indeed lack knowledge, and some sensitivity, over what is clearly a hot button issue, and that I and others can take this as an opportunity not to dig in, but rather to open up to the stories and experiences of those in the disabled community. I appreciate those who took the time to write in. I wish I'd had the chance to respond sooner, but until today I was not able to go through all the mail I'd received.
>
> So to those who were hurt by my posts on this issue, I ask you please to accept this apology. To those who think I shouldn't have to apologize, I

* That comment was removed along with the original post, eventually, but a screen capture used in a blog post is available at http://rampyourvoice.com/2014/08/19/the-george-takei-disabled-meme-controversy-the-offense-response-public-apology/.

want to remind you that I get to decide what I apologize for, so there's no need to come to my defense.*

By most accounts, the apology was surprisingly sincere (for a celebrity) and seemed to reflect a legitimate learning experience for the actor. One blogger called it "classy, down-to-earth, articulate."† The apology reflects the fact that the meme seemed out of line with the mission of Takei's Facebook work, so the apology has the effect of bringing Takei's position on disability into alignment with his other views.

READING A MEME

Before I examine the role of the image in social media, I want to see what meaningful information I can gather from reading the image itself. The image must be read on its own terms, as it comes with no contextual information. We do not know who took the photograph, who added the text, or anything about the woman in the image. As a still image with no context, the wheelchair serves as a cue to the viewer that this woman is disabled. Most people with disabilities do not use a wheelchair, and there are times when a nondisabled person might use a chair, but the *image of the wheelchair* is a signifier of disability. It is the image used to label parking spaces and other resources that are designated for people with disabilities. So regardless of what we can know about the person, we have a strong indication that we are meant to interpret the image as portraying a person with a disability.

The next major signifier is the word "miracle." In the context of George Takei's post, the word works in tandem with his claim that the woman pictured is filled with the holy spirit(s). These are references to Christianity, but they indicate a very specific form of Evangelical Protestant Christianity associated with televangelism and mega-churches. Consumers of American popular culture are accustomed to seeing images of church members coming forward in response to a call from the minister, sharing testimony about strife and a declaration of faith, and then receiving a prayer from the minister for a miracle of healing. Perhaps the congregant falls over, an indication of

* The apology can be found at https://www.facebook.com/georgehtakei/posts/1026144020748384. I have archived it at http://archive.is/9wkWq.

† http://robinstoynest.com/Toys/2014/08/11/another-gay-icon-misses-the-mark-with-disability-humour/.

receiving the holy spirit, and then the minister declares that a miracle has taken place and the worshipper has been healed. It sounds like a sacred moment, except that many of these ministers are considered scam artists and their followers are presumed to be naïve and desperate, due in part to their physical conditions and in part to their financial conditions. So ultimately the image of the miracle-working televangelist is an image of a charlatan conducting his profane business in the heart of a sacred space. Televangelists are the proverbial money-traders in the temple who need to be thrown out, and the way that we have done that in contemporary society has been to ridicule them in popular culture.

But there is no miracle-working priest in this image, only a woman supposedly receiving a miracle in the liquor aisle. Our pop culture contempt has shifted from the charlatan to the faithful. When we look at the woman in this image, we might be inclined to think of the narrator in the Janis Joplin song "Mercedes Benz," asking the "Lord" to buy her, in successive turns, a Mercedes Benz, a color TV, and a night on the town. Perhaps she sings "Prove that you love me, and buy the next round" as she reaches for her bottle of choice. In the absence of a minister, we are left treating the miracle recipient as the scam artist.

The image taps into fears that people with disabilities cannot be trusted. The presumption is that they are faking or exaggerating their disabilities in order to receive government benefits. In an incident in 2016, for example, a conservative tow truck driver who was faulted for refusing service to and abandoning a disabled woman due to her Bernie Sanders bumper sticker noted that "there's a huge difference between being disabled and drawing disability" (quoted in Liebelson 2016). His statement reflects a widely held notion in American culture that there are two kinds of disabled persons. Those who are *being disabled* have real conditions that are part of the essence of their bodies. In sociology, we use the term **"essentialism"** to describe beliefs that explain human identity as inscribed on our bodies and presumed to be real or unchanging. Those who are *drawing disability* are frauds who fake their disability for the sake of government benefits. The distinction implies that all people who draw disability are frauds. In American popular culture, those who are *being disabled* are presented as heroes who overcome great adversity and never let their bodies limit what they can do. Those who are *drawing disability* are presented as scam artists draining federal funds.

So when the woman in the image stands up to reach for a bottle on the top shelf, the message is clear: she is a fraud who bought a wheelchair in order to gain access to disability benefits, and now she is using those taxpayer dollars to purchase alcohol, which reveals the truly corrupt nature of her soul. Had she reached for a loaf of bread or a bottle of water, the picture would never have been taken, even though the act of standing would seem no less miraculous.

Of course we don't know if the woman in the image is drawing disability at all. One woman commented on Facebook:

> The woman in the picture is my personal friend's mother. When it became a meme a few years ago she thought it was the funniest thing ever. Her mother is not disabled, she was recovering from ankle surgery.*

I cannot verify the veracity of the post, but that is beside the point. The comment on Facebook reflects the fact that when we see a woman standing up from a wheelchair to reach for a bottle of liquor, there are a variety of possible meanings to what we are seeing:

1. She could be a person with a disability who has difficulty with movement and uses a wheelchair for mobility, but who is nevertheless able to stand.
2. She could be a person with an injury, but who does not identify as disabled, who has difficulty with movement and uses a wheelchair for mobility but is nevertheless able to stand.
3. She could be a person with neither a disability nor an injury who, for reasons only she knows, uses a wheelchair for mobility. Perhaps she is an actress preparing for a role as a person with a disability.
4. She could be a fraud who is drawing disability but is not disabled or injured in any way.
5. She could be a person with a disability, or an injury, who is indeed experiencing a miracle.

All of these, except perhaps the last, are reasonable interpretations of that moment. But this controversy is not about a moment, it is about an image. When someone takes a photograph of that moment and captions it "THERE HAS BEEN A MIRACLE IN THE ALCOHOL ISLE," that person is foreclosing several possible interpretations and imposing a meaning of their own

* An archive copy of the page can be found at http://archive.is/9wkWq.

choosing: that the woman is indeed a fake, wasting her disability check on booze.

The many meanings of alcohol are important here, too. Do people with disabilities have the right to drink? Do people who receive government assistance have the right to drink? Alcohol consumption is not quite universal, but it is common across the world and throughout history. Alcohol represents celebration and leisure, but in American popular culture it also represents vice and a lack of self-control. I contend that if we simply remove the wheelchair from the image, what's left might not be meme-worthy, but many viewers would still bristle at the image of what appears to be a lower income person buying alcohol. Of course they would have to rely on assumptions about her clothing to make a conclusion about her social class, which is obviously fraught with danger, but we make conclusions based on clothing and appearance all the time. However, if we remove the wheelchair and place her in business attire or a stylish dress, the image would offer no cause for concern or judgment.

In other words, American popular culture tends to treat leisure and celebration as a privilege that is earned through financial success. The poor, who perhaps are more in need of leisure and escape than anyone else, are expected to be austere. They have not earned the right to leisure. Further, we who are middle or upper class often believe that we have earned the right to judge them because we presume they survive thanks to government benefits that are funded by our tax dollars.

Have I read too much into this image? I don't think so. Consider the interpretation offered by one disability blogger:

> It says your illness and your experience is a joke. When they laugh at such an image they are essentially saying you, your illness, your challenges, pain etc. are meaningless. When those who use a wheelchair but can still mobilise independently over short distances see such an image it is hard not to take offence. We know the mental and emotional challenge it can take to simply accept the need for a wheelchair. We know that a wheelchair means *difference* at an age where most are simply out living life, starting careers, studying, having children or travelling. We know that every time we head out into the world someone will find our life a joke. Or, if you are unlucky enough to be this woman, you and your situation become a beacon for global mockery.*

* http://bobisdysautonomia.blogspot.com.au/2014/03/this-is-not-funny.html.

Images are social structures. They enable image makers to share meaning and enable viewers to interpret meaning. The meanings may be multiple, but they are not limitless. The image itself constrains interpretation to a list of possible meanings, and viewers determine which of those meanings they believe based on how much the interpretation resonates with comparable messages coming from other social experiences. The disability/miracle meme resonates with the familiar image of the fraudulent evangelist and insecurities about the fraudulent disabled.

METHODOLOGICAL MOMENT: Interpretive Sociology and Thick Description

In the preceding section I have used the methods of **thick description** and **interpretive sociology** to unwrap the wide range of meanings that are embedded in the disability/miracle meme. Interpretive sociology was first outlined by Max Weber in his two-volume work *Economy and Society: An Outline of Interpretive Sociology*, published in 1922 (Weber 1978). According to Weber, all social actors, which is to say all people, are driven by motivations that are filled with meaning, and these meanings are shaped by everyday interactions with other people, institutions, and the whole social milieu. Thus: "[I]t is the task of the sociologist to be aware of this motivational situation and to describe and analyze it, even though it has not actually been concretely part of the conscious intention of the actor; possibly not at all, at least not fully" (Weber 1978, 10). Did the person who created the "Miracle in the Alcohol Isle" meme consciously intend that the image would have all of the meanings that I have described here? Perhaps not, but the image carries those meanings nonetheless, because they are woven into the fabric of American culture, just as the meme maker is also woven into that fabric.

The anthropologist Clifford Geertz picked up the mantle of interpretive analysis from Weber and used it to develop his method of thick description. He explains: "Believing, with Max Weber, that man is an animal suspended in webs of significance he himself has spun, I take culture to be those webs, and the analysis of it to be therefore not an experimental science in search of law but an interpretive one in search of meaning" (Geertz 1973, 5). Geertz's method of thick description is a form of interpretation that focuses on social discourse, fleeting details, and microscopic

continues

METHODOLOGICAL MOMENT:
Interpretive Sociology and Thick Description *continued*

analysis. It involves close readings, but there is an important distinction between *reading closely* and *reading into*. I have tried to focus here on a close reading that identifies key meanings that actually are embedded in this image. The idea that meaning is open to interpretation is often misunderstood as a statement that an image (or text) can mean absolutely anything. In truth, the act of interpretation involves reading the details of an image and trying to understand the meaning of those details within a given cultural context. In that sense, rather than reading into the image, I have tried to read out of it.

One unique aspect of conducting interpretive sociology in virtual spaces is that the importance of the original context is minimized or even negated. I do not want to ignore the fact that the woman in the disability/miracle meme is a real person who lives somewhere in this world, has a name and feelings, and may or may not be aware of her presence in this controversy. But I also have no way of tracking her down and no way of tracking down the photographer or the meme maker (the person who added the text may or may not have been the photographer). So as a virtual ethnographer, deeply concerned with the issue of context, I have limited access to the original context for this image. But the technological reproduction of the image allows it to be viewed in a multitude of new contexts, offering a wide range of new possible interpretations and impacts. My work as a virtual ethnographer in this chapter has been to interpret the image through a range of possible lenses.

To take the project even further, I could interview a random sampling of people to ask them how they interpret the image and perhaps contrast those views with a random sampling of persons with a disability. I could even arrange to do those interviews online, presenting them with the meme in a setting that resembles how they might stumble upon the image while surfing through Facebook. Another form of thick description in virtual ethnography is to observe people as they use the Internet and social media, which is different from observing the media itself, as I do in this book. All are legitimate forms of virtual ethnography, but each comes with its own unique challenges.

READING DISABILITY

Is the woman in the disability/miracle meme actually disabled? It seems like a fair question, but "actually disabled" is our first stumbling block. Disability is not a medical category and is not diagnosed by doctors, despite the perception that the word is a medical term. In reality, "disability" is a political and cultural term. Politically, disability refers to a bureaucratic process of determining which individuals qualify for certain accommodations that are often referred to as benefits or entitlements. A doctor may play a role in confirming this qualification, but not in the form of a medical diagnosis. At the federal level in the United States, the definition of "disability" is variable and changing. Currently the following language is used by the American Community Survey (ACS), conducted by the US Census Bureau:

> - Hearing difficulty: deaf or having serious difficulty hearing.
> - Vision difficulty: blind or having serious difficulty seeing, even when wearing glasses.
> - Cognitive difficulty: Because of a physical, mental, or emotional problem, having difficulty remembering, concentrating, or making decisions.
> - Ambulatory difficulty: Having serious difficulty walking or climbing stairs.
> - Self-care difficulty: Having difficulty bathing or dressing.
> - Independent living difficulty: Because of a physical, mental, or emotional problem, having difficulty doing errands alone such as visiting a doctor's office or shopping.
>
> Respondents who report any one of the six disability types are considered to have a disability.*

Using this definition of disability, the ACS estimates that 12.3 percent of Americans are considered disabled, as of 2014.† This definition is not based

---

* http://www.census.gov/people/disability/methodology/acs.html.

† http://factfinder.census.gov/faces/tableservices/jsf/pages/productview.xhtml?pid=ACS_14_5YR_S1810&prodType=table.

on a list of conditions, but rather on a series of questions about how respondents interact with the world around them.

The definition of disability used by the ACS is narrower than that used by another census report, the Survey of Income and Program Participation (SIPP). The SIPP report on disability explains its disability definition as follows:

> People who have disability in the communicative domain reported one or more of the following:
>
> 1. Was blind or had difficulty seeing.
> 2. Was deaf or had difficulty hearing.
> 3. Had difficulty having their speech understood.
>
> People who have disability in the mental domain reported one or more of the following:
>
> 1. Had a learning disability, an intellectual disability, developmental disability or Alzheimer's disease, senility, or dementia.
> 2. Had some other mental or emotional condition that seriously interfered with everyday activities.
>
> People who have disability in the physical domain reported one or more of the following:
>
> 1. Used a wheelchair, cane, crutches, or walker.
> 2. Had difficulty walking a quarter of a mile, climbing a flight of stairs, lifting something as heavy as a 10-pound bag of groceries, grasping objects, or getting in or out of bed.
> 3. Listed arthritis or rheumatism, back or spine problem, broken bone or fracture, cancer, cerebral palsy, diabetes, epilepsy, head or spinal cord injury, heart trouble or atherosclerosis, hernia or rupture, high blood pressure, kidney problems, lung or respiratory problem, missing limbs, paralysis, stiffness or deformity of limbs, stomach/digestive problems, stroke, thyroid problem, or tumor/ cyst/growth as a condition contributing to a reported activity limitation. (Brault 2012)

The language above is used to determine the presence of a disability. If a respondent indicates "yes" to any of these questions, they are then asked to indicate if they are actually *unable* to engage in any of the activities described. If unable to engage in any of those activities, the respondent is then identified as severely disabled. SIPP's broader definition of disability results in a significantly higher calculation of the proportion of Americans who are disabled. According to SIPP data from 2010, 18.7 percent of Americans reported having a disability and 12.6 percent reported having a severe disability. These are roughly the same numbers as found in the 2005 SIPP report (Brault 2012). Table 4.1 summarizes the key findings from the census regarding disability. Note that the last column uses 2011 ACS data to indicate that nearly one-third of recipients of government assistance report having a disability.

TABLE 4.1. Key Census Findings Regarding Disability in America

	SIPP 2005	SIPP 2010	ACS 2014	ACS 2011
Percent of Americans with a Disability	18.7% (12.0% with a severe disability)[1]	18.7% (12.6% with a severe disability)[1]	12.3%[2]	30.4% of recipients of government assistance[3]

[1]*Source:* Brault (2012).
[2]*Source:* US Census Bureau American Fact Finder, http://factfinder.census.gov/faces/tableservices/jsf/pages/productview.xhtml?pid=ACS_14_5YR_S1810&prodType=table.
[3]*Source:* Boursiquot and Brault (2013).

I quote the two definitions of disability at length because these definitions, like the disability/miracle meme, are social structures that are infused with meaning. The variance in the definitions highlights the fact that disability is a social construct. When we call something a social construct, that in no way means that it is not real. Rather, calling it a social construct is a way of identifying what kind of reality it is. Disability, though based on the experience of embodiment, is a social reality rather than a biological reality. From the political perspective, disability is social because it serves a function that is grounded in policy making: determining who qualifies for certain entitlements and measuring the proportion of the population that is eligible.

From a cultural perspective, the function of disability is to create a two-tiered classification of human bodies: disabled and nondisabled. Nondisabled bodies are presumed normal, while disabled bodies are rendered pathological, deficient, and in need of intervention. If this seems harsh, remember that disability is a historically new concept and that in earlier periods of history people with disabilities were often sold into freak shows or subjected to institutionalization and isolation.

Why have a two-tiered classification of human bodies? Disability is one of many systems that help to distribute resources like education, income, wealth, and power in unequal ways across society. Disability is part of what Patricia Hill Collins calls the "matrix of domination" (1990, 18), along with race, class, and gender, and a whole range of interlocking systems of inequality. In other words, the *function* of disability cannot be understood apart from a critical analysis of how disability intersects with issues of power.

CRIP THEORY

Organized widespread disability activism appeared in the 1970s. Perhaps the most prominent moment in disability activism was the "We Will Ride" Denver bus protests of 1978, led by the Americans Disabled for Accessible Public Transit (ADAPT). These protests slowly began to effect change, starting with the introduction of lifts on buses in a number of cities around the nation. The activism continued throughout the 1980s and eventually resulted in the 1992 Americans with Disabilities Act (ADA), a sweeping legislative fiat that is meant to guarantee equal access in employment, education, commercial spaces, transportation, and communications technology for people with disabilities. As policy changes have moved people with disabilities more into mainstream American life, many radical disability activists and leaders have fought to retain the uniqueness of disability identities and to celebrate the queerness of disability culture.

The academic discipline of disability studies developed in the 1980s and has a variety of intersections with disability politics. Campuses have often served as a site for disability protests, particularly with regard to educational access. Campus classrooms have also increasingly become spaces in which questions of disability can be explored. Disability studies is an interdisciplinary field that includes aspects of both the humanities and social sciences, as well as perspectives from law, education, communications, and natural sciences.

Crip theory is one of the many contributions that have been made to scholarship by disability studies. Like radical disability politics, crip theory embraces the margins of disability life. "Crip" is short for cripple, which is a deliberate, powerful, and divisive word. "Cripple" is a derogatory term that has been used to insult many people with disabilities. After a long history in the margins and in freak shows, why would people with disabilities now embrace terms like cripple or crip?

Many do not. Many people with disabilities are eager for full participation in American life—at work, at school, at home, and in the community—and have no interest in highlighting or celebrating their disabilities. But others treat disability as a core part of their identity, something that makes them unique and gives them a special vantage point on the world. They argue that disability is a badge of honor and a culture of pride. They see the mainstreaming of disability as an assault on their culture, history, values, and identity.

The embrace of "crip" as a label for an important theoretical perspective in disability studies reflects a commitment to the radical perspective and a denial of the assumption that people with disabilities just want to be like everyone else. Like the use of "queer" in queer politics or queer theory, crip is intended to be polarizing and is chosen precisely because it demands a conversation about radical disability politics. That conversation asks difficult questions like the following:

- Why should deaf people get cochlear implants? What's wrong with being deaf?
- Why should pregnant women have tests to see if they will deliver a child that has disabilities? Is the abortion of fetuses with disabilities a kind of genocide against disability culture?
- How can we talk about disability in a way that avoids treating disabled people as pathetic victims in need of sympathy?
- Where does disability sit in the matrix of romance and sexuality? Does having desire for a person with a disability equate to fetishizing the disability? How do people with disabilities express their sexual desires in a culture that is both squeamish about sex and discriminatory against disability?

The radical character of crip theory is perhaps best exemplified in a spoken word performance by the artist and activist Cheryl Marie Wade, who is also known as the "queen mother of gnarly." She says:

> Culture. It's about passing the word. And disability culture is passing the word that there's a new definition of disability and it includes *power*.
>
> Culture. New definitions, new inflections. No longer just "poor cripple." Now also "CRIPPLE" and, yes, just "cripple." A body happening. (Wade 1994)*

Embracing the word "crip" is also a signifier that crip theory is dangerous. The word invokes both a derogatory term for people with disabilities *and* a notorious gang that is based in Los Angeles, with wings in major cities across the United States. The connection is not a coincidence. The Crips were originally called the Cribs, a name that referred to the young age of the members, who seemed to join straight out of the crib. In the early 1970s it became common for leaders in the gang to walk with canes, which was meant to mark their status as "pimps." Walking with a cane also made them "cripples," and the merger of Crib and cripple yielded Crip.

Crip activism and crip theory are as dangerous as a gang, not because of violence but because of the power of their ideas and the ways those ideas force all of us to question our assumptions about the body and the meaning of being normal.

One of these dangerous crip ideas is Robert McRuer's concept of "**compulsory able-bodiedness**" (McRuer 2006, 1). McRuer, an English professor and a leading scholar in disability studies, explains how the concept reveals the connections between disability and sexuality, between crip and queer:

> [T]he system of compulsory able-bodiedness, which in a sense produces disability, is thoroughly interwoven with the system of compulsory heterosexuality that produces queerness: in fact, compulsory heterosexuality is contingent on compulsory able-bodiedness, and vice versa. The relatively extended period, however, during which heterosexuality and able-bodiedness were wedded but invisible (and in need of embodied, visible, pathologized, and policed homosexualities and disabilities) eventually gave way to our own period, in which both dominant identities and nonpathological marginal identities are more visible and even at times

* An excellent video performance of "Disability Culture Rap" is available on YouTube in two parts. Part 1 is at https://www.youtube.com/watch?v=j75aRfLsH2Y. Part 2 is at https://www.youtube.com/watch?v=WTO2vn0dkaU.

> spectacular. Neoliberalism and the condition of postmodernity, in fact, increasingly need able-bodied, heterosexual subjects who are visible and spectacularly tolerant of queer/disabled existences. (2006, 2)

Not an easy explanation to follow, to be sure. Compulsory able-bodiedness describes a social system that is obsessed with identity categories and needs workers and consumers to fit into these categories in clear ways. McRuer claims that compulsory able-bodiedness is interlocked with compulsory heterosexuality in a system of inequality that is primarily concerned with consolidating power and resources in the hands of a wealthy minority. Marginalized sexualities spent the twentieth century in the closet, and marginalized disabilities spent the twentieth century in freak shows and institutions. Both of these overlapping groups have moved from invisibility to visibility. Visibility is not the same as liberation. The visibility of queer and disabled bodies has yielded new forms of policing those bodies.

The disability/miracle meme is one of those forms of policing. It sends a powerful missive about disabled bodies. That missive does not disregard all disability out of hand; rather, it spells out the terms of what it means to be the right kind of person with a disability. Those terms start with an insistence that nondisabled people have the right to police disabilities. In a wheelchair, but able to stand? Your disability is not authentic. Even if an argument can be made for the authenticity of the disability, the behavior of the disabled body is an additional site of social policing. The realness of the disability must be performed ad nauseam. As one disability blogger explained, in a reflection on the disability/miracle meme:

> I went for years without using "handicapped" parking spaces because I was afraid of what people would think when I got out of my car and walked into a store. I use a permit now, but I still feel weird and embarrassed when I catch someone looking at me for an extra few moments as I leave my car on foot. I feel like I have to explain myself, which would just be weird, so I don't. Instead I just have a moment of anxiety. Which isn't horrible or anything, but it's something I don't need.*

---

* http://disabilitythinking.blogspot.com/2014/08/the-george-takei-controversy-my-two.html.

So even if the woman in the meme has an acceptable story to explain why she is able to stand but uses a wheelchair, she is nevertheless expected to perform her disability by remaining seated at all times, so as to avoid confusing the nondisabled audience of her performance. The perspective in the photograph tells us who that audience might be: everyone. If someone is behind you, and you cannot see them and do not know they are there, you must still maintain the performance.

The consequences of not maintaining the performance are vast. First, the individual is ridiculed in the public forum of social media—a forum in which she is rendered silent. There is no central Internet node where she can focus her defense and speak against her accusers. Second, the pictured woman stands in for all people with disabilities. Through this meme, they are given notice: "You are suspect and under surveillance." Third, the meme tells the bulk of its viewers that they are normal, legitimate, and preferred, because of all the ways they are not like this woman. The image affirms their able-bodiedness. Fourth, the meme and associated social media discussion (comments, likes, shares, etc.) contribute to a public policy discussion that threatens to revoke the strides made by disability activists over the past several decades. Although the meme says nothing explicit about disability benefits, it rests on a presumption that the audience will assume with the meme maker that the pictured woman is a fraud who uses the wheelchair in order to gain access to taxpayer-funded disability entitlements. The message is that disability is a fraud, and the able-bodied taxpayer is the victim.

If the disability/miracle meme demonstrates the dangers of getting off-script in the performance of disability, **inspiration porn** models the ideal path for visible disabilities. Inspiration porn refers to any celebration of the exceptional success of disabled bodies. To find an example, conduct an image search for the question "What's your excuse?" What comes up are lots of memes of disabled bodies, many of them missing limbs, achieving great feats in basketball, weight lifting, gymnastics, and other sports.

Inspiration porn is another form of compulsory able-bodiedness. The presumed viewer is an able-bodied person who is meant to feel insignificant in their achievements in comparison to the unexpected and unusual success of the inspiring disabled bodies. Inspiration porn is designed to whip the able-bodied into shape, literally and figuratively. Literally, these images whip able bodies into shape by getting them to the gym—and engaging in the broad range of consumption associated with getting fit. Figuratively, inspiration porn whips able bodies into shape by demanding productivity at work and beyond. But in policing able bodies toward a very specific performance of compulsory able-bodiedness, inspiration porn also sends strong messages about disability. It says that disabled bodies can be spectacular—to use McRuer's word—but only when they accomplish superhuman feats and only when the able portion of the body is spectacularly beautiful. Thus, we have a recent proliferation of disabled models—male and female—many of whom are veterans or athletes. The visibility of their bodies marks a cultural shift from the invisibility of disability in the twentieth century, but that visibility enables new strategies for policing. As indicated in the comparison of the disability/miracle meme to inspiration porn, the policing of compulsory able-bodiedness impacts all bodies. It impacts them in different ways, but ultimately demonstrates that all bodies are subject to scrutiny and control by the matrix of domination and oppression.

Another aspect of crip theory that is useful for examining the disability/miracle meme is Alison Kafer's **political/relational model of disability**, as presented in her book *Feminist Queer Crip* (2013). The political/relational model is an alternative to the medical model that is still the most common framework for understanding disability, but it is also an expansion on the social model that has been articulated by scholars of disability studies. The **medical model of disability** asserts that disability is strictly an issue of bodily impairment that necessitates medical intervention. The **social model of disability** asserts that disability is an issue of social policies and cultural attitudes that necessitates social change. Kafer's concern about the social model is its tendency to discount the embodied character of disability and the range of relationships that disabled bodies can have with the institution of medicine. She explains:

> [A] political/relational framework recognizes the difficulty in determining who is included in the term "disabled," refusing any assumption that it refers to a discrete group of particular people with certain similar essential qualities. On the contrary, the political/relational model of disability sees disability as a site of questions rather than firm definitions. (Kafer 2013, 10–11)

From this political/relational perspective, I argue that the primary problem depicted in the disability/miracle meme is that the woman pictured has to stand from her wheelchair to reach the product she wishes to purchase. As one blogger who also uses a wheelchair explains:

> It's a freaking person wanting to get a freaking drink, and if you're a decent person, if you see me standing up and struggling to reach something in a store, you'll ask if I need help and if you can get something for me. If I say "no, I got it," you need to respect that and walk away, but chances are I will be grateful that I don't have to do the complicated dance of motor movements that is parking my chair in a spot that's not blocking anything or annoying other people, turning my chair off, unbuckling my seatbelt, making SURE my chair is off (because I roll around at top speed and crashing into store displays generally makes employees very annoyed with me), standing up (which may or may not involve adjusting pieces of my chair so that I have room to stand up), grabbing what I want and bringing it down without knocking anything else off the shelf, and sitting back down.*

Her use of the wheelchair likely, but not necessarily, indicates an embodied condition that limits her movements, but her inability to reach the item she wants indicates a problem in her relationship to the social environment. She is a consumer, wishing to purchase a product, but the space of consumption was not designed with her body in mind. This was no less true of the Denver bus protestors lead by ADAPT. Buses were not designed for their bodies, but through political action they were able to change the design of the social space of transportation, and in so doing they changed their relationship with the social environment.

If it happens that the woman is not disabled, whatever that might mean to her or to us as viewers, that in no way changes the disability implications of the image. As a centerpiece for debate, disability has been signified in the image regardless of the actual context. As Kafer indicates above, disability is not a binary identity—disabled/able-bodied—but rather a complex system that impacts all of us, if unequally. Regardless of the pictured woman's bodily condition, she is rendered disabled in the photograph in service to a debate about fraud—a debate that furthers the cause of compulsory able-bodiedness.

---

* http://thatcrazycrippledchick.blogspot.fr/2013/12/this-is-what-disability-binarism-looks.html.

Kafer also suggests the concept of "crip time" as a lens for understanding the dynamics of disability. Crip time refers to a sense that people with disabilities need accommodations of more time or may frequently arrive late, and the claim that disability-related events often start late. Kafer transforms the joke into a theoretical tool to highlight the way that disability is in many ways a relationship with time: a disabling event in the past, a healing moment in the future. "I am speaking here about a *curative imaginary*, an understanding of disability that not only *expects* and *assumes* intervention, but also cannot imagine or comprehend anything other than intervention" (Kafer 2013, 27). In the case of the disability/miracle meme, the future has arrived in the form of the miracle. The miracle marks the end of time for the disabled body, like an embodied enlightenment. In this case, the intervention is metaphysical, rather than medical, and in being metaphysical is also implied to be fictional. As a fictional cure, the not-pictured authentic disabled body is presumed incurable, trapped in time in a broken body. In contrast, the woman in the picture is presumed to be always and already healed and therefore without need for a cure, but also corrupt.

CRIP SOCIOLOGY

The sociological analysis of disability is still a very thin field. The bulk of sociological studies of disability are found within medical sociology and, like disability studies, focus on trying to determine what exactly disability is and how best to understand it as a social institution. By comparison, there is very little work from the sociology of culture that examines disability cultures, nor is there much work in the field of social movements looking at disability activism.

There is even less to report on in terms of the study of disability and social media. Although there is a rapidly developing body of social media research, almost none of it has considered the impact of social media on disability or the ways people with disabilities are using social media. One study examines participation levels in Facebook and LinkedIn groups related to various aspects of both disability and aging, but largely concludes that these groups are an area of untapped potential for these communities (Baker et al. 2013). A meta-analysis by Caton and Chapman (2016) found only ten studies that had examined the use of social media by people with intellectual disabilities. Most used either questionnaires or qualitative analysis (interviews and focus groups). Although one of the studies had 114 participants (all students in the Netherlands), the rest had between 3 and 20 participants and yielded very little generalizable information. They conclude from the studies that although social media provides some positive opportunities for people with intellectual disabilities—opportunities to build relationships, experience self-expression, learn new skills, and relax—there are also a number of barriers for these people: safety, accessibility, miscommunication, media literacy, and marginalization.

There is one truly cultural study that happens to be relevant for this chapter. Katie Ellis (2014) conducted an analysis of the social media responses to a contestant on season 1 of Australia's *The Voice* who was visually impaired. That contestant's name is Rachael Leahcar, and she took third place that season. In its advertising and editing, the show played on the double entendre of the "blind audition," in which judges face away from the contestants, a gimmick meant to emphasize that this show, unlike others, focuses on the true talent indicated by the voice, not on nonmusical issues such as looks. Despite the official focus on the voice, the show chose to frequently emphasize Leahcar's visual impairment. However, Leahcar is not "fully blind," and this became a major issue in some of the online discussion, with fans of the show arguing that she wasn't "blind enough" to merit being "the blind contestant." Ellis found a range of themes in these online discussions. The first theme is that Leahcar is inspirational. This sounds positive, but if she is inspirational for her blindness, and not for her music, then it can hardly be considered progressive. Ellis references tropes of supercripples and sweet innocents, drawing on the work of disability film scholar Martin Norden (1994). The implication is that people with disabilities have to be perfect and work harder than anyone else in order to achieve success. The second and third themes identified by Ellis are two sides of a coin. On one side, some people argued that Leahcar had an unfair competitive edge because of her blindness—an implication that she would unfairly advance just because of the sentimental value of her story. On the other side of that coin, other commenters argued that she deserved that advantage because of the obstacles she had had to overcome that were not faced by other competitors.

The final issue that Ellis raises, which really shows the significance of social media, is that Leahcar was able to participate in these online discussions and present her own perspective on these debates about her talent. She was able to explain the true nature of her disability and help viewers to better understand the range of visual impairments. Unlike in scripted television programs and films, where people with disabilities are often represented in ways they have no say over, reality television and social media allowed this particular person with a disability to represent herself.

CONCLUSION

I argue that the disability/miracle meme is an example of bad art that rehashes misguided confusions about what disability is and whom disability impacts. It is art because it is a cultural object that is bound up with layers of meaning, produced as a kind of trained craft involving a mixture of technical expertise and creativity. Media scholar Patrick Davison takes the position that "[a]n internet meme is a piece of culture, typically a joke, which gains influence through online transmission" (2012, 122). As a piece of culture, the meme falls into the category of humor, which we rarely associate with art. But humor is just as creative as other forms of art. This piece of humorous art was made by a long-forgotten artist who, though probably still living, has been lost to the sands of time. But his work lives on. The meme had already traveled the circuits of the online world more than once before it catapulted to new audiences with the help of George Takei. Takei is then an artist himself who helps to launch the work of other artists, particularly comedic ones.

As Shifman (2011) points out, what makes a cultural object a meme is the mimetic practice. The ideal type meme is typically an image that circulates with a broad range of captions placed over it by a slew of meme makers or a phrase that circulates imposed on a broad range of images. The concept of meme presumes an original that is followed by an array of copies. But now the mimetic process is of a standardized meme: an image with one phrase across the top and another across the bottom. A number of apps allow users to make memes, including Mematic, Meme Generator, Meme Producer, Caption Meme, and many others. While most of these apps allow users to grab widely recognized meme images, they also allow users to use their own images in the production of a meme. Instead of meme-ing an original, we are meme-ing the very idea of the meme.

The disability/miracle meme is not only an image that is a copy with no original; it is also a reproduction of ideas about disability that have no authentic origins. Disability fraud is not widespread (Neas 2014). Disability is a multidimensional continuum rather than a strict binary. People who use wheelchairs are not necessarily bound to them. Standing from a wheelchair does not make one a fraud.

Unpacking these images and these meanings is a crucial tool for social change because we are embedded in countless cultural messages every day, and many of them have as little connection to social reality as the disability/miracle meme. If we do not stop to question them when we can, they become part of our collective wisdom that ultimately becomes our collective folly.

5

GamerGate: Gender Perspectives on Social Media

On August 27, 2014, a Twitter user by the name of Adam Baldwin sent a short, cryptic message composed almost entirely of a hashtag: #Gamer-Gate.* Below the tag were links to two YouTube videos posted on the account

*Much of this chapter is derived from my contributions to a book chapter that I co-authored with Amanda Turner (Kidd and Turner 2016).

of someone named Internet Aristocrat. The videos were titled *Quinnspiracy Theory: In-N-Out Edition*, parts 1 and 2. When the tweet is viewed on a desktop computer, Twitter adds a preview of the video player with an image of an In-N-Out Burger franchise. The caption beneath the video reads "Whose [*sic*] a guy gotta fuck around here to get some fries with this?"

What is **GamerGate**? GamerGate is essentially a culture war for the soul of the gaming industry. On the one hand, we have a nerd-centric gaming culture that is historically male dominated, whose members have been watching gaming transform as it goes mainstream and as women begin to join the ranks. On the other hand, we have a critique of gaming driven by feminist cultural critics who are increasingly gamers themselves, as players, designers, and game journalists (Hathaway 2014). As the GamerGate Wiki site states: "Gamergate is a worldwide scandal."* Like many epics, GamerGate is a story of love, sex, and jealousy (Hathaway 2014). But its origins are unique and unlike any of the epic tales of old. It starts with one woman's passion for coding and her battle with depression.

DEPRESSION QUEST

Zoë Quinn released the game *Depression Quest* in 2013. It is a text-based game that is designed to demonstrate the experiences of depression, also designed with the intent of helping people fight the effects of depression. Its style is reminiscent of the Choose Your Own Adventure novels, but the most important choices are the ones that the designer has stricken through. Those options cannot be selected by the player, and they highlight the fact that good options often feel unavailable to people who suffer from depression.

Depression Quest is found online at www.depressionquest.com, but it has also been released through Greenlight, a component of the online gaming platform Steam. Greenlight is a tool by which the Steam community can review new games and help good games find a wider audience. In an interview for *Vice* magazine, Quinn described what happened when she first released *Depression Quest* on Greenlight:

* The site has been taken down. An archive of the timeline can be found at https://web.archive.org/web/20150310043424/http://wiki.gamergate.me/index.php?title=Timeline.

> When it hit Greenlight, people were leaving foul comments there, and suddenly I started getting stuff sent to my email. "Oh I saw your game on Greenlight and I hope you kill yourself." I guess somebody who thought they were really clever figured out my address and sent a very detailed rape threat to my house. That was when I decided to pull it off [Greenlight]. (Kotzer 2014)

The article, entitled "Female Game Designers Are Being Threatened with Rape," was published on January 23, 2014, and was written by gaming journalist Zack Kotzer. As GamerGate eventually unfolded later in 2014, the field of gaming journalism would turn out to be a central issue. While many would respond to this by scoffing at the very concept of gaming journalism, others would argue that if there is no integrity in gaming journalism, then there is no integrity in journalism at large and no integrity in gaming. A few weeks before Kotzer's article appeared in *Vice*, another gaming journalist included *Depression Quest* in a piece he published online at the site Rock, Paper, Shotgun. That piece, written by Nathan Grayson and published on January 8, 2014, consisted of little more than a list of fifty new games released on Greenlight. The games were not reviewed or rank ordered. However, the list was illustrated with a screen capture from *Depression Quest*. At the end of the opening paragraph, the last line before the list reads: "Anyway, standouts: powerful Twine darling *Depression Quest*, surrealist Thief usurper Tangiers, and sidescrolling epic Treasure Adventure World" (Grayson 2014a). Twine is an open-source platform used in game development, including *Depression Quest*.

On social media, Quinn alleged that *Depression Quest* was particularly attacked by members of **Wizardchan**, is an online discussion board, found at wizchan.org, which describes itself as follows:

> Wizardchan is a Japanese-inspired image-based forum (imageboard) for male virgins to share their thoughts and discuss their interests and lifestyle as a virgin. The name of our website is inspired by the wizard meme, which refers to someone who has maintained his virginity past the age of 30. In contrast to other imageboards, Wizardchan is dedicated exclusively to people who have no sexual experience and may be NEET or hikkikomori.*

* As quoted on the opening page of Wizardchan, https://wizchan.org/.

NEET stands for not in education, employment, or training. *Hikikomori* is a Japanese term for socially withdrawn. Wizardchan users have denied the claims that they attacked *Depression Quest* and allege that Quinn invented the attack to garner more press for her game.

The trail to GamerGate went quiet for a couple of months, until Rock, Paper, Shotgun posted a video on its YouTube account at the end of the Game Developers Conference (GDC) in San Francisco.* The video appeared on March 22, 2014, and featured Nathan Grayson sitting on a bed interviewing Hayden Dingman from *PC World*; Lucas Pope, the developer of the game *Papers, Please*; Zoë Quinn, developer of *Depression Quest*; and Matthew Ritter, developer of the game *Boon Hill*. They seem to be sitting around someone's bedroom, having a casual conversation about their current game interests. Each person is featured for a few minutes. Quinn talks for about three minutes (in a thirty-minute video) about sharing her game at the GDC. She discusses a talk she gave about what it is like to release a game that is so personal. The discussion of *Depression Quest* is pretty limited. At one point, the other interview participants congratulate Quinn on her success. When she expresses discomfort with the positive comments, Ritter says, "We take it back. Your game sucks." But when you watch the interview, it's clear that he is joking and the general spirit is one of support for Quinn. But there is no indication that the other participants have even played the game.

GAME_JAM

The next major event in the path to GamerGate happened in the week that followed the Rock, Paper, Shotgun video. Quinn was recruited to participate in a reality television show called *GAME_JAM* that would pit teams of game developers against each other as they raced to create new games. The premise of the show is a core element in indie game culture, the **game jam**. The show was being sponsored by Mountain Dew and produced by a production company called Polaris (owned by Maker, which is owned in turn by Disney) (C. Campbell 2014). The host for the show was Matti Lesham, whose previous credits include, according to the Internet Movie Database (IMDB), *Dewmocracy* (2008), "[a] web-based fantasy game that allows gamers to create a

* The video is available on YouTube at https://www.youtube.com/watch?v=xIKEJBHbLgg.

Mountain Dew soft drink, including its flavor, color and label."* Each team of developers also included a YouTube star, such as the video blogger (or vlogger) JonTron, of the *JonTronShow*.†

Production of *GAME_JAM* did not go well, according to pretty much everyone involved. Not surprisingly, the reality television style of the show resulted in pressures to create conflict between gamers. When these conflicts failed to materialize, Lesham began asking competitors questions about whether women could succeed in gaming. He is quoted in one article about the production as follows:

> "Two of the other teams have women on them. Do you think they're at a disadvantage?"

> And then:

> "Do you think you're at an advantage because you have a pretty lady on your team?" (Grayson 2014b)

Participants left the set soon after this incident and refused to take part in the production any further. The production was derailed, and the show never happened.

The article that I use above to quote Lesham was written by Nathan Grayson, so it provides the next key point in a series of connections between Grayson and Quinn that would later become the linchpin for GamerGate. By this time, Grayson had started writing for *Kotaku*, a gaming blog owned by Gawker.

After *GAME_JAM* fell apart, Quinn took to her blog, *Dispatches from the Quinnspiracy*, to reflect on the experience:

> It's a weird time for games, and it can be easy to lose sight of that when you're working in the industry. . . . I've taken every speaking gig offered to me because I've read so much on how having someone who looks like you being visible in places you'd like to be in someday can do really powerful stuff for traditionally marginalized groups. (Quinn, 2014)

---

* His filmography can be found on IMDB at http://www.imdb.com/title/tt1139308/?ref_=nm_flmg_prd_3.

† His YouTube channel is found at https://www.youtube.com/user/JonTronShow/.

She did not directly address the show, which she explained was a result of a contractual obligation. But clearly the show's failure led her to examine the culture of gaming, including indie gaming, and the intersecting issues of gender.

Quinn noted in Grayson's article that the experience made her want to start her own game jam, and she began using the name Rebel Jam to refer to that goal. She was accused of derailing *GAME_JAM* as a way of promoting Rebel Jam.

THE FINE YOUNG CAPITALISTS

Throughout 2014 Zoë Quinn was also engaged in a somewhat public battle with a group that identifies as The Fine Young Capitalists (TFYC). On *Wikipedia*, TFYC are described as radical feminists (*Wikipedia* 2015b). But an article on CinemaBlend describes them simply as profeminist (Usher 2014). The group operates as an anonymous collective whose goal is to help women and minorities become more involved in gaming. The origins of the group are described in a YouTube video that features the group's founder, Matthew Rappard.* He is the only publicly identified member of the group, and he claims that he has only gone public as a result of Zoë Quinn and others sharing his personal information online—a practice referred to in the Reddit and 4chan communities as **doxxing**.

So an anonymous profeminist organization, founded by a male, and possibly consisting of mostly men, set out to reward female game designers. They recruited the help of a Colombian "transmedia production company" called Autobótika to help them launch a campaign. A video on TFYC's YouTube page features Autobótika's Lola Barreto, which gives the impression that women are actively involved in the campaign. Perhaps they were; it is difficult to ascertain the group's demographics. But there is no clear indication that women were active with the group from the start. In a defense of TFYC on their Tumblr account, Barreto is one of several women listed, even though she is part of Autobótika (The Fine Young Capitalists 2014). In one interview, Barreto clearly stated that she was not part of TFYC and that her company was contracted for its services (Morley 2014). The central premise of the group is that men, a group that is privileged in gaming, can reach

* The video is available on YouTube at: https://www.youtube.com/watch?v=yXHylDeOa0w.

out and lend a hand of support to help more women and other "underrepresented labor"* become game developers. Rappard did say in an online video that there were women involved as well, but those women were not named. The campaign that they launched with Autobótika solicited ideas for games from women. The women whose ideas were considered the best were then matched with concept artists to storyboard the game (Morley 2014). These storyboards were then made available online so that a broad audience could vote on which of the games should actually get made, with the plan being to make the games and sell them, giving 8 percent of the proceeds to the women who created the games and the rest of the money to charity.

Quinn became aware of TFYC's project in February 2014 and contacted them with concerns. First, she was bothered that they were basically asking women to work for free, as they volunteered their creative gaming ideas (Seraphita 2014). Rappard stated in his YouTube video that he did not understand why this was a problem, because the group was essentially trying to help women, and the winner would be offered 8 percent of the proceeds. Quinn's critique does seem legitimate though, as they were basically using a contest to generate free research and development ideas. Later in the year, Stephen Daly at Gameranx published an op-ed that shared Quinn's concerns (Daly 2014).

Second, Quinn asked questions about TFYC's policy regarding trans people. The question wasn't random. They had a stated policy on their website. The name of the HTML document is "TransgenderPolicy," and the headline at the top of the policy reads "Are you a boy or a girl?" The policy is as follows:

> Although it has become an Internet meme, the question "Are you a boy or a girl?" is actually quite a complicated question. As TFYC is based in Canada we use the theory of self identification, where a person will be considered a man or a woman based upon on their own view of how they should be perceived in society. This can bother some people for some reason, so to put the record straight let's lay out what exactly that means. The only question regarding gender we ask is.
>
> Participant has self identified as Woman before the date of March 11, 2014.†

* The video and online campaign can be found on Indiegogo at: https://www.indiegogo.com/projects/the-fine-young-capitalists—2#/.

† The policy is described http://www.thefineyoungcapitalists.com/TransgenderPolicy.

Quinn claimed that the policy was transphobic. Rappard defended the policy, saying it was a necessary way to prevent men from gaining access to the award by suddenly claiming that they identify as women. In an e-mail to a journalist, Rappard said "the text was approved by a lawyer and signed by a sociology student."*

The theory of self-identification seems to be a fairly progressive approach. However, the concern that men would embrace a trans identity and declare themselves women simply to gain access to this award is unfounded and hints at a fear that trans identities could destabilize social action.

Zoë Quinn took her concerns to Twitter. Rappard says that it was at this point he was doxxed, when Quinn's friend and associate Maya Felix Kramer released his name and Facebook account on Twitter. He says that Quinn's reply to that tweet effectively alerted her followers as well, making her complicit with the doxxing. The launch of the fund-raising campaign for TFYC was delayed as a result. Quinn tweeted: "I love how a conversation between me and @legobutts resulted in accidentally killing an exploitative startup's website."† @legobutts is the Twitter handle for Maya Felix Kramer.

The launch was delayed into the summer. Rappard says that during this time Quinn was contacted and even offered a chance to work with TFYC as a consultant, but she rebuffed their offers.

By the time the fund-raising campaign launched, the battle between Zoë Quinn and TFYC had been waged fairly publicly, especially on Twitter and 4chan. Two of the boards on 4chan, /pol/ or Politically Incorrect and /v/ or Video Games began organizing donations to TFYC, explicitly to spite Zoë Quinn. According to Rappard, the 4chan portal on the giving site IndieGoGo was the strongest source of donations for their program. The Fine Young Capitalists and the 4chan users worked out a deal whereby the 4chan /v/ board could place its logo on the resulting game *and* choose the charity that would receive the donated proceeds from the game. They were even allowed to create a character that would be inserted into the winning game. The character they created is named Vivian James.‡ 4chan users selected the Colon

* A screen capture of an e-mail explaining this is found at http://knowyourmeme.com/photos/816444-quinnspiracy.

† A screen capture of the tweet is found at http://imgur.com/PFO1zJB,CU55Sd5,OH8fIpw,Dwm6vvx#1

‡ An image and overview of Vivian James are available at http://knowyourmeme.com/memes/vivian-james.

Cancer Alliance as the charity recipient. CCA was one of six choices presented in a 4chan poll,* the others being the Prostate Cancer Foundation, the Mankind Initiative (described as a "charity for abused men"), Survivors UK ("male rape and sexual abuse support"), the Jewish Internet Defense Force (a group described on *Wikipedia* as "an organization that uses social media to mobilize support for campaigns against websites and Facebook groups that promote or praise what it regards as Islamic terrorism or anti-Semitism" [2015a]), and the Friends of the Israel Defense Forces (a New York City–based organization that provides support for veterans of the Israel Defense Forces). The selection of possible charities is telling. If Zoë Quinn is seen as a social justice warrior—a hot button term in this debate—then these charities are meant to present an alternative vision of social justice that emphasizes the victimization of men.

4chan is an online image and message board that was started in 2003 by a fifteen-year-old named Christopher Poole. The primary purpose of 4chan is to share images and to create dialogue about those images. It was modeled on Japanese websites, particularly 2chan, and originally focused on Japanese popular culture. Its original catchphrase, according to an August 18, 2005, screen capture was: "What you need, when you need it."†

4chan allows users to post images without registering. They can use any identity they choose, or they can post entirely anonymously. 4chan has been linked to the worldwide anonymous collective of hacktivists (hacker activists) known as Anonymous, and it is widely described as their original creation point. Anonymous has been linked to campaigns against Scientology and the Westboro Baptist Church, as well as attempts to direct greater media attention to a number of crimes (Gilbert 2014). 4chan explains its concept of Anonymous on an FAQ board:

> "Anonymous" is the name assigned to a poster who does not enter text in to the [Name] field. Anonymous is not a single person, but rather, represents the collective whole of 4chan. He is a god amongst men.‡

---

* An image capture of the straw poll can be found online at http://knowyourmeme.com/photos/816470-vivian-james.

† The page can be viewed through the Web Archives at https://web.archive.org/web/20050818191647/http://dp.information.com/?a_id=35&domainname=4chan.com.

‡ The FAQ is found on the 4chan website at http://www.4chan.org/faq.

A stroll through 4chan's boards reveals a sustained interest in Japanese anime and manga, as well as a variety of adult boards. Its most popular board is the random board, known popularly as /b/ (because that is the URL extension where it is found, i.e., http://boards.4chan.org/b/). Frequent users of /b/ call themselves /b/tards, a play on the slur "retards," and they are known for making heavy use of the word "fag."

The character created by the 4chan users for the game selected by TFYC is named Vivian James. She will appear in the game *After Life Empire*, which is being developed by Autobótika. The Fine Young Capitalists have a video about the game development on their YouTube account. In the video, five game designers and technicians—four males and one female—discuss the process of developing the game. The women who created the game are not named, but one of the men in the video comments on them. The comment is in Spanish but is translated in the subtitles as: "What I like about this project is that the ideas come from women."*

The Fine Young Capitalists have come under fire for taking money from 4chan (Daly 2014), but at the request of 4chan users, they are now making videos about female game designers and have already released videos about Anna Kipnis† and Corrinne Yu.‡ More recent projects by TFYC are being funded by an online porn stream, in partnership with the porn star Mercedes Carrera.

TL;DR

As the controversy over TFYC reached its zenith in August 2014, Zoë Quinn faced a new battlefront, this one much more personal than the others. This is the same month in which Quinn re-released *Depression Quest* on Steam's Greenlight service, after pulling it a year earlier due to harassing comments. As all of this was happening, her romantic relationship with boyfriend Eron Gjoni was ending. They had taken a break, gotten back together, and then

* The video is available on YouTube at https://www.youtube.com/watch?v=FCRuu82DxcI.

† The video is available on YouTube at https://www.youtube.com/watch?v=QAHdntHbPM8.

‡ The video is available on YouTube at https://www.youtube.com/watch?v=OQk_z_vnGGg.

called it quits again. Gjoni is also a game developer and was very aware of Quinn's struggles with *Depression Quest*, *GAME_JAM*, and TFYC.

He started a blog to publicly express his anger toward his ex-girlfriend, naming the blog *The Zoë Post*. The first post on the blog, dated August 16, 2014, was titled "TL;DR." **TL;DR** is a shorthand term used on Reddit and other sites (Sheets 2012). It stands for "Too Long; Didn't Read." If you jump in midstream to a lengthy thread, you need a summary to catch you up and save you from reading the full thread. Look for a post labeled "TL;DR," and you should find a summary of the thread up to that point. Gjoni's post about his relationship was meant to provide a summary of their breakup. He opened with a concise statement of his feelings toward Quinn:

> I dated Zoë Quinn. I thought she was the most amazing, kind hearted person in the world.
>
> Turns out she was bullshitting pretty much everything I fell in love with her for, and is actually an unbelievable jerk. (Gjoni 2014)

Gjoni listed twenty-four things he was holding against Quinn, including an accusation that she had a sexual affair with games journalist Nathan Grayson. In fact, he identified five men (some named, some left anonymous) who he believed Quinn slept with during their relationship or during a period when they were on a break but had a supposed commitment not to sleep with others. "TL;DR" was one of nine posts that Gjoni published on August 16 on *The Zoë Post*. The others are the "too long" versions, which elaborate on the breakdown of the relationship in great detail.

Within days the blog made national headlines. *Daily Dot* broke the story on August 20. Its coverage of the story highlighted the ways that an online gaming community had used Gjoni's blog to construe a claim that Quinn had traded sex for professional success:

> All week, gamers have accused Quinn of trading sexual favors for career advancement from industry professionals and positive reviews from gaming journalists. Despite the lack of evidence for either of these claims—again, Gjoni's post never makes either allegation, and the gaming journalist he names never reviewed Quinn's game, Depression Quest—the idea has taken firm hold within the gaming community. (Romano 2014)

Vice published an article less than two weeks later that featured an interview with Gjoni, calling him "the guy whose tell-all blog entry about his ex-girlfriend sparked the recent flare-up of the notorious Quinnspiracy debacle" (Pearl 2014). The *Vice* article did note that Gjoni allied himself with the social justice side of the controversies, but separated that issue from his personal romantic problems with Quinn.

METHODOLOGICAL MOMENT: Collecting and Sharing Virtual Ethnographic Sources Through Social Media

Unlike most other forms of ethnography, virtual ethnography allows us to reproduce many of the experiences we observe and to make these moments available to others. You cannot reproduce a moment on the street, except perhaps through a video recording, but the presence of a camera would likely change the interaction. Online and in social media, however, moments can be captured and shared with others. But the ephemeral nature of these spaces means that we need to be diligent in capturing the moment. Here are some tools that we can use in this process:

1. Screen captures. One method for grabbing images and text from the Internet and social media is to use the screen capture function that is available on computers, tablets, and phones. On a computer, the screen capture options include a cross-hairs function that allows the user to capture a specific portion of the screen. Capturing the full screen is a good way to record a collection of elements that may not appear together in any other moment. For example, the ads that appear online and in social media vary from person to person, and they are not likely to stay the same on a particular page over time. Capturing the screen in a given moment allows us to study the combination of particular content and particular ads in a specific moment. Screen captures are also a great way to visually grab specific tweets (although tweets can also be linked to individually), to save images on Instagram (which does not have an internal "save image" option), to seize a playlist from Spotify, and much more.
2. Image collections on Flickr or Google Photos. Image collections are a great way to share screen captures and other types of images in an environment that can be organized and curated.

continues

METHODOLOGICAL MOMENT: Collecting and Sharing Virtual Ethnographic Sources Through Social Media *continued*

3. Playlists on YouTube. A researcher studying video culture online can capture the videos being observed into a playlist that can function as a database for ethnographic observation.
4. Boards on Pinterest. Pinterest boards are one of my favorite resources for capturing, curating, and sharing information and for capturing moments in virtual ethnography. Pinterest allows users to create collections that include multiple types of content that can either be found online or uploaded to Pinterest. This content can include images and videos. Technically, as of the publication of this book, there is no option to include a link. But if a web page has an image on it, that image can be pinned to a board, and clicking the image will take the viewer to the original link. Pinterest allows the user to include comments for each item that is pinned, which allows for curation of the board. Screen captures can also be uploaded to Pinterest boards. An example Pinterest board that uses information from this chapter is available at https://www.pinterest.com/popculturefreak/gamergate/.
5. Prezi. Prezi is an online presentation system that allows presentations to be shared publicly. Prezis can include music, videos, images, and text. Prezi provides another way to collect and share observations and moments from virtual ethnography and allows the user to create a path for viewers to step through the information. An example Prezi that uses information from this chapter is available at https://prezi.com/uxk0mpe9z_bm/gamergate/.

MUNDANEMATT AND THE INTERNET ARISTOCRAT

After the launch of *The Zoë Post*, gamers began using the details offered by Gjoni to piece together a case against Zoë Quinn. YouTuber MundaneMatt posted a nearly sixteen-minute video later the same day, August 16. He opens with a lament about the accusations of sexism that have been leveled against the gaming industry. Then he turns to *The Zoë Post* as evidence, he believes, that the accusations of sexism are coming from a corrupt relationship between gaming journalism and **SJW** gamers. SJW stands for "social justice warriors," a term that is often used with contempt in a community that is now known as the GamerGate community, a group of gamers who want to rid the gaming industry of questions related to gender, race, and inequality.

MundaneMatt's video was titled *Hell Hath No Fury Like a Lover's Scorn (Zoë Quinn and Eron Gjoni)*. He reads the "TL;DR" from *The Zoë Post* and then begins his case against Zoë Quinn, asking: "How much of Zoë's coverage for Depression Quest lately has been from actual merits—you know, 'she earned it'—or people she was fucking to get it?"* He argues that Quinn is (1) sleeping with reporters to generate positive coverage of her work and (2) sleeping with reporters to protect herself from negative coverage. He cites Grayson's pieces on Quinn from Rock, Paper, Shotgun and *Kotaku* as proof that the sexual relationship was generating coverage for Quinn. However, he never reads from those sources. The RPS piece, as mentioned above, is just a list of fifty new games released through Greenlight. The *Kotaku* piece was about *GAME_JAM*. But it seems to be the existence of these pieces, and not their tone, that infuriates MundaneMatt.

In MundaneMatt's YouTube video, we hear his voice but we don't see his face. The visual part of the video is a screen capture from *Depression Quest*. Quinn used that screen capture to claim to YouTube that the video violated her rights under the Digital Millennium Copyright Act of 1998 (DMCA). The video was removed a day after it was posted but then restored a week later when YouTube determined that the DMCA claim was invalid.

While the video was down, and partly in response to the video's removal, another YouTuber posted his case against Zoë Quinn in a pair of videos. Internet Aristocrat posted *Quinnspiracy Theory: The Five Guys Saga* and *Quinnspiracy Theory: The In-N-Out Burger Edition*† on August 19 and August 22, respectively. The name of the videos is based on an element from *The Zoë Post*. Reflecting on the fact that he had a list of five guys with whom Quinn had allegedly cheated, Eron Gjoni had joked that he couldn't stop thinking of her as "burgers and fries." Thus, Internet Aristocrat named his first video after the Five Guys burger chain and chose a second hamburger restaurant, In-N-Out Burger, for the second video. At one point in the first video, he even posted pictures of the five men in question and stepped through their links

* The video is available on YouTube at https://www.youtube.com/watch?v=O5CXOafuTXM.

† The video is available on YouTube at https://www.youtube.com/watch?v=TezNpsXvUoo.

to Zoë and how those links suggested problems in the worlds of gaming and journalism.

Internet Aristocrat largely repeated the arguments put forward by MundaneMatt. In one of the videos he says, "Gaming journalism has reached a low point. . . . It started to travel off into the areas of social justice and feminism and opinion pieces, and op-eds that had nothing to do with gaming."* In comparison to MundaneMatt, Internet Aristocrat is even more focused on using the controversy to expose problems in journalism. He uses apocalyptic language, comparing problems in gaming journalism to Watergate and saying, "We watch as the fifth estate burns in front of our eyes." He suggests that if Quinn and Grayson had a sexual relationship, perhaps another *Kotaku* editor, Stephen Totilo, was sleeping with cultural critic Anita Sarkeesian.

In keeping with his focus on journalism, Internet Aristocrat gives more attention to Grayson than did MundaneMatt, calling Grayson "the biggest fucking issue that we're looking at." He discusses the same RPS and *Kotaku* articles that were mentioned by MundaneMatt, also failing to actually read from them to indicate how the articles present Quinn's game favorably. He adds a discussion of an item he found posted on Reddit by a user named SillySlader, who was later revealed to be Matthew Rappard,† describing Quinn's takedown of TFYC. The video is a case not only against Quinn, but also against those he considers SJWs. Perhaps his frustration is best summed up in the line: "They have ruined our hobby." It should be noted that Internet Aristocrat has since removed his YouTube and Twitter accounts, although the videos are reproduced elsewhere, and he has functionally left GamerGate, saying that he is uncomfortable with the notoriety and with the viciousness that occurs online (The Ralph Retort 2014).

Another video released on August 19 was called *Lies, Damned Lies and the Video Game Press*, by Sargon of Akkad. Sargon was also angry about both Zoë Quinn and gaming journalism, but he targeted his attacks toward SJWs:

> The fundamental problem with social justice in video games is that social justice revolves around the concept of demonizing straight white men. As

*The video is available on YouTube at https://www.youtube.com/watch?v=dH1052F2ZaY.

† The connection between Rappard and SillySlader is examined in a Zoë Quinn blog post "How Not to Run Your Games Education Programs," http://blog.unburntwitch.com/post/103251119644/how-not-to-run-your-games-education-programs.

> you can imagine, since the video games industry was created by straight white men, this leaves social justice warriors on the outside. Or at least, it should do if blatant lying, nepotism, bigotry, and corruption hadn't overrun the video game press.*

Sargon expresses grave concerns about how SJW journalism has misconstrued the very concept of gaming. He picks apart published data that indicate women are half of all gamers by pointing to other reports that indicate men and women play very different games. High numbers of women, for example, play Candy Crush and Farmville. "No one who calls themselves a gamer plays Farmville or Candy Crush." He insists that gaming only truly refers to competitive games and that women are averse to such games because of "inherent biological differences." What does he think true gamers want? "They want to be left alone to enjoy their games and they want objective video game reviews."

On August 20 *Kotaku* spoke up about the controversy and the implied role of its employee, Nathan Grayson. The blog concluded that he never reviewed *Depression Quest* and that he had only written about Quinn in the article about *GAME_JAM*, in March, prior to the beginning of Grayson's romantic relationship with Quinn in April 2014 (Totilo 2014). The post on *Kotaku* was by editor Stephen Totilo.

ME JAYNE

We finally get to the hashtag that launched a thousand tweets: #GamerGate. That hashtag was sent in a tweet by the actor Adam Baldwin. Baldwin has 114 film, television, and video game credits to his name, according to IMDB,† but in nerd culture he is best known for playing Jayne Cobb on the science fiction show *Firefly*. *Firefly* had just fourteen episodes, in 2002–2003, but it acquired a huge cult following that led to a film in 2005 called *Serenity*. Baldwin's character offered a particular archetype of masculinity, despite the name Jayne, that was gruff, quiet, and resistant to change. It was a personality that suited Baldwin as well. He opposes gay marriage, is skeptical about climate change,

* The video is available on YouTube at https://www.youtube.com/watch?v=bAJYmrKR8WE

†Baldwin's filmography can be found on IMDB at http://www.imdb.com/name/nm0000284/?ref_=tt_cl_t5.

and is a gun enthusiast who is an occasional contributor to conservative site Breitbart. (Breitbart posted an article about GamerGate on September 1, 2014, with the headline "Feminist Bullies Tearing the Video Game Industry Apart" [Yiannopoulos 2014].) Baldwin is active on Twitter, with over 209,000 followers. That's an increase from the 186,000 followers reported on August 28, 2014 (McNally 2014). His Twitter feed is filled with political observations and stances against gay rights and feminism.

On August 27, 2014, Baldwin tweeted links to both of Internet Aristocrat's videos, along with the hashtag (#) GamerGate. The size of Baldwin's Twitter audience allowed this issue to reach a much wider audience, well beyond the limits of gaming culture. Baldwin is credited with essentially breaking the story with his simple tweet.

That same day, Anita Sarkeesian received a series of violent threats on Twitter. Anita Sarkeesian is a feminist media critic who operates as a public intellectual using social media spaces like YouTube, Tumblr, and Twitter. She holds a master's degree in social and political thought from York University in Toronto, where she graduated in 2010. In 2009, while still a student, she launched the **Feminist Frequency** project, which began as a website that offered feminist media and media criticism. Her videos have covered a range of topics in commercial popular culture, including applications of the Bechdel Test to the Academy Award nominees and feminist critiques of children's toys. She gained significant public attention in 2012 when she began a Kickstarter campaign to pay for a series of videos called Tropes vs. Women in Video Games. Her goal was to raise $6,000. She raised over $150,000. The video series, and other similar series that she has released since, have been very popular, and they are often used in college classrooms. Sarkeesian has appeared on numerous media outlets, including a widely seen interview with Stephen Colbert on the *Colbert Report*. Sarkeesian had just released a new video on August 25, 2014, two days before the threats appeared.

The threats that Sarkeesian received allude to rape and murder, and they reference her home address and the address of her parents. The account was listed as Kevin Dobson (@kdobbsz), and it was a newly created account. Sarkeesian tweeted a pic of the tweets, called authorities, and fled her home. Initially the group that came to be known as GamerGate insisted that she had posted the offending tweets herself. Two months later, GamerGaters claimed to have tracked down the harasser and discovered that he was a games journalist in Brazil (Schreier 2014). The timing of the incident in conjunction with Baldwin's tweet made GamerGate a story that superseded the series of events surrounding Zoë Quinn. Quinn also fled her home around this same time, after receiving multiple threats of rape, violence, and murder, and she stayed away from her home for several months (Lee 2014). She spoke with the *Guardian* from England in December 2014: "What am I going to do—go home and just wait until someone makes good on their threats? I'm scared that what it's going to take to stop this is the death of one of the women who's been targeted" (Stuart 2014).

In September 2014 Quinn, along with several journalists and a few Internet detectives, scoured the boards of 4chan to trace back the origins of GamerGate. The findings are summarized in an article on *Ars Technica* (Johnston 2014). The boards indicate that a few posters coordinated the controversy on 4chan and used fake Twitter accounts—known as sock puppets—to generate online attention. One 4chan user, OperationDunk, congratulated the group on their success in generating media attention, saying: "It took a few days of 4–5 of us doing it but it's taking off." According to the discussion boards, the group planned out a new hashtag to add to the conversation: #NotYourShield. The implication was that the women they called social justice warriors were using male gamers as a shield against attacks on their own integrity. 4chan responded by producing logs of its boards, claiming that the full logs would exonerate it. Blogger David Futrelle examined the logs and came to the following conclusion:

> The 4channers express their hatred and disgust towards her; they express their glee at the thought of ruining her career; they fantasize about her being raped and killed. They wonder if all the harassment will drive her to suicide, and only the thought of 4chan getting bad publicity convinces some of them that this isn't something they should hope for. (Futrelle 2014)

One week later, on September 17, 2014, 4chan began shutting down all discussion of GamerGate. Threads in which the term was mentioned were deleted, and users who posted about it were reportedly banned from the site (Gaming Admiral 2014).

8CHAN

The next major event in the GamerGate saga occurred in October, when indie game developer Brianna Wu tweeted pics of a meme that someone had sent her. The meme—of the sort often found at memegenerator.com—pictures a little boy who seems angry and close to tearing his hair out. Text appearing above and below his head uses tweets from Wu to present a series of jokes about GamerGaters:

- Above: GamerGate is not
  Below: About oppressing women
- Above: This is about corruption
  Below: Tweets 500 things attacking women
- Above: Says "go start your own game studio"
  Below: To a woman who owns a game studio
- Above: Lectures women on how to respond
  Below: To the problems he causes
- Above: Fighting an apocalyptic future
  Below: Where women are 8% of programmers, and not 3%
- Above: Bases entire identity in video games
  Below: Feels like a badass (Scimeca 2014)

Wu tweeted out the meme on October 9, 2014, at 2:39 p.m. Immediately GamerGaters took the meme and flipped the script, prompting Wu to send a new tweet at 6:44 p.m. that read: "A fan made a meme of 6 of my Tweets. #Gamergate spent day filling it with 36 pages of garbage."* The new variants of the meme were created by users of **8chan**, an offshoot and competitor to 4chan. When 4chan had banned conversations about GamerGate in September, many users simply migrated to 8chan, because 8chan promised not to impose any rules other than the law. Child pornography is banned on 8chan, but not much else. The quick response from GamerGaters to Wu's tweeted meme was, at that point, all fun and games.

By the next evening, it was a different story. A newly created Twitter account called Death to Brianna (@chatterwhiteman) sent a series of threatening messages directed to Wu's Twitter account @spacekatgal. Some highlights:

- "@spacekatgal Guess what bitch? I know where you live. You and Frank live at."
- "@spacekatgal I'm going to rape your filthy ass until you bleed, then choke you to death with your husband's tiny Asian penis."

---

*The tweet can be seen at https://twitter.com/Spacekatgal/status/520344200249090048.

- "@spacekatgal If you have any kids, they're going to die too. I don't give a fuck. They'll grow up to be feminists anyway."

At 8:57 p.m. on the night of October 10· Brianna Wu tweeted an image of the tweets from Death to Brianna, with the message: "The police just came by. Husband and I are going somewhere safe. Remember, #gamergate isn't about attacking women" (Scimeca 2014). Death to Brianna was shut down by Twitter.

Wu's story was the basis of an episode of *Law & Order: Special Victims Unit* that aired on February 11, 2015. The episode was called "Intimidation Game." In an essay on Bustle just before the episode premiered, Wu described how the intimidation she felt from a long series of threats had impacted her career. "The reality is, this circus has sucked every bit of joy from a career I once felt destined for. . . . There's not a single day I don't ask myself why I'm here" (Wu 2015). Since the initial threats came in October 2014, Wu has received over forty more threats and has reported all of them to the police.

OPEN CARRY

Just days after the threats against Brianna Wu, a new threat was made against Anita Sarkeesian. She was scheduled to speak about women in video games at Utah State University on October 15, 2014. The school received three different threats in the days leading up to the event. One threat, received on October 13, promised that unless the talk was canceled there would be a "Montreal Massacre-style attack," referencing the 1989 tragedy when Marc Lepine killed fourteen women under the banner of "fighting feminism" (Hern 2014). A second threat, received on October 14, claimed affiliation with GamerGate. Then a third threat came in that claimed to be from a USU student, saying:

> Anita Sarkeesian is everything wrong with the feminist woman, and she is going to die screaming like the craven little whore that she is if you let her come to USU. I will write my manifesto in her spilled blood, and you will all bear witness to what feminist lies and poison have done to the men of America. (Quoted in Alberty 2014)

Since the threats promised violence, and one of them mentioned guns and pipe bombs, Sarkeesian asked for metal detectors at the talk. The school refused, saying that Utah's open carry laws prohibited them from removing any weapons they might find. An additional Utah law restricts schools from banning weapons. Sarkeesian says that she could not guarantee the safety of her audience, so she canceled the talk.

THE END OF GAMING

The FBI confirmed in December 2014 that it was investigating GamerGate and the threats that have been associated with it (Rogers 2014). So far (2016), there have been no arrests related to the threats against Quinn, Wu, or Sarkeesian.

According to some, the beginning of GamerGate was the end of gaming as we know it. The GamerGate wiki page, which is clearly maintained by GamerGaters, provides a list of ten articles and blog posts that declare the death of gaming.* On Gamasutra, Leigh Alexander stated: "'Gamer' isn't just a dated demographic label that most people increasingly prefer not to use. Gamers are over. That's why they're so mad" (Alexander 2014). Also on Gamasutra, Devin Wilson offered what he called a "Guide to ending gamers" (Wilson 2014). He presented a series of eighteen steps that gamers can take to transform the gaming culture, including more self-reflection about the games they play, and ending with "we all grow up." *Kotaku* predicted that GamerGate would be the end of the gamer identity (Plunkett 2014). Other articles raised grave concerns about the subculture of male gamers (Chu 2014).

Of course gaming has not ended. Mainstream commercial games are just as successful as ever. Indie gaming persists as well. GamerGate may not have transformed the gaming journalism culture as GamerGaters had hoped, and it may not have eradicated misogyny from gaming culture the way that feminist critics may have wished. But it has brought mainstream media attention to gaming culture and has helped to renew attention to gender disparities across cultural genres. The world of gaming is now heavily intertwined with the anonymous world of social media and the Internet. That has created a culture in both places that is rampant with bullying and threats—an upsetting but logical result of the culture of anonymity. Anonymity, like the hacktivist group Anonymous, can be powerful and can effect change that might not otherwise happen. But it is difficult to hold accountable.

* This site has been removed. An archive of the page can be found at https://web.archive.org/web/20150310043424/http://wiki.gamergate.me/index.php?title=Timeline. The list of articles is under the entry for "28 Aug 2014."

Jennifer Allaway, now a graduate of Willamette University, conducted a study of gender issues in gaming as part of a funded undergraduate research project. She interviewed 34 games professionals and conducted a survey of 344 respondents. She then began a new project, using an online survey method, studying the role of diversity in game development. In a post on Jezebel from October 13, 2014, she said she was close to completing her data collection when GamerGate caught wind of it (Allaway 2014). She received an e-mail on September 25 warning her that she had been targeted for "vote-brigading," which is a coordinated attack of something posted on social media to get it voted down or taken down. One discussion I found of the practice described it as "the Reddit form of a lynch mob."* In Allaway's case, vote brigading resulted in a lot of fake survey responses. She explained: "In under four hours, the developer survey jumped from around 700 responses, which had been collected over the course of a month, to over 1100 responses. The responses . . . ranged in their degree of racism and misogyny, but they all ridiculed the project with dishonest mockery" (Allaway 2014). The new surveys that she collected were filled with phrases like "suck my dick" and "kill yourself." Allaway concludes that GamerGate is a hate group, with Eron Gjoni as its initial leader, a series of recruitment practices online, propaganda tools that include YouTube videos and memes, and a practice of dehumanizing its victims.

Erik Kain, a gaming blogger for *Forbes*, has argued that GamerGate is not a hate group, but rather a consumer movement. He credited GamerGaters with organizing a revolt against a deeply unsatisfying marketplace by loyal consumers who deserve better. GamerGate, he argued, is "the natural outcropping of upset consumers who have long been at odds with the video game media" (Kain 2014). Is GamerGate a hate group, or a consumer movement? Can it be both?

Turning the lens from GamerGaters to feminist critics of the gaming industry, how do we make sense of the women who embrace a gamer identity while also challenging what that identity means? Do the women who make and play indie games like *Depression Quest* also participate in what GamerGaters call hardcore point and shoot games? If these women are part of gamer culture, what are the common threads across that culture? How does feminist

---

* This comment was found in a Reddit discussion board retrieved June 28, 2015, at http://www.reddit.com/r/OutOfTheLoop/comments/24d8cj/whats_vote_brigading_and_why_is_it_illegal/.

participation in the gaming industry transform the practice of feminism? Can games be a useful tool for addressing questions of inequality?

CONCLUSION

This case study has shifted our focus from resistance identities to project identities, to use the language of Manuel Castells that I discussed in chapter 1. Resistance identities, like those found in queer social media celebrities and the disability activists who critiqued the disability/miracle meme, are focused on defending individuals and groups against the oppressive impacts of hegemonic structures that privilege what Castells refers to as legitimizing identities: those that benefit most from the matrix of domination and oppression. Project identities do more than defend, they transform—or they at least seek social transformation.

In this case study we have at least one project identity at work, and perhaps two. The women who are leading the charge in both critiquing existing video games and creating new ones are seeking to transform the way that gender works within the field of video games—in terms of who makes video games, who plays them, and what the content and characters look like. These women are using art as a tool of social change, from the video games they design to the videos that Anita Sarkeesian has produced to give her audience new tools for thinking about women in video games. They are also using social media as one of their sets of artistic tools, including blogs, Twitter, and YouTube.

Are GamerGaters enacting a project identity or a legitimizing identity? That is a tricky question. On the one hand, many GamerGaters appear to be unemployed or underemployed, presumably living in their parents' basements, if Wizardchan is an accurate reflection of the movement. That would lead me to conclude that GamerGaters are part of a project identity seeking to transform the gaming field in exactly the opposite direction to that sought by the women game developers and game critics. On the other hand, GamerGate has been partially led by the successful actor Adam Baldwin, and the flames have been fanned by journalists at Breitbart. That leads me to believe that GamerGaters are actually just a backlash seeking to shore up the dominance of legitimizing identities, particularly of straight white men.

Are GamerGaters artists? They have generated a tremendous amount of creative, if also destructive, content online in the form of YouTube videos, tweets, memes, and much more. Their discussions on Reddit, 4chan, 8chan, and Wizardchan constitute a kind of creative support group that generates energy and ideas for the project.

For both groups, social media has been incredibly effective as a creative and political tool. Social media has allowed Anita Sarkeesian to reach a massive audience with her work. Although she chose a path away from academia, toward a more public form of scholarship, her work is widely used in college classrooms. Her ideas are widely discussed, and she is likely a major influence on a new generation of gamers and game developers. Social media has allowed a seemingly ragtag assortment of male gamers to organize and fight back against feminist influences in gaming. And sadly, it has worked, in the sense that some women have left gaming entirely as a result of GamerGate. But social media has also been a very powerful tool for those who have fought back against GamerGate, and it has enabled them to expose the movement for the backlash that it is.

6

Occupy Wall Street: Class Perspectives on Social Media

All day, all week, occupy Wall Street!

With this chant, coined by rapper Lupe Fiasco, began the social movement that, though considered a failure by many, is likely responsible for the presidential candidacy of Bernie Sanders. **Occupy Wall Street** officially began with the first occupation on September 17, 2011. The protests were intended to take place on Chase Manhattan Plaza in front of the headquarters of JP Morgan Chase, a block and a half from Wall Street but even closer to the Federal Reserve Bank of New York. However, police barricaded the plaza and would not allow protestors in. The first alternative was to move to Bowling Green, a public park a few blocks south that is also surrounded by the titans of the financial industry. But police had also shut that down to keep out the protestors. As one protestor pointed out on CNN, they had even surrounded the iconic Charging Bull statue, a symbol of Wall Street that happens to resemble the bull logo of Merrill Lynch, with barricades. Said one protestor: "A success? It's already happening. They corralled a bull. And that's pretty much a huge symbolic statement."*

Fortunately for the protestors, there was a third option that police could not so easily shut down: Zuccotti Park. Zuccotti Park is north on Broadway from Bowling Green, just a block from Chase Manhattan Plaza in one direction, and a block from the 9/11 Memorial in the other direction. It is a publicly accessible park that is privately owned by Brookfield Properties, a major global real estate development firm that owns a number of major properties in the financial district of New York City. The park had been named Liberty Plaza Park when it was first built in 1968 by U.S. Steel. But in 2006, after renovations to repair damage resulting from the attacks of 9/11, it received its new name, after the chairman of Brookfield Properties, John Zuccotti. So a park with infamous ties to American finance strangely became the only possible host to protests against that very financial world, precisely because of the private ownership of this public space.

An estimated one thousand people participated in the first day of protests (Week 2011). Some estimates are much lower, and others are up to two thousand. About sixty people camped in Zuccotti Park on that first night. The protestors remained in Zuccotti Park for nearly two months, before they were finally removed by police on November 15, 2011. Occupy Wall Street spawned the even larger Occupy movement, which held protests in numerous cities across the United States and in more than eighty countries (White 2016).

ONE DEMAND

Although Occupy has always identified as a leaderless resistance movement, it did not erupt from nothing. Occupy Wall Street was functionally organized

* CNN, "2011: Occupy Wall Street Begins," https://www.youtube.com/watch?v=GgJ5f9ZqOFc.

by the magazine *Adbusters* and the associated Adbusters Media Foundation. *Adbusters* was founded in Vancouver in 1989 by Kalle Lasn and Bill Schmalz. According to its website, "Adbusters is a not-for-profit magazine fighting back against the hostile takeover of our psychological, physical and cultural environments by commercial forces."* A first glance at *Adbusters* might lead you to think it is a magazine full of ads, but then you realize that the images are not selling anything. *Adbusters* uses the style of advertising to present ideas, something it refers to as "culture jamming." Its goal is to turn commercial culture on its head and expose it for what it is: crass, corrupt propaganda and commercial exploitation. The magazine is published every other month and is now also available for purchase online as a digital pdf.

A writer for *Adbusters*, Micah White, worked alongside Kalle Lasn in creating a series of viral campaigns that were driven by hashtag memes. White discusses how those early campaigns became a blueprint for Occupy Wall Street in his 2016 book *The End of Protest: A New Playbook for Revolution*. Some of the earlier campaigns included #NOSTARBUCKS and #BuyNothingDay, but these campaigns had marginal success. "[R]ather than be discouraged, I became convinced that our idea of a contagious action spread through a hashtag was simply ahead of its time. We failed because we were too early. I remember feeling that Kalle and I were living in the future of activism and being confident that if we tried again the people might catch up" (White 2016, 13). That next try would be Occupy Wall Street.

On July 13, 2011, *Adbusters* posted a call to action on its blog.† At the top is a collage featuring multiple copies of the same image: a dancer balancing on one leg on top of the Raging Bull statue in Bowling Green park, New York. A yellow rectangle across the center of the image features the hashtag that also serves as the call to action: #OCCUPYWALLSTREET. The post is addressed to "90,000 redeemers, rebels and radicals." The post describes a sea change in activism that is "a fusion of Tahrir with the acampadas of Spain," referring to the Egyptian uprising of January 2011 and the Spanish Indignados movement of May 2011. That influence of Egypt in particular would be echoed months later in an interview with economist Jeffrey Sachs:

* http://www.adbusters.org.

† The post is archived at https://web.archive.org/web/20110717094726/http://www.adbusters.org/blogs/adbusters-blog/occupywallstreet.html.

> I was in Egypt after Tahrir Square, talking to young people who had accomplished something completely amazing. Two thousand eleven was a year of global upheaval—I'd seen it everywhere. And a number of times in the spring, I said in interviews: Don't be so sure that this can't happen here. Because the precursors—of inequality, of a sense of injustice—apply to the U.S. (Lalinde et al. 2012)

The blog post calls for readers to join together in lower Manhattan on September 17, 2011, to "set up tents, kitchens, peaceful barricades and occupy Wall Street for a few months. Once there, we shall incessantly repeat one simple demand in a plurality of voices." The post does not commit to what that simple demand should be. Instead, it makes a suggestion and invites readers to use the comments section to offer suggestions and critiques. The suggested message is:

> [W]e demand that Barack Obama ordain a Presidential Commission tasked with ending the influence money has over our representatives in Washington. It's time for DEMOCRACY NOT CORPORATOCRACY, we're doomed without it.

Although Occupy members have a wide range of ideological commitments—including pro-environmentalism, antiracism, and anticolonialism—the movement committed early on to having a singular message that focused on economic inequality. At times the economic inequality that concerns them is framed as an inequality between two groups of humans—the wealthiest 1 percent and the remaining 99 percent—which has yielded the core concept of **The 99%**. But at other times it is framed as an inequality between corporations and humans. There is a logical association between the top 1 percent and the corporations they lead, and through which they acquire and manage their wealth. On the other hand, if we swap out some or all of the humans, the corporations still stand, and therefore the inequality still stands.

Another interesting aspect of the call to action is the fusion of street protests with social media action. On the one hand, they are very clearly calling for in-person, on the streets, face-to-face action. But the headline is a hashtag. The call to action is not a dichotomous either-or—streets or tweets—but an insistence that old style protests modeled on the Boston Tea Party could pair well with new media tools for tactical coordination.

So the call was issued. Over the two months that followed, the movement clearly began to pick up steam. Weekly planning meetings, called general assemblies, began on August 2. The first meeting was held in conjunction with another protest group, New Yorkers Against Budget Cuts, and took place in Bowling Green under the gaze of Charging Bull. A *Vanity Fair* article described the emerging consensus-based debate and decision-making style as "a sort of anarchist version of Robert's Rules of Order that allows anyone to speak and gauges feedback via hand signals. The system had been used successfully in Spain, but many of the New York activists who showed up that day were unfamiliar with the concept" (Lalinde et al. 2012). A poster for the second general assembly featured the phrase "We are the 99." This eventually became the core message of the movement. The anthropologist David Graeber is credited with the phrase. "On August 4, we came up with the 'We are the 99 percent' idea. I just threw it out there. I'm sure a lot of people were thinking it—I just suggested it to the group. It was a reference to all those people who were talking about the 1 percent" (quoted in Lalinde et al. 2012). Although the phrase was now in play, a blog post on August 11 indicated that the group was still working to identify the specific demand to focus on:

> Strategically speaking, there is a very real danger that if we naively put our cards on the table and rally around the "overthrow of capitalism" or some equally outworn utopian slogan, then our Tahrir moment will quickly fizzle into another inconsequential ultra-lefty spectacle soon forgotten. But if we have the cunning to come up with a deceptively simple Trojan Horse demand . . . something profound, yet so specific and doable that it is impossible for President Obama to ignore . . . then we just might have a crack at creating a decisive moment of truth for America.*

This blog again poses possibilities for the core message without identifying a finalist. One option is to continue the call for a commission on the corruption of politics by the financial industry. Another option is the so-called Robin Hood rule, which would take money from wealthy corporations and redistribute it to the poor. Finally, there is the option of reviving the Glass-Steagall Act. The Glass-Steagall Act refers to a set of banking regulations enshrined in the Banking Act of 1933 that restricted the intermingling

* https://www.adbusters.org/action/occupywallstreet/occupywallstreet-update/.

of Federal Reserve Banks with commercial banks. "Most critically, Glass-Steagall made it illegal for a bank that held FDIC-insured deposits to invest in anything other than government bonds and similarly low-risk vehicles" (Goldstein 2016). Glass-Steagall kept banking relatively low risk. But those provisions were repealed in 1999 by the Gramm-Leach-Bliley Act, and that repeal is often blamed for the economic recession that began in 2007. The consistent thread is still economic inequality and the tremendous power of financial corporations.

On August 16, 2011, *Adbusters* announced that the Spanish Indignados would join with them in solidarity by occupying the Madrid Stock Exchange.* The same post also described a planned movement in Washington for October. The developing picture was that Occupy Wall Street was not intended to be a one-city event, but rather a worldwide movement.

The next major announcement about the movement came on August 22, 2011, when **Anonymous** proclaimed it would be joining the movement through a video released by the group on YouTube. Over backdrop scenes of protests and street clashes, and against an orchestral war song, a digitized voice reads:

> Hello citizens of the internet. We are Anonymous. On September 17th, Anonymous will flood into lower Manhattan, set up tents, kitchens, peaceful barricades, and occupy Wall Street for a few months. Once there, we shall incessantly repeat one simple demand in a plurality of voices. We want freedom. This is a non-violent protest. We do not encourage violence in any way. The abuse and corruption of corporations, banks, and governments ends here. Join us. We are Anonymous. We are legion. We do not forgive. We do not forget. Wall Street, expect us.†

It is not clear in this script whether the one demand is "we want freedom" or is simply still yet to be determined. My best guess is that it was still being debated and worked out in the general assemblies taking place in New York. The protestors in the video are all wearing the Guy Fawkes mask associated with Anonymous—the same mask that is worn by the character V in the 2005

*https://www.adbusters.org/action/occupywallstreet/spanish-indignados-join-occupywallstreet/.

† AnonOps, "Occupy Wall Street—Sep17," https://www.youtube.com/watch?v=zSpM2kieMu8.

film *V for Vendetta*. Gregg Housh, a spokesman for Anonymous, explained that the group needed to find masks in order to protect their anonymity during street protests:

> One of the [discussions] we were having was "With everyone going to the streets, we need to cover our faces if we want to remain anonymous." So we started spitballing, throwing out a bunch of ideas. [Guy Fawkes] was one of them. We called around to all of the costume shops and comic-book shops in most of the major cities worldwide—from Moscow and Paris to New York. We realized that the *V* [*for Vendetta*] mask was in every major city in the world. It was cheap and available. (Quoted in Lalinde et al. 2012)

Guy Fawkes is a famed English conspirator who was arrested on November 5, 1605, for attempting to blow up Parliament. That date is known alternately as Guy Fawkes Day or Bonfire Night and is marked by burning effigies of Guy Fawkes. His reason for wanting to blow up Parliament came down to the issue of religion, as he hoped for England to return to Catholicism. But his name is associated now with conspiracy and the potential for a small group to ignite a social revolution.

Anonymous released the video on YouTube, through an Occupy blog post, and via Twitter:

> @AnonOps: Do you have your tents ready for #OCCUPYWALLSTREET? >> SPREAD THE WORD! >> http://anonops.blogspot.com/2011/08/occupy-wall-street-occupywallstreet_10.html . . . #AnonOps#Anonymous.*

An *Adbusters* blog post on September 6 made an oblique reference to the "We are the 99%" concept, referring to "The 99% that will no longer tolerate the greed and corruption of the 1%."† But even this blog post continued to ask for ideas about the core message. It also dismissed the first idea, the call for a presidential commission to examine the influence of corporate donations on politics:

---

* https://twitter.com/anonops/status/105667927113596928.

†https://www.adbusters.org/action/occupywallstreet/does-the-american-left-have-the-guts-to-pull-this-off/

> [A]nother ineffective commission? Forget it. Waste of time. They're made up of self-interested insiders. That would never satisfy the demands of these radicals. And if Obama did appoint a commission, it'd just be a ploy to delay and disburse angry revolutionaries.
>
> Remember: In Tahrir Square, "Mubarak must go" was the "one simple demand." That outcome was easy to measure. But so far with Occupy Wall Street the demands are vague. No clear rallying cry. That uncertainty adds risk and danger for both sides.*

At this point, *Adbusters* was not just asking for ideas, but also sounding the alarm. The movement was less than two weeks away from occupation and still had no clear message. Based on the model of Tahrir Square, the protestors had good reason to fear a risk of failure. Another post on the *Adbusters* blog the next day indicated that the task of choosing a demand was being punted to the occupation itself:

> On September 17, 20,000 of us will descend on Wall Street, the iconic financial center of America, set up a peaceful encampment, hold a people's assembly to decide what our one demand will be, and carry out an agenda of full-spectrum, absolutely nonviolent civil disobedience the likes of which the country has not seen since the freedom marches of the 1960s.†

Clearly the "one demand" played a central role in the push to occupy Wall Street, but it was still an empty box, waiting to be filled in. The next blog post, on September 13, focused on what to do if police blocked protestors from gathering near Wall Street, made no mention of the one demand at all.

On September 15, two days before occupation began, an *Adbusters* blog declared: "Hey President Obama . . . get ready for our one demand!"‡ However, the text of the blog raised doubts that Occupy would succeed in finding an agreed-on demand:

> What if, try as we might, we just can't come up with only one demand? Well, then maybe we can decide together on an END THE MONIED

* Ibid.

† https://www.adbusters.org/action/occupywallstreet/occupywallstreet-less-than-two-weeks-away/.

‡ https://www.adbusters.org/action/occupywallstreet/hey-president-obama-2/.

> CORRUPTION OF AMERICA MANIFESTO–a rousing compendium of our most urgent demands. And on the seventh day of our occupation we publicly deliver our manifesto to the White House and to the American media, letting Obama know that we won't leave Wall Street until he responds.*

The blog posts highlights one of the unique difficulties of sustaining a leaderless movement. No one in Occupy Wall Street, *Adbusters*, or Anonymous could simply declare what the one demand should be, but some people within these groups had nevertheless succeeded in declaring that one demand was the best tactic. Clearly this eleventh-hour post was a way to prepare for the possibility that a single demand would never be found. A final post on September 16 reminded participants that a **people's assembly** would be held in the afternoon, at the occupation, to finally decide on a demand.† No demand materialized at the people's assembly on day 1, nor did it in the days that followed.

The Occupy protestors finally released their one demand on day 5 of the occupation, through a post on their website—or rather, they released a list of "one demands":

> On September 21st, 2011, Troy Davis, an innocent man, was murdered by the state of Georgia. Troy Davis was one of the 99 percent.
>
> *Ending capital punishment is our one demand.*
>
> On September 21st, 2011, the richest 400 Americans owned more wealth than half of the country's population.
>
> *Ending wealth inequality is our one demand.*
>
> On September 21st, 2011, four of our members were arrested on baseless charges.
>
> *Ending police intimidation is our one demand.*
>
> On September 21st, 2011, we determined that Yahoo lied about occupywallst.org being in spam filters.
>
> *Ending corporate censorship is our one demand.*
>
> On September 21st, 2011, roughly eighty percent of Americans thought the country was on the wrong track.

---

* Ibid.

†https://www.adbusters.org/action/occupywallstreet/occupywallstreet-orientation-guide/.

Ending the modern gilded age is our one demand.

On September 21st, 2011, roughly 15% of Americans approved of the job Congress was doing.

Ending political corruption is our one demand.

On September 21st, 2011, roughly one sixth of Americans did not have work.

Ending joblessness is our one demand.

On September 21st, 2011, roughly one sixth of America lived in poverty.

Ending poverty is our one demand.

On September 21st, 2011, roughly fifty million Americans were without health insurance.

Ending health-profiteering is our one demand.

On September 21st, 2011, America had military bases in around one hundred and thirty out of one hundred and sixty-five countries.

Ending American imperialism is our one demand.

On September 21st, 2011, America was at war with the world.

*Ending war is our one demand.**

By my count that is eleven demands, all identified as the one demand. How do they justify this? By declaring in a note preceding the post: "Our use of the one demand is a rhetorical device." Redefining the one demand strategy as a rhetorical device gave them a way to declare success and move forward, despite not producing the single demand they had seemingly been promised. But it also left them without the tool that the founders had believed was so critical to the success of their models in Egypt and Spain. In the weeks, and then months, that followed, competing factions of protestors continued to work toward cohesive statements of Occupy demands, including one known as the Liberty Square Blueprint† and another labeled the 99 Percent Declaration.‡ Both were written by enormous teams of protestors, and both had an open-ended character that makes it difficult to find a final list of

---

*http://occupywallst.org/article/a-message-from-occupied-wall-street-day-five/.

† https://web.archive.org/web/20120425135529/http://www.freenetworkmovement.org/commons/index.php?title=Liberty_Square_Blueprint.

‡ https://web.archive.org/web/20120228052013/http://www.the99declaration.org/.

demands or goals. The 99 Percent Declaration had twenty-one demands in February 2012,* but then just six in April,† and was back up to twenty in July.‡

Lacking a single demand, the message of Occupy Wall Street became the slogan "We are the 99%." This slogan is based on the idea that 1 percent of the population controls an unfair and unacceptable proportion of the world's wealth and has unique access to positions of power. The idea of "the 1 percent" is synonymous with wealthy men, often white, who sit on massive fortunes and corporate empires and have little connection to the everyday lives of the middle and working classes. They are associated with the mistakes and malfeasance that tripped the world economy into a recession in 2007. They are the beneficiaries of government bailouts, and many of them managed to claim large bonuses even as the companies they led left many without jobs or homes.

* Ibid.

† https://web.archive.org/web/20120425134312/http://www.the99declaration.org/.

‡ https://web.archive.org/web/20120703044611/http://www.the99declaration.org/.

METHODOLOGICAL MOMENT: Privacy and Anonymity in a Public Space

The Internet and social media create an odd mix of public and private, allowing some users to maintain tremendous anonymity while others have their most private secrets exposed to the world. danah boyd explored this topic at length in her 2014 book *It's Complicated: The Social Lives of Networked Teens*. The young people she studied expressed a desire for privacy in their online interactions, particularly privacy from their parents. Although most were technically aware of the public nature of social media, they still maintained an expectation of privacy.

boyd was studying teenagers, but I think it would be a mistake to assume that it is any different with adults. Although some adults may be very mindful of the public nature of social media, others may have not considered the issue at all. This public/private concern is an issue for two major reasons, as explained by Robert V. Kozinets in his book *Netnography* (2010). First and foremost, it is an issue that we need to consider as we think about our **research ethics** and the implications of our studies. Do the research subjects—the people being studied—know that their work is

continues

METHODOLOGICAL MOMENT:
Privacy and Anonymity in a Public Space *continued*

being observed and could be used in academic scholarship? Do they think of the work they are posting as public in nature? If they believe, or might believe, that they are posting under an expectation of privacy, are they going be given an opportunity to consent to participation in research? Will their identity be protected?

Second, the public/private issue raises the possibility that virtual ethnography will need to be reviewed and approved by an **institutional review board** (IRB). These boards exist at universities and other centers of research (school districts typically have their own IRBs) to protect the interests of human subjects and to minimize the harm that a human research subject might experience as a result of the research itself. The IRB issue might seem one and the same as the ethical issue, but that is not necessarily the case. Depending on the design of the virtual ethnographic research, an IRB may not deem the research to fall under its auspices, either because it views the research as not producing generalizable claims (which leads some IRBs to deem it as not research) or because the design focuses more on an analysis of existing content and less on online interactions. In the latter case, such an IRB is treating the Internet and social media as a publicly available text, rather than a space of interaction. In cases in which a research design is not subject to review by an IRB, the researchers are still morally and institutionally obligated to act in an ethical manner toward their research subjects. Most important, they should seek to minimize any harm that their research subjects might face as a result of the research.

Ethics is not as simple as a yes or no question. It requires making complicated decisions and focusing on the issues of minimizing harm to the research subjects. In the case studies that I present in this book, I had to weigh whether the participants in these stories viewed their social media posts as public documents that were attempting to reach a public audience, as opposed to a private audience of specific individuals. To that question, the answer was a consistent yes. In some ways the usual concerns were flipped on their heads in these case studies. Because my research subjects were trying to reach a public audience as artists and activists, denying them their authorship of these posts seemed to be the more unethical route to take.

In addition, I had to consider the issue of anonymity and whether the identities of these individuals could truly be protected. It would actually

continues

METHODOLOGICAL MOMENT:
Privacy and Anonymity in a Public Space *continued*

be very misleading to attach a fake profile name to a tweet or post that could be easily found with a simple Google search. Most of the individuals discussed in this book were also heavily discussed in the news media, so using pseudonyms would ultimately be fruitless.

However, for research in which the public character of the postings or of the subjects is less clear, scholars need to consider ways to protect the privacy of their subjects. Kozinets sums up the dilemmas that are created by the metaphors we use to think about the Internet:

> The internet is not really a place or a text; it is not either public or private. It is not even one single type of social interaction, but many types: chats, postings, comments on mass-trafficked blogs, sharings of soundclips and videos, telephone conversations shared using **VOIP** protocols. The internet is uniquely and only the internet. As we reason about it, we need to keep our guiding metaphors in mind. (2010, 142)

Ultimately, Kozinets is arguing that we should leave these metaphors behind and focus on developing a set of research protocols that are tailored to the Internet itself and the many different types of interactions within the Internet, rather than modeling our research practices on those developed for other types of subjects. Just as the legal system has had to catch up to the new issues raised by the Internet and social media, so also do our research methods and our research ethics need to catch up to the unique issues engendered by these platforms.

THE METHODS OF OCCUPATION

Occupy Wall Street, and the broader Occupy movement, deployed a range of tactics both on the ground and in social media. Some of these were learned from previous social movements, such as the Arab Spring and the *acampanadas* movement in Spain. Others were learned through a series of actions taken by *Adbusters*. Micah White's book, which is less a memoir of Occupy than a handbook for activism, indicates that he and Lasn are committed to a long-term, lifetime search for how to make social change a reality. Following are a few of their primary tactics.

Occupation

One of the key strategies that Occupy learned from the revolution in Egypt was to occupy a strategic and visible public place. **Occupation** of spaces is by no means a new revolutionary tactic; in many ways it is one of the oldest tactics of protest. But occupation can *seem* less logical in a globalized and networked world. Occupation—actually showing up for the revolution—marks the investment of one's body in the cause. Social media activism, often denigrated as mere slacktivism (click, like, share, move on), can seem like a total divestment from the cause. But Occupy, like Egypt, found a way to merge occupation tactics with social media strategies.

Occupy held Zuccotti Park for just shy of two months—from September 17 to November 15, 2011. Although a threatened police raid on October 14 nearly shut the protest down, when the city backed off it only strengthened the resolve of the occupiers, who saw that they could successfully stand up to the government and the police. According to Michael Levitin, who published the movement's unofficial newsletter *The Occupied Wall Street Journal*, "That was the major turning point. After that, the tents went up. They had had this rule where we could stay in the park—but no sitting on tarps, no bags, no benches. But after that night it was complete defiance. The city loved us. The country loved us" (quoted in Lalinde et al. 2012).

A precursor to occupation was the student sit-ins made famous in protests against the Vietnam War and numerous causes since. As Micah White notes, these sit-ins were held in elite spaces that were unavailable to the public and easily ignored by the media. The logic of Occupy was to make the revolution publicly available—protestors were encouraged to leave behind jobs and homes and live in tents in the park—and annoyingly visible. The leaders of the very organizations they protested against had to reroute their commutes to work and see the protests through their office windows.

People's Assemblies

The occupation strategy was partly inspired by the seizing of Tahrir Square in Egypt and partly the seizing of the square at Puerta Del Sol in Madrid, Spain, by protestors in the Indignados movement, also known *acampanadas*. Another tactic that Occupy learned from the Indignados was the people's assembly, also referred to at times as a general assembly. Throughout 2011, and prior to the call for Occupy, the Indignados had been holding massive protests in Spain, particularly in Madrid. Like the Occupy movement that would follow, the Indignados lacked a single demand, but shared a set of overlapping characteristics such as being young, unemployed, and angered by government cuts to welfare.

Lacking leaders and specific focuses, the Indignados relied on a method of assembly to discuss their positions and develop shared platforms. Similarly, Occupy relies on a method of people's assembly that began well before the first occupation. These assemblies emphasize consensus building and the value of all perspectives. They use breakout working groups of smaller numbers, determined by self-selection, to refine points and develop proposals. These proposals are then presented to the full assembly, and members respond using a set of hand gestures:

Agreement: Hands up, fingers up and waving.
Disagreement: Hands down, fingers down and waving.
Unsure: Hands flat, fingers horizontal and waving.
Clarification (requested or offered): Hand curled in the shape of the letter C.
Point of Process (conversation has strayed from procedure): Hands forming a triangle between the index fingers and thumbs (with thumbs forming one line).
Block (hard disagreement): Arms crossed to form an X.*

Not surprisingly, making progress in a general assembly is difficult, but participants spoke well of the process. David Graeber describes how he helped to form the general assembly process in New York:

> It was supposed to be a general assembly, but instead we had a top-down leadership group that was going to make all the decisions. They were going to make speeches, and then we were going to march under waving banners. Who fucking cares?
>
> I started tapping people on the shoulder who looked like they were as annoyed as I was and said, if we actually did a real general assembly, would you come? We ended up forming a circle, and at that point everyone defected from the rally. (Quoted in Lalinde et al. 2012)

* Some of these hand signals are summarized at the website for the New York City General Assembly, http://www.nycga.net/resources/general-assembly-guide/.

Participant Sandra Nurse, who had been invited by a friend, explained her experience with the assembly: "I'd never been to a general assembly before. I wasn't aware of this process they used, so it seemed bizarre. But it was also fascinating (quoted in Lalinde et al. 2012).

Leaderlessness

As a challenge to arbitrary and unfair social hierarchies, Occupy sought to avoid such hierarchies in its own structure. *Adbusters*, under Kalle Lasn and Micah White, launched the call for people to Occupy, but they were not the leaders of the organization. The organization had no leaders in the usual sense, although leadership was demonstrated at various points by a variety of participants. There is no board of directors for Occupy Wall Street, no executive leadership, and not even a mailing address. Also, there are no gatekeepers of membership. There are no dues and no forms to fill out. Anyone with a spirit of solidarity with Occupy can simply declare himself or herself a participant. Occupy is a deliberately horizontal organization, in contrast to the vertical hierarchies of corporations that are mimicked in nonprofits and most voluntary associations.

> Uncritical openness was Occupy's downfall: the general assemblies were paralyzed by the inability to distinguish between true and false. Participants who had been with Occupy for a day were given a say equal to that of committed activists who had founded the first encampments. (White 2016, 112–113)

Hashtags

Adbusters has used **hashtags** as an ordering principle for a range of campaigns. Occupy inherited that technique and spawned a number of hashtags, the most common of which are #OWS, #Occupy, and #OccupyWallStreet.*

---

* A note on hashtag conventions: the capitalization of some or all letters is purely for emphasis or clarity. Capitalizing an entire one-word hashtag can be effective, but capitalizing all of a multiple-word hashtag is much less so, given the lack of spacing between words. In those cases, it is more common to capitalize the first letters of each word. Whether some, all, or none of the letters is capitalized, the hashtag still has the same indexing impact. Clicking on #OCCUPYWALLSTREET, #OccupyWallStreet, and #occupywallstreet will take the Twitter user to the same list of tweets.

What is the value of a hashtag? A hashtag functions as a kind of indexing system. It organizes a tweet or post into a category or set of categories. But in doing so, it also connects that post to other posts with the same hashtag. This creates a kind of backdoor network within platforms that allows people who do not know each other and may not connect with or follow each other to participate in the same conversation. Clicking on the hashtag presents the user with a reverse chronological list of tweets bearing that hashtag.

Granted, the search function can also find tweets with the same terms that might be used in a hashtag, but it is also going to turn up a lot of unrelated tweets as well, which has the effect of creating a lot of noise in the network, to the point of making the conversation hard to follow. Hashtags remove most of that noise, except for a portion that remains due to deliberate hacking of the tag. These are people who add irrelevant hashtags to their posts, either for comedic effect or in hopes of hijacking an audience from one issue to pay attention to another issue. When Beyoncé released her visual album *Lemonade*, a conversation developed in social media that was indexed with the hashtag #Lemonade. A coffee chain in my city seized the opportunity to advertise its new lemonade. A local frenzy of tweets with #Lemonade added some confusing noise to a worldwide conversation about a striking new album. It had the effect of drawing curious people to the chain's account who would possibly becoming followers or customers. So hashtags do not remove all of the noise, but they remove much of it, and that allows the conversation to be more coordinated. In Twitter, the option to click on "Top" within a hashtag search allows the user to just "listen" to those tweets that have garnered the most attention.

In addition to allowing for coordinated and indexed conversations, hashtags also allow conversations to grow and spread in unpredictable ways. Hashtags allow for the rhizomatic growth of social movements. **Rhizomes** are underground networks of stems for certain plants. These networks emerge out of existing plants, but they are able to produce new buds of their own and to survive when cut off from the original plant. Ginger is a great example of a rhizome. In social theory, the philosophers Gilles Deleuze and Felix Guattari have suggested the rhizome as a metaphor for understanding the spread of ideas. They contrast the horizontal, decentralized system of the rhizome with the vertical and centrally organized system of the tree.

> Let us summarize the principal characteristics of a rhizome: unlike trees or their roots, the rhizome connects any point to any other point, and

> its traits are not necessarily linked to traits of the same nature; it brings into play very different regimes of signs, and even non-sign states. . . . It is comprised not of units but of dimensions, or rather directions in motion. It has neither beginning nor end, but always a middle (milieu) from which it grows and which it overspills. . . . Unlike the graphic arts, drawing or photography, unlike tracings, the rhizome pertains to a map that must be produced, constructed, a map that is always detachable, connectable, reversible, modifiable, and has multiple entranceways and exits and its own lines of flight. (Deleuze and Guattari 1987, 21)

The rhizomatic structure that Deleuze and Guattari are describing provides an excellent metaphor that applies both to some forms of social media and to some forms of social movements, including Occupy. Hashtags are the building blocks of rhizomatic conversations carried out in Twitter and in other platforms that allow for tagging. I can control my profile as a Twitter user, but I cannot control a hashtag, even if I create it. If I start a conversation with a hashtag, my withdrawal from the conversation cannot cause the conversation to end. If I disagree with the direction a conversation takes, my power to change the direction is not greater than that of any other participant. The hashtag may create numerous local conversations that can function independently of an original or global conversation.

Similarly, in rhizomatic social movements, there is no central trunk that controls the movements of branches, but rather an organic multidimensional series of interconnected lines of action. Being leaderless, Occupy was naturally rhizomatic. Each participant directed their own line of action within the movement, coordinating with and only with other participants who shared the same interest.

Memes

Memes are not necessarily separate from hashtags, but they reflect a unique way of using them. A hashtag in and of itself is not a meme. If a company creates a hashtag and largely controls how it is used—or if no one else shows an interest in using it—then it's just a marketing device or a communication tool. Memification happens when actors other than the hashtag originator apply the hashtag to circumstances that differ from the original context. Further memification happens when those actors shift the hashtag in some way to make it unique to them, even as it still indicates a connection to the original. #OWS and #OccupyWallStreet are just hashtags. The memification happens when others start adding #OCCUPY to their own political activities and forms of protest, and when the hashtag itself gets amended.

> Local activists joined the wider movement by appending the name of their city to the word Occupy. Each occupation had its own flair while maintaining a shared ideal of participatory, consensual democracy. During the height of our movement, every protest called itself Occupy. To be taken seriously, one needed only use the meme. And the movement spread more quickly because few people knew the origin of the idea. For most participants, Occupy simple appeared out of nowhere, making it easier for them to take ownership of the meme. . . . People learned that by invoking Occupy their protests would quickly attract eager participants and curious media attention. Eventually anything from protesting development near Berkeley (Occupy the Farm), to providing hurricane disaster relief (Occupy Sandy) could be a part of the Occupy umbrella. Building from fluke events to become the lingua franca for a variety of passions and causes, our new social protest behaviour had gained history-making weight. (White 2016, 22–23)

To be clear, there are three forms of memification at work here. First, there is the addition of the hashtag #Occupy to posts on social media about a wide range of concerns, going well beyond those that had been discussed in general assemblies in New York City. For example, pulling up the hashtag on Twitter as I write this in 2016, I see that #Occupy is still used very frequently, including this June 5, 2016, tweet from @justiceunited: "Shut Down the Democratic National Convention: Corporate Democrats rigged the primary election . . . #occupy #news."* Second, there is the modification of #Occupy to include a range of additional issues or locations, including #OccupyPhilly, #OccupyArt, and #OccupyDisney (all real examples). Third, there is the invocation of Occupy outside of the realm of social media and therefore without the hashtag. This includes the names of the various Occupy groups around the world and other ways that Occupy has become a cultural reference point.

*https://twitter.com/justiceunited/status/739642830230949889.

Occupy has appeared in televisions shows from *South Park* to *30 Rock* and received shout-outs from Miley Cyrus and Jay-Z.

Memes are an extension of the rhizomatic character of both Occupy and its particular social media strategies. Occupy is deeply rooted in the work of local chapters and allied organizations, but it is not completely dependent on them. Moreover, the successes and failures of the global Occupy umbrella have a limited impact on these rhizomatic extensions. If Occupy shuts down on a global or national level, the local branches can continue operating. Organizations that predate Occupy or are otherwise unaffiliated can easily be added to the Occupy umbrella in a number of ways: they can add the Occupy hashtag to their campaigns, they can add Occupy to the their names, they can ally with Occupy organizations, and they can use Occupy's online InterOccupy tool to share their activities with the Occupy network.* InterOccupy provides individuals with resources to find Occupy groups in their area and provides groups with the tools to start a new Occupy "hub."

This overview of Occupy strategies is not exhaustive but highlights the most widely used and most unique aspects of Occupy strategies as they compare to earlier social movements in the United States. Occupy was not a hacktivist movement, because it insisted on a two-pronged approach of online organization and on-the-streets action. "Offline and online action are necessary but not sufficient for revolution. The lesson of Occupy Wall Street was that meme warfare is only as effective as the underlying theory of social change" (White 2016, 217). I discuss Occupy's theory of social change in the next section as a way of reflecting on what it can teach us about both the lessons of Occupy and the future role of social media in movements for social change.

THE END OF OCCUPATION

Was Occupy a success or a failure? The answer depends on how you measure. First, Occupy is not over. There are cells of activists who still identify with Occupy all over the world. So the ideas carry forward with them. Moreover, Occupy was hugely successful in generating greater discourse about social inequality in the United States and globally. Bernie Sanders's supporters for his 2016 presidential bid represent a remnant of Occupy. It is frequently pointed out that his supporters were very young, aligning them with the

* http://interoccupy.net

Occupy demographic far more than supporters for any other candidate. The themes of his campaign seem to have been pulled straight out of the Occupy playbook. His top five issues, according to his website, were (1) "income and wealth inequality," (2) tuition free college, (3) "getting big money out of politics and restoring democracy," (4) "creating decent paying jobs," and (5) "a living wage."* Bernie Sanders may have lost the nomination to be the presidential candidate of the Democratic Party, but his campaign shifted the ways that front-runner Hillary Clinton had to talk about those same issues of inequality. That shift may have softened the demands of Occupy, but it also brought them to a mainstream of Americans who could never imagine protesting in tents in a park but are absolutely impacted by economic inequality.

In many important respects, Occupy failed. It never produced a single demand, and none of the demands that it did produce over time were met. Micah Hill has a very interesting perspective on the failures of Occupy:

> Occupy Wall Street was a ***constructive failure*** but not a *total failure*. Occupy demonstrated the efficacy of using social memes to quickly spread a movement, shifted the political debate on the fair distribution of wealth, trained a new generation of activists who went on to be the base for movements ranging from campus fossil fuel divestment to Black Lives Matter protests. . . . However, an honest assessment reveals that Occupy Wall Street failed to live up to its revolutionary potential. . . . I call Occupy Wall Street a constructive failure because the movement revealed underlying flaws in dominant, and still prevalent, theories of how to achieve social change through collective action. (White 2016, 26–27)

White argues that Occupy could not possibly have succeeded in the face of a new operating terrain for major governments. Occupy's strategies presumed a democratic system that would respond to the demands of the people. However, governmental forces are now stronger than ever at pushing back against that will, as evidenced by the militarization of the police. "Western governments are not required to comply with their people's demands, even if those demands are articulated by a historic social movement backed [by] millions of people in a social movement" (White 2016, 36). This leads White to insist that new models for social change are needed. He predicts that the days of marching are over.

* https://berniesanders.com/issues/.

What does White see as the new model for social action? The short version is this: *revolutionaries better pray!* Existing theories of social change, he argues, have vacillated between voluntarism (good ideas and leadership can change the world) and structuralism (the world changes when specific conditions are met). Both of these approaches are materialist in nature, in that they focus on social change in the world that we can see and touch. We are missing alternative ideas from the spiritual world that would allow social change to occur through divine intervention or personal enlightenment.

As a sociologist, I struggle to take White's "new playbook for revolution" seriously. Guided by the historical materialism of Karl Marx and other scholars whose work shaped the discipline of sociology, I do not know how to treat spiritual factors as variables that can have a predictable relationship with the organization of modern society. If there is no predictive capacity, then I do not see how spiritual practices can be useful in a playbook for social change. However, I feel compelled to note that I finished reading White's book on the day after the worst mass shooting in American history,* at the Pulse Nightclub in Orlando, Florida. That evening I went to a candlelight vigil held at City Hall in Philadelphia. I noted that colleagues from the sociology department were there, as well as undergraduate and graduate students. I could not help but think then that maybe sociologists are not as closed to spiritual considerations as we assume. The sociology of religion tells us that humans are, by nature, "moral believing animals," to use a phrase from sociologist of religion Christian Smith (2009). We know from the work of Emile Durkheim that religion plays an important role in building solidarity and trust between people and across societies (Durkheim 2008). So perhaps religion and spirituality also have a role to play in social change; perhaps there are ways that we can examine this role through a sociological lens.

Toward the end of White's book he lists eight "principles of revolution" that he believes should guide the work of those who choose to follow his new playbook for revolution. Spiritual matters show up in various ways across the eight principles, most especially in the principle labeled "Spirit." Here, he argues that there is "an ephemeral force that exceeds the material—the esprit de corps, or the loyal group spirit that gives strength to the social body—and

* This claim is not counting those mass shootings committed by agents of the state, such as when federal troops killed perhaps as many as three hundred Lakota at Wounded Knee.

the side that can harness the people's primal heroism will often be the victor" (White 2016, 225). What does not appear in the eight principles—in any way, shape, or form—is social media. He does not decry social media; he simply does not discuss it in his forward-looking model of social change. One of the principles in the list of eight is "Innovate," but his discussion of this principle is not driven by technology in any way. He defines innovation as "acting differently from our adversary and our predecessors" (White 2016, 222) and says we can achieve this by unifying material and spiritual approaches to social change. Twitter receives nary a mention.

It is striking that a founder of one of the most profound global protests, noted for its use of social media, devotes so little attention to technological tools as he looks toward the revolutions of the future. In the middle of his book, during a discussion of the leaderless movement strategy, White offers this strongly worded caution about the Internet, which I think would also include social media:

> In the early stages of a new movement, the Internet is crucial. However, over time the Internet becomes detrimental because protests start to look better online than in real life. By sharing beautiful photos of dismal events, people start to prefer the online experience to real-world participation. The result is that we become spectators of our own protests and momentum collapses. So the Internet is a double-edged sword: it is a weapon that is not fully under our control, and it is very difficult to wield effectively. (White 2016, 131)

CONCLUSION

Thanks to Micah White's reflections on Occupy, we can safely conclude that at least one major leader within that movement had strong reasons for doubting the long-term value of social media as a tool for social change. But we can also see that Occupy absolutely embraced social media as a significant tool in its arsenal early in the development of the movement. Occupy is not a definitive test of the value of social media, but it should count as *a* test among many, and this particular test seems to give social media a failing grade.

Occupy leaders used social media as more than a communications tool for sharing information with their participants. They used it as an artistic medium to tell new stories about social inequality and about the power of the people to step up, fight back, and build a new world. Occupy stands as an example of project identity because of the focus on social change, as outlined in the many demands that the movement considered over time—demands that would lead to sweeping changes not just in the political order, but also in the realms of commerce, the media, and education.

7

Black Lives Matter: Racial Perspectives on Social Media

"Black Lives Matter" is the phrase that launched the hashtag that became a movement. Started in 2013 in response to the acquittal of George Zimmerman for the killing of Trayvon Martin, it is now an international movement with chapters around the world, mostly across the United States. It has been both celebrated and vilified, with offshoots both online and off. **Black**

Lives Matter has become synonymous with protests around the country in response to police shootings of black Americans; with protests at the rallies of presidential candidates; and with a shooting in Minneapolis, Minnesota, where on November 23, 2015, five participants of a Black Lives Matter protest were injured after a group of men opened fire. Early reports indicated that the men were part of a white supremacist movement. The protesters had organized in Minneapolis's 4th Precinct after the November 15 police killing of twenty-four-year-old Jamar Clark.

How did this movement come to be? Why did it appear more than a decade into the twenty-first century? What are its links to other movements, including earlier race-based social movements? And what is the relationship between Black Lives Matter and social media? Can the success of Black Lives Matter be attributed to social media? What does #BlackLivesMatter reveal to us about the racial currents of social media? And is this movement ultimately transforming how we see and use social media? We begin with an origin story.

A LOVE NOTE TO BLACK PEOPLE

In a video interview posted to the website of *USA Today*, Alicia Garza tells the origin story of the Black Lives Matter movement, dating back to the acquittal of George Zimmerman for the death of Trayvon Martin on July 13, 2013:

> I was at a bar with friends and we were waiting for the verdict and when we heard that George Zimmerman had been acquitted, it was as if we had all been punched in the gut. Trayvon could have been my brother. And so I immediately felt not only enraged but a deep sense of grief that I can't protect him. It really has to do with a society that has a really sick disease, and that disease is racism. So I started writing a love note to black people on Facebook, saying that it wasn't our fault and it didn't have anything to do with pulling up your pants or voting or education or any of that—that fundamentally what it has to do with is systemic racism, and what I said was something to the degree of: "Black people I love you. I love us. Our lives matter. We matter. Black lives matter." (Guynn 2015)

Before Black Lives Matter became either a hashtag or a movement, it was a turn of phrase in a love letter from a black woman to black communities after the experience of sitting in a bar in Oakland, stunned by the verdict of "not guilty" for George Zimmerman.

Garza's friend, Patrisse Cullors, read the posts and began sharing them, adding the hashtag #BlackLivesMatter (Day 2015). In the days that followed Garza, Cullors, and a third friend named Opal Tometi, all activists and organizers, decided to coordinate their feelings of dismay into action. These actions happened both on the streets and online. They started by creating Tumblr and Twitter campaigns around the hashtag #BlackLivesMatter. "Garza made protest signs with block capital letters and put them in the window of a local shoe shop. Cullors led a march down Rodeo Drive in Beverly Hills with a banner emblazoned with the same hashtag. The slogan started gaining traction" (Day 2015).

In the year that followed Zimmerman's acquittal, the hashtag #BlackLives Matter was used increasingly on social media, as the social movement by the same name gained members across the country. On August 9, 2014, police officer Darren Wilson shot and killed an unarmed black teenager named Michael Brown in Ferguson, Missouri. Garza, Cullors, and Tometi organized a freedom ride to Ferguson as part of the campaign. "When they reached Ferguson, Garza was astonished to see her own phrase mirrored back at her on protest banners and shouted in unison by people she had never met" (Day 2015). This was over a year after the movement started and after a long series of activism events that invoked the hashtag, but with minimal media attention.

The lack of media attention would begin to change after Ferguson, but not quickly. The Black Lives Matter Ride for Justice for Mike Brown arrived in Ferguson on Labor Day weekend, at the end of August 2014. It was framed as "a call to action, a slogan under which Black people can unite to end state sanctioned violence both in St. Louis, but also across the United States of America. In addition, it aims to end the insidious and widespread assault on Black life that pervades every stage of law enforcement interactions; be it in custody or in our communities."* Black Lives Matter partnered with organizations already working on the ground in Ferguson, such as the Organization for Black Struggles (OBS) and Missourians Organizing for Reform and Empowerment (MORE) (Mused 2014). Although many smaller news sites and blogs covered the Ride for Justice, larger news outlets did not. The *New York*

*http://theshabazzcenter.net/event/the_blacklivesmatter_ride_for_justice_for_mike_brown.html.

Times had mentioned, a week earlier, that some protestors in Ferguson had signs reading "Black Lives Matter" (Eligon 2014), but it didn't cover the Ride for Justice over Labor Day weekend.

Although *Huffington Post*'s Black Voices launched the social media campaign #MyBlackLifeMattersBecause in August 2014 (Dickerson 2014), the *New York Times* and other mainstream media outlets treated Black Lives Matter as a chant and a slogan on a sign, but not as a movement, throughout the Ferguson protests. Intriguingly, in light of events that have occurred since, on October 13, 2014, a *Times* story described the chants on the streets as follows: "'Black lives matter!' the crowd chanted. 'All lives matter!'" (Davey and Blinder 2014). An Associated Press story on November 15, 2014, demonstrates how little the media was paying attention to this movement, even more than six weeks after the Ride for Justice: "In Boston, a group called Black Lives Matter, which has chapters in other major cities, is organizing a rally in front of the police district office in the Roxbury neighborhood the day after an indictment decision" (Marcelo 2014). Even as the media was preoccupied with the phrase "Black Lives Matter," the actual movement and its history really weren't on the media's radar. New protests erupted around the country. On November 22, 2014, twelve-year-old Tamir Rice was fatally shot by Cleveland police officer Timothy Loehmann. On December 3, 2014, a Staten Island grand jury decided not to indict officer Daniel Pantaleo for the death of Eric Garner. The full list of cases is long. A May 2015 story on BuzzFeed gave the following names and locations of police shootings of unarmed black people from April 2014 to May 1015:

- Dontre Hamilton, Milwaukee, April 30, 2014
- Eric Garner, New York, July 17, 2014
- John Crawford, III, Dayton, August 5, 2014
- Michael Brown, Ferguson, August 9, 2014
- Ezell Ford, Clarence, CA, August 11, 2014
- Dante Parker, Victorville, CA, August 12, 2014
- Tanisha Anderson, Cleveland, November 13, 2014
- Akai Gurley, Brooklyn, November 20, 2014
- Tamir Rice, Cleveland, November 22, 2014
- Rumain Brisbon, Phoenix, December 2, 2014
- Jerame Reid, Bridgeton, NJ, December 30, 2014
- Tony Robinson, Madison, March 6, 2015

- Phillip White, Vineland, NJ, March 31, 2015
- Eric Harris, Tulsa, April 2, 2015
- Walter Scott, Charleston, April 4, 2015
- Freddie Gray, Baltimore, April 19, 2015 (Quah 2015)

This list of sixteen names doesn't reflect a flurry of new police shootings; rather, it illustrates a flurry of new media attention to an ongoing problem.

As anger and activism increased around the country throughout December 2014, Black Lives Matter signs continued to appear, and increasingly the media understood those words to reflect a movement and not just a slogan.

AN OVERVIEW OF THE MOVEMENT

One aspect of Black Lives Matter that is particularly striking is that the movement is active both online and off—in the tweets *and* the streets. This is not a movement of "slacktivism" in which participants simply click "like" or "retweet" and go about their day, a charge levied against the Kony activism of 2012, nor is it an anonymous, faceless movement like GamerGate. The leaders of Black Lives Matter are identified by name, and their faces are visible both in social media and in face-to-face (and face-to-media) activism.

Black Lives Matter is a deliberately and explicitly intersectional movement. That might seem counterintuitive given that the movement clearly focuses on black lives and racial inequalities, but the leaders and participants seem to consistently hold to an intersectional focus. **Intersectionality** is a social science paradigm that examines the ways that racism, classism, sexism, and other forms of oppression work as interlocking systems. Day (2015) quotes Garza speaking about how intersectional thinking has impacted the leadership of Black Lives Matter: "'We have a lot of leaders,' insists Garza, 'just not where you might be looking for them. If you're only looking for the straight black man who is a preacher, you're not going to find it.'" Black Lives Matter sees racial inequalities as deeply connected to issues of gender, sexuality, transgender identity, class, and the whole gamut of oppressive structures that also work to create privilege for others—what sociologist Patricia Hill Collins has called "the matrix of domination" (1990, 18).

Its website presents a history of the movement, written by Garza, under the heading "A HerStory of the #BlackLivesMatter Movement." The opening paragraph reads as follows:

> I created #BlackLivesMatter with Patrisse Cullors and Opal Tometi, two of my sisters, as a call to action for Black people after 17-year-old Trayvon Martin was post-humously [*sic*] placed on trial for his own murder and the killer, George Zimmerman, was not held accountable for the crime he committed. It was a response to the anti-Black racism that permeates our society and also, unfortunately, our movements.*

A lot of things are happening in this paragraph that should be noted. First, Garza is naming the founders of the movement. That is significant. Black people, women, and queer people are often rendered invisible in history, including in the history of major social movements. Second, Garza is naming the precipitating events that foreground the creation of this movement. The movement is not an abstraction, and the slogan is not a generic idea. They constitute a response to a specific moment in history, set in a specific geographic context, involving identifiable individuals and institutions (Trayvon Martin and George Zimmerman; the criminal justice system of Sanford, Florida, etc.). Much of the response to the Black Lives Matter movement lost sight of that specificity and that history. That critique applies to both positive and negative responses, but especially to the counter-slogan #AllLivesMatter, which held no reference to historical events, contexts, people, or institutions.

The "Herstory" presented on the BlackLivesMatter website also discusses "the theft of Black queer women's work." Garza discusses the ways that the slogan has been appropriated by numerous groups, with little or no acknowledgment of the history behind the words. "We completely expect those who benefit directly and improperly from White supremacy to try and erase our existence. We fight that every day. But when it happens amongst our allies, we are baffled, we are saddened, and we are enraged." White supremacy is not the only source of this theft. She also points to heterosexism and patriarchy, further indicating the movement's commitment to intersectional approaches.

Thirteen "guiding principles" of the movement are identified on the website:

1. Diversity
2. Restorative justice
3. Unapologetically black

*http://blacklivesmatter.com/herstory/.

4. Globalism
5. Black women
6. Collective value
7. Transgender affirming
8. Black villages
9. Empathy
10. Black families
11. Queer affirming
12. Loving engagement
13. Intergenerational

Each includes a description, all of which can be found on the website.* This list reflects both intersectional values and a commitment to specificity and context over abstraction. This movement is rooted in black communities in ways that emphasize the need for black visibility, women's visibility, trans visibility, queer visibility, disability visibility, and visibility of all age groups.

The website for the movement lists twenty-seven chapters across the country (and one in Canada).†

The first archived appearance of the website is captured on Archive.org as being on October 8, 2014.‡ The site that is archived from that date is essentially just a splash page announcing that the site is coming soon, on October 12. It also directs visitors to the Black Lives Matter Tumblr page, which has remained active since.§ The first post-launch archive of the site is from November 7, 2014.¶ On the "Demands" page for the site on that date, the leaders indicate a five-part agenda that starts with the specific circumstances of Ferguson, Missouri, but broadens to encompass nationwide goals for the years ahead:

- We will seek justice for Brown's family by petitioning for the immediate arrest of officer Darren Wilson and the dismissal of county prosecutor Robert McCullough. Groups that are part

*http://blacklivesmatter.com/guiding-principles/.

†http://blacklivesmatter.com/find-chapters/.

‡https://web.archive.org/web/20141008133241/http://blacklivesmatter.com/.

§http://blacklivesmatter.tumblr.com/.

¶https://web.archive.org/web/20141107235403/http://blacklivesmatter.com/.

of the local Hands Up Don't Shoot Coalition have already called for Wilson's swift arrest, and some BLM riders also canvassed McCullough's neighborhood as a way of raising the public's awareness of the case.

- We will help develop a network of organizations and advocates to form a national policy specifically aimed at redressing the systemic pattern of anti-black law enforcement violence in the US. The Justice Department's new investigation into St Louis-area police departments is a good start, but it's not enough. Our ride was endorsed by a few dozen local, regional and national organizations across the country–like the National Organization for Women (Now) and Race Forward: The Center for Racial Justice Innovation–who, while maintaining different missions, have demonstrated unprecedented solidarity in response to anti-black police violence. We hope to encourage more organizations to endorse and participate in a network with a renewed purpose of conceptualizing policy recommendations.
- We will also demand, through the network, that the federal government discontinue its supply of military weaponry and equipment to local law enforcement. And though Congress seems to finally be considering measures in this regard, it remains essential to monitor the demilitarization processes and the corporate sectors that financially benefit from the sale of military tools to police.
- We will call on the office of US attorney general Eric Holder to release the names of all officers involved in killing black people within the last five years, both while on patrol and in custody, so they can be brought to justice–if they haven't already.
- And we will advocate for a decrease in law-enforcement spending at the local, state and federal levels and a reinvestment of that budgeted money into the black communities most devastated by poverty in order to create jobs, housing and schools. This money should be redirected to those federal departments charged with providing employment, housing and educational services.*

---

*https://web.archive.org/web/20141023044545/http://blacklivesmatter.com/demands/.

Again, we see that the movement roots its abstract ideas in local and temporal specifics. Any claims about race in America are based in an understanding of the deaths of Trayvon Martin and Michael Brown (although by this point, much of the focus online was on Brown). A page focused on the events of Ferguson pairs seven local demands with four national demands, another indicator of how the movement rooted broad goals in the local and the specific.*

The early version of the movement's website also showed an emphasis on using hashtags as a tool of activism, listing twelve specific hashtags as a way of organizing ideas and information within a complicated set of intersectional lenses. Those tags are, in order: BlackWomenMatter, BlackGirlsMatter, BlackGayLivesMatter, BlackBiLivesMatter, BlackBoysMatter, BlackQueerLivesMatter, BlackMenMatter, BlackLesbiansMatter, BlackTransLivesMatter, BlackImmigrantsMatter, BlackIncarceratedLivesMatter, and BlackDifferentlyAbledLivesMatter.

The blog on the site,† still preserved in archives, featured posts and reposts (from major media outlets) of essays about Ferguson, the Black Lives Matter movement, and the history of racial politics and activism in the United States. Following are some of the post titles:

"'The Politics of Jesus' and "#BlackLivesMatter": Ferguson as Movement"‡

"5 ways to never forget Ferguson—and deliver real justice for Michael Brown"§

"Ferguson Forward: 'Black Lives Matter' Brings Heartbroken Helping Hands to St. Louis"¶

"Al Sharpton does not have my ear: Why we need new black leadership now"**

* https://web.archive.org/web/20141023044807/http://blacklivesmatter.com/ferguson.

† https://web.archive.org/web/20141128070337/http://blacklivesmatter.com/blog.

‡ https://web.archive.org/web/20150129231635/http://blacklivesmatter.com/the-politics-of-jesus-and-blacklivesmatter-ferguson-as-movement/

§ https://web.archive.org/web/20150129231638/http://blacklivesmatter.com/5-ways-to-never-forget-ferguson-and-deliver-real-justice-for-michael-brown/.

¶ https://web.archive.org/web/20150129231649/http://blacklivesmatter.com/349/.

** https://web.archive.org/web/20141225045554/http://blacklivesmatter.com/al-sharpton-does-not-have-my-ear-why-we-need-new-black-leadership-now.

METHODOLOGICAL MOMENT: Key Principles in Virtual Ethnography

Throughout this book I have provided a series of snapshots of virtual ethnography, the method that I employ in this analysis. Below, I offer a few key principles that should guide the ethnographic process, both online and off, with particular attention to how these principles impact ethnography in the digital environment.

1. *The ethnographer needs to be immersed in the field.*

   You cannot simply jump onto the Internet or onto a social media platform, make a few observations, and jump back out. There are nuances to the interactions that take place in these communities that are analogous to unique local cultures. A weekend visit to a foreign city would not give me the expertise to make scholarly claims about the culture of that city. Similarly, a small sample of tweets or a few days on Facebook are not sufficient for making claims about the culture of social media.

   Virtual ethnographers should develop a discipline of spending several hours per week in their digital environments. This time should be spent in a mixture of directed and nondirected searching. While directed searching—focusing on particular themes and questions—is necessary to ultimately answer questions and complete an analysis, nondirected searching—clicking a reading just to see what is there—is necessary to truly develop an understanding of the complex terrain.

2. *The ethnographer needs to avoid cynicism.*

   Complaints about the selfie generation—the PBS show *Frontline* has called it the "like generation"—and gripes that nothing of substance happens online are distractions from our scholarly enterprise. Our job is to ask questions and be open to all possible answers, including those that defy our preconceived notions about the Internet and social media. The value of social media is not for us to determine; rather, our role is to observe the value that social media has for its many participants. What the cynical mind might think of as a waste of time turns out to be high art for many social media creatives.

   This principle holds true when we study the social media underworld. Many of our experiences online may lead us to regard some Internet users as **trolls**, but that does not mean we should be dismissive

continues

METHODOLOGICAL MOMENT:
Key Principles in Virtual Ethnography *continued*

of them as people. We need to approach sites like Wizardchan and 4chan with curiosity and an open mind.

3. *The ethnographer needs to get off the beaten path.*
Although ethnographers need to develop a level of knowledge comparable to "the locals," they also need to do the things that locals forget to do. Locals stay on the same paths in their everyday lives, but meaningful realities can often be found on the adjacent paths that locals neglect. An ethnographer in a business setting should ask about what's in the storage room. An ethnographer in a church should ask about the items hidden behind the altar. The online ethnographer should also explore forgotten twists and turns. What new conversations can we discover if we play with misspelling our search terms? What backstory can I find if I cross-reference a story on Facebook with the Twitter accounts of those involved? How can I fill in gaps in the biographies of major actors in my study by examining their profiles on LinkedIn? One irony of the Internet is that although it makes so much information publicly available, little of that information is ever seen because we are not actively sifting through it.

The day-to-day work of conducting online ethnography looks like this: me sitting at my desk or in a coffee shop, headphones on, reading through posts on Twitter, Facebook, LinkedIn, Pinterest, Reddit, 4chan, 8chan, Google+, and many other platforms; then turning down side streets and alleys by searching alternate hashtags, cross-checking user profiles on multiple sites, and even doing that one thing we are always told never to do: reading the comments.

SOCIAL MEDIA AND THE PHENOMENON OF BLACK TWITTER

Black Lives Matter has a multidimensional relationship with social media. Social media has played a profound role in increasing the visibility of racial inequalities, particularly police brutality against black people. Many of these events have been captured on video by smartphones and posted to YouTube and other social media sites, generating a national outcry against actions by the police that would otherwise have been ignored. Social media allows individuals to create media that captures or describes these events and to share those accounts with the their exponentially expanding networks.

Furthermore, social media has provided a structure that allowed a rhetorically forceful phrase—Black Lives Matter—to become both a meme and a movement. Many organizations have developed in the past few years as part of what is often referred to as "the new civil rights movement" (including an organization called the New Civil Rights Movement). But none has had the visibility of Black Lives Matter. If social media did not exist, we still would have powerful civil rights organizations, and we might even have one called Black Lives Matter, but their embrace of social media has allowed them to capture public imagination and to have a powerful place in public discourse:

> [I]f you wanted a megaphone for a movement spearheaded by young people of color, you'd be hard-pressed to find a better one than Twitter, whose users skew younger and browner than the general public, which often has the effect of magnifying that group's broad priorities and fascinations. (Demby 2014)

The term "**black Twitter**" is often used to describe the ways that black social media users embrace the medium as a space for discussing black culture and debating black politics. Discussing black Twitter with my students, I discovered some of my nonblack students believed it was literally an alternative app like Snapchat or Whatsapp, because they have heard the phrase so often but have so little concept of what it is. Black Twitter is not a distinct app but rather a cultural notion of one of the ways that culture gets used by black communities.

Black Twitter attained mainstream media attention in 2010 when Farhad Manjoo discussed it in an article on Slate. Manjoo focuses on the use of **blacktags**: hashtags that reflect a black discursive practice on Twitter. These are often not tags about blackness or race. Manjoo (2010) gives the examples of #wordsthatleadtotrouble, #ilaugheverytime, #annoyingquestion, and #wheniwaslittle. If a so-called blacktag is not about blackness, how do we know that it is part of black Twitter? On some level, we don't. Social media affirms the social boundaries that exist in the offline world, but it renders them more porous. There is no guard at the gates of black Twitter. But the racial boundaries remain. Manjoo raises the point: "While you begin to see some nonblack faces after a trending topic hits Twitter's home page, the early participants in these tags are almost all black. Does this suggest a break between blacks and nonblacks on Twitter—that real-life segregation is being mirrored online?" The evidence we have so far on that question points to a resounding "yes."

A digital racial divide exists in usage of Twitter that shows higher usage rates among blacks—counter to the standard perception of digital divides that technology works strictly in favor of privileged folks like whites, men, and nondisabled persons. Hargittai and Litt (2011) examine Twitter adoption using original longitudinal data in which they surveyed participants in 2009 and again in 2010, with 505 participants completing the survey at both times. They find that black participants are more likely to use Twitter than white participants and more likely to have adopted Twitter during the period of analysis. They also find that people with higher Internet skills are more likely to use Twitter, as well as people who are interested in celebrity culture and entertainment news. Interest in news or politics, however, has no correlation with Twitter use.

A study by the Pew Internet and American Life Project reveals similar findings about racial differences in Twitter adoption. Although the study found that only 13 percent of Internet users were also Twitter users, a full 25 percent of black Internet users were also Twitter users, based on data from 2011 (Smith 2011). We can compare this to only 9 percent of white Internet users and 19 percent of Hispanic Internet users. Furthermore, black Twitter users also use Twitter more *often* than other groups. "One in ten African-American internet users now visit Twitter on a typical day—that is double the rate for Latinos and nearly four times the rate for whites" (Smith 2011, 3). In an earlier report, the same author found that black Twitter users are also more likely to use Twitter on their mobile devices than are other racial groups (Smith 2010). A report by Ogilvy Public Relations Worldwide and The Center for Social Impact Communication at Georgetown University (2011) found that Twitter and other social media play an important role in getting black citizens involved in social issues, more so than for whites.*

*As a counterpoint, it is worth noting that access to the Internet via phone reduces the ways that we can use the Internet. Heavy reliance on phone access by black Internet users has been shown to diminish their overall benefit from the Internet (Washington 2011).

Social media segregation is not just a result of usage rates. It also reflects deliberate strategies of racial groups. danah boyd (2011) has a described a kind of "white flight" that emerged in 2006–2007 as more users began adopting Facebook, even as MySpace continued to be a prominent social networking site. Facebook users were more likely to be white and more likely to be affluent. In focus groups, boyd's white respondents described MySpace as "ghetto." "What distinguishes adoption of MySpace and Facebook among American teens is not cleanly about race or class, although both are implicated in the story at every level. The division can be seen through the lens of taste and aesthetics, two value-laden elements that are deeply entwined with race and class." She notes a preference for MySpace among black and Latino teens and a preference for Facebook among white and Asian teens. Economically, Facebook also had an early association with specific universities and later high schools. "In essence, the 'glitter' produced by those who 'pimp out' their MySpaces is seen by some in a positive light while others see it as 'gaudy,' 'tacky,' and 'cluttered'." While Facebook fans loved the site's aesthetic minimalism, others viewed this tone as "boring," "lame," and "elitist." boyd calls the move from MySpace to Facebook a kind of digital white flight.

#ALLLIVESMATTER

As Black Lives Matter gained visibility in Ferguson, an immediate pushback came in the form of a short counter-phrase: "**All Lives Matter**." All Lives Matter is a hashtag, and a response to the Black Lives Matter movement, but it is not a movement itself. The phrase "all lives matter" has a complicated history and an even more complicated politics. As stated previously in this chapter, protesters in Ferguson at times chanted: "Black lives matter! All lives matter!" In California, an organization called Bay Area All Lives Matter was formed at the end of August 2014 as part of the expanding network of Black Lives Matter groups. An August 26, 2014, post on the *Ms.* blog, coauthored by Ai-Jen Poo and Black Lives Matter founder Alicia Garza, used the title "On Women's Equality Day, ALL Lives Matter" (Poo and Garza 2014). So the phrase "black lives matter" was always tied to the idea that *all* lives matter. But "all lives matter" quickly diverged from "black lives matter" and took on its own meaning and politics.

On September 6, 2014, students at the University of Virginia gathered for a rally against police brutality, organized to show solidarity with protestors in Ferguson. One participant, in her blog, described hearing an onlooker yell "all lives matter" in a sarcastic tone, in response to the group's chant "black lives matter."* According to news coverage of the event, "all lives matter" was also one of the chants in the protest (Kass 2014). So we have an onlooker, disdainful of the protest, selecting a piece of the protest's rhetoric and flipping the meaning of that rhetoric. In her hands, and the hands of many others who have declared that "all lives matter" as a protest against Black Lives Matter, "all" becomes a way of pronouncing Black Lives Matter to be racist simply for having named a racial group.

In late October 2014 a Black Lives Matter awareness week clashed with an antiabortion campaign using the slogan "all lives matter" (Lindsay 2014). Posters with the former slogan were pulled down and replaced by posters with the latter slogan mixed with statistics on abortion. No person or group claimed responsibility (Xu 2014).

For the original movement, declaring that black lives matter was a way of saying both that all lives should matter and that black lives have been systematically devalued. For the counterprotest (though it never became a movement), declaring that all lives matter has been a way of silencing the Black Lives Matter movement, minimizing the role of race in the examination of police brutality, and amplifying the leadership of whites in moments of cultural conflict. Let me explain that last statement. Although some black leaders have embraced the slogan "all lives matter," it has primarily been the rhetoric of white leaders (politicians, pastors, commentators), who seem to think it shows them to be more reasonable and measured than the angry black protestors chanting "black lives matter." "All lives matter" also has the effect of turning the debate into an issue of rhetoric—this language versus that language—rather than an issue of specific events that unfold in historical moments. "Black lives matter" is an action: an attempt to make true that which has been denied by the state. "All lives matter" is an abstraction: an attempt to render invisible the racial identity of racial politics.

Alicia Garza speaks against the "all lives matter" slogan on the "Herstory" page of the Black Lives Matter website. She does not declare that the broader slogan is wrong. Rather, she highlights the fact that "all lives matter" is typically used to silence black activism and erase the blackness of the movement. "#BlackLivesMatter doesn't mean your life isn't important—it means that

---

*https://wtfkellyc.wordpress.com/2014/09/06/on-the-importance-of-black-lives/.

Black lives, which are seen as without value within White supremacy, are important to your liberation. Given the disproportionate impact state violence has on Black lives, we understand that when Black people in this country get free, the benefits will be wide reaching and transformative for society as a whole."* She goes on:

> When we deploy "All Lives Matter" as to correct an intervention specifically created to address anti-blackness, we lose the ways in which the state apparatus has built a program of genocide and repression mostly on the backs of Black people. . . . We perpetuate a level of White supremacist domination by reproducing a tired trope that we are all the same. . . .
>
> When you drop "Black" from the equation of whose lives matter, and then fail to acknowledge it came from somewhere, you further a legacy of erasing Black lives and Black contributions from our movement legacy.†

The explanations that Garza gives are much more sophisticated than the defenses of "all lives matter" that are presented online or in the media. Those defenses really boil down to rhetoric and the fear that white people, despite retaining control over the political and economic institutions in the country, might somehow be oppressed under the banner "black lives matter." One celebrity, standing in solidarity with the movement, explained his position humorously on Twitter: "#BlackLivesMatter doesn't mean other lives don't. Like people who say 'Save the Rainforests' aren't saying "Fuck all other types of forest."‡

The journalist Harvey Simon called this a "PR problem" on the part of the movement, in an essay posted to the *Huffington Post* (Simon 2015). His suggested solution to this problem was for the group to simply add the word "too," as in "Black Lives Matter Too." What Simon seems to misunderstand is that the folks declaring that "all lives matter" as a counterprotest to "black lives matter" aren't simply confused by the phrase. That would imply that they would join the movement if it just fixed the name issue, but all evidence is to the contrary—these are folks who stand against the principles of Black Lives Matter by focusing either on the value of white lives in general or on the value of police over and above the citizens they are sworn to protect.

---

*http://blacklivesmatter.com/herstory/.

† Ibid.

‡ https://twitter.com/mattmcgorry/status/622511182004367360.

ALL LIVES MATTER GETS REDDITED

Reddit, so often associated with the dark side of social media, has played an interesting role in the Black Lives Matter movement and All Lives Matter counter-rhetoric. Deep in Reddit, Redditors—those frequent users of Reddit—have a range of deep discussions, some of which are quite fruitful. On multiple occasions, Redditors have posed questions about the problems with saying "all lives matter." These conversations have been more productive and democratic than Reddit is typically credited for. At least one even caught the eye of the media (Roose 2015).

When user Bigred2989 posted a question to the Reddit board /explainlikeimfive/ on July 19, 2015, they probably did not anticipate generating 1,694 responses or 1,736 Reddit points (as of November 29, 2015). But it was the top response that caught the media's attention, with a score of 7,390 Reddit points. The question?

> ELI5: Why is it so controversial when someone says "All Lives Matter" instead of "Black Lives Matter?"*

The opening characters ELI5 are just a reference to the board: Explain Like I'm Five. This is an explainer board on which people pose questions and expect responses to be clear and considered. There is even a detailed explanation of the board's culture and editing policies:

> explainlikeimfive establishes and enforces a number of rules to maintain a quality subreddit that allows for quality discussion that is largely uncensored and open. However, we do remove comments and submissions for various reasons to ensure that the quality of the subreddit lives up to its status as a default subreddit.†

This introduction is followed by a list of thirteen rules that include "be nice" (rule 1), "explanations must be layman-friendly" (rule 4), and "respect the spirit of the subreddit" (rule 13). So perhaps it should be no surprise that the ensuing conversation was civil and quickly produced an answer that other

---

*https://www.reddit.com/r/explainlikeimfive/comments/3du1qm/eli5_why_is_it_so_controversial_when_someone_says/.

† https://www.reddit.com/r/explainlikeimfive/wiki/rules.

redditors seemed to find quite helpful. That answer came from Redditor GeekAesthete:

> Imagine that you're sitting down to dinner with your family, and while everyone else gets a serving of the meal, you don't get any. So you say "I should get my fair share." And as a direct response to this, your dad corrects you, saying, "*everyone* should get their fair share." Now, that's a wonderful sentiment—indeed, everyone should, and that was kinda your point in the first place: that you should be a part of everyone, and you should get your fair share *also*.
>
> Just like asking dad for your fair share, the phrase "black lives matter" also has an implicit "too" at the end: it's saying that black lives should *also* matter. But responding to this by saying "*all* lives matter" is willfully going back to ignoring the problem.*

The response was extraordinarily positive, although we need to bear in mind that the board is edited. But here are some of the comments that Geek Aesthete generated:

- "You just changed my mind on the statement bud, I will bring up your argument to friends who haven't seen the light. I get it now. The goddamn implicit 'too.' Fucking genius."†
- "Seriously. This guy just ** single handedly changed my opinion on this[.]"‡
- "Wow. I honestly never thought of it this way."§

Perhaps inevitably, the idea that Black Lives Matter implies a "too" at the end led to debates about whether "Too" should be added to the movement

* https://www.reddit.com/r/explainlikeimfive/comments/3du1qm/eli5_why_is_it_so_controversial_when_someone_says/ct8pei1

† https://www.reddit.com/r/explainlikeimfive/comments/3du1qm/eli5_why_is_it_so_controversial_when_someone_says/ct91792.

‡ https://www.reddit.com/r/explainlikeimfive/comments/3du1qm/eli5_why_is_it_so_controversial_when_someone_says/ct98yyf.

§ https://www.reddit.com/r/explainlikeimfive/comments/3du1qm/eli5_why_is_it_so_controversial_when_someone_says/cuwgq0q name. But these debates also resulted in productive conversations about why adding "Too" is not only unnecessary but also wrongheaded. For example:

> The phrase has power because of its directness: Black lives matter. Period, full stop. Adding an explicit "too" at the end would weaken the statement by acknowledging (and legitimizing) the default position that when we talk about "lives" we are talking about non-minorities unless we state otherwise. "Black lives matter too" = "black lives matter in addition to the lives of people we normally care about." Not much of a rallying cry.*

My point in including this discussion is to consider the ways that social media allow us to address problems in new ways, even when those problems may themselves be the result of social media. In this case, the rhetorical power of the phrase "black lives matter" was confused for rhetorical weakness; the power is in the debate that the phrase has generated, yet so many people think that the debate itself is a sign of the ambiguity or weakness of the phrase. But if we "fix" the ambiguity, what is the prompt to continue having the conversation?

RACIAL PROTEST WITHOUT RACE

The "all lives matter" retort is a form of **color-blind racism** that fits many of the parameters outlined in Eduardo Bonilla-Silva's book *Racism Without Racists* (2013). Sociologist Bonilla-Silva examines the contours of what he calls the "new racism" of post-1960s America. This new racism is characterized by covert racial discourse, the avoidance of racial language, fears about reverse racism, and a surprising return to racial practices that mirror Jim Crow–era racism. This last element may seem hyperbolic, but it is quickly supported by an analysis of racial disparities in the correctional system, capital punishment, police brutality against blacks, economic outcomes, educational opportunities, residential segregation, and many other variables that define modern life and indicate the durability of racial inequality.

Bonilla-Silva defines race as a social construction that creates a social reality. That means he is rejecting the impulse to dismiss racial analysis simply

---

* https://www.reddit.com/r/explainlikeimfive/comments/3du1qm/eli5_why_is_it_so_controversial_when_someone_says/ct9mc5j.

because of its socially constructed nature. Social constructions are not myths, although there are myths associated with many social constructions, including race. Social constructions, like race, are powerful realities whose materiality is composed of sociological elements. The myth associated with race is that its nature is biological rather than social. Putting that myth aside should not lead to dismissing the concept of race or the reality of racial inequality. As Bonilla-Silva points out, the concept of race has created a **racial structure**, which he defines as "the totality of the social relations and practices that reinforce white privilege" (2013, 9). Racial structure does not change easily, but it can change, in part because of the conflict between competing **racial ideologies**. Bonilla-Silva defines racial ideologies as "the racially based frameworks used by actors to explain and justify (dominant groups) or challenge (subordinate race or races) the racial status quo" (2013, 9). In the case of the Black Lives Matter movement, we see a clearly defined racial ideology that is defined to challenge the status quo. It is met with the color-blind racist ideology of the "all lives matter" retort.

We can further apply Bonilla-Silva's framework by stating that "all lives matter" utilizes a frame of abstract liberalism and styles of avoidance and projection. According to Bonilla-Silva, "Dominant **racial frames** . . . provide the intellectual framework used by rulers to navigate the always rocky road of domination and . . . derail the ruled from their track to freedom and equality" (2013, 74). He identifies four racial frames that are common in the new racism: abstract liberalism, naturalization, cultural racism, and minimization. The significance of these frames is that they are used to either deny racial inequality or, more often, to simply justify it without acknowledging that its source might be racism. For example, the frame of naturalization claims that racial segregation is the result of natural human impulses that will persist despite our attempts to combat racism. Although it utilizes the sociological concept of homophily, this frame ignores the fact that we do not divide naturally into racial categories. The pull of like to like is still driven by nonbiological forces, including racism. The frame of cultural racism is used to argue that racial inequalities are the result of bad values held by specific groups. In other words, it is *their* choices and not *our* racism that create these inequalities. The frame of minimization acknowledges some degree of inequality but insists that it is in a persistent decline. The material reality of black Americans may be better today than it was several decades ago, but as the scholar points out, "their chances of catching up with whites are very slim" (Bonilla-Silva 2013, 74).

"All lives matter" fits best within the frame of abstract liberalism. Abstract liberalism promotes racial blindness, with its emphasis on liberal ideals such as "equality of opportunity" and "freedom of choice." Under this logic, real outcomes do not matter so long as the groups under comparison started with equal opportunities. Given this level playing field, actors may still make choices that lead to very different outcomes. The problem with abstract liberalism is not the liberalism, but the abstraction. Any focus on equality of opportunity should be on the real opportunity differences of actual groups, which means a willingness to name and analyze those groups. Any focus on freedom of choice should recognize that if the *range* of choices made by actors in one group is widely variant from the range of choices made by actors in another group, there are likely systemic forces at work that are constricting those choices.

In addition to frames of color-blindness, Bonilla-Silva also explains the styles of expression in the new racism. He describes five styles in particular: avoidance, semantic moves, projection, diminutives, and incoherence. Since I am applying avoidance and projection to "all lives matter," I return to those below. "Semantic moves" refers to short phrases that are meant to deflect accusations of racism, such as the phrase, "I'm not a racist, but. . . ." "Diminutives" refers to the use of words like "little" and "small" to describe racial realities or racist feelings. "Incoherence" refers to the incapacity to formulate ideas related to race, resulting in stammering and poor sentence formation.

The style of avoidance describes an avoidance of both racist and racial language for fear that it violates the rules of color-blindness. Shifting the word "black" to "all" is a very clear case of avoidance, particularly when it is deployed by those who claim to be allies of the antiracism movement. The implied argument is that the best way to value black lives is to value all lives. As the saying goes, a rising tide lifts all ships. But if our concern is for the inequality between the ships, lifting all of them does nothing to address that inequality. If our society consistently devalues black lives—as indicated by incarceration rates, execution rates, income differences, and many other data points—the solution is not simply to value all lives more.

The style of projection describes the insistence that the real racists are the racial minorities who insist on the persistence of racial categories and appear to threaten the opportunities of white people through practices of reverse racism. Shifting the word "black" to "all" is a form of projection, particularly when it is deployed by those who stand opposed to black antiracist movements. The argument is that "Black Lives Matter" somehow devalues nonblack lives, or that it constitutes a movement for black supremacy. This style obscures the reality of white supremacy under which the Black Lives Matter movement has appeared and ignores the participation of antiracist whites in the movement. It explains black political gains as white social losses, and the only racial equality it allows for is the status quo.

Bonilla-Silva's work is best used to explain both current racial realities and the backlash against the Black Lives Matter movement. However, it also sheds light on the movement itself. In the conclusion of his book, he outlines the conditions that are needed for fighting color-blind racism: (1) black people and their allies need to form the core of a new civil rights movement, (2) antiracist whites need to challenge color-blind racism from within, (3) counter-ideologies need to be formed to work against the frames of color-blindness, (4) the myth of color-blindness needs to be persistently exposed, (5) whiteness must be challenged at every turn, and (6) the movement must embrace militancy. He sums up the point nicely: "What is needed to slay modern-day racism is a new, in-your-face, fight-the-power civil rights movement" (Bonilla-Silva 2013, 308). These words have carried over from the first edition of *Racism Without Racists*, published in 2003, so they predate the Black Lives Matter movement by a decade, yet they also seem to be calling the movement into being.

CONCLUSION

The spring of 2015 was dubbed Black Spring by a pair of law professors writing for *Al Jazeera* (Beydoun and Ocen 2015). They were deliberately connecting the black activism in the United States with Arab activism in the Middle East from 2010, known as the Arab Spring:

> In the Arab World, the intersection of poverty and stigmatised religion, sectarian status or tribe is at the crux of persecution. The economics of Arab dictatorships was simple: Emaciate the opposition as a means to capitalise power. Although lacking the racial dimension of the American dialectic, the process is similar to how white supremacy and the maintenance of racialised wealth and poverty functions stateside. (Beydoun and Ocen 2015)

What struck these writers most, though, was the very different responses from white America and the American media to each movement. The Arab

Spring was praised as an outburst of democracy, while the Black Spring was demonized as a threat to democracy. These authors made no mention of social media, but the power of the medium was as much a connection between the Arab and Black Springs as the politics of the message. In both cases, the use of new media has generated new conversations—new possibilities and pitfalls—for old and ongoing social divides.

Black Lives Matter, like Occupy Wall Street, is a prime example of a project identity because of its emphasis on widespread, multidimensional social transformation. It has embraced the value of social media as a powerful resource, while also emphasizing coordinated action in the streets. Black Lives Matter did not begin with a political manifesto, but rather with Alicia Garza's "love letter to black people." It has emphasized the use of creativity and appeals to the heart, in addition to political action. There is even a dedicated website for the art of the movement, found at http://art.blacklivesmatter.com, which features a range of posters, videos, and other projects.

The ongoing crisis of police shootings and killings of black citizens seems likely to maintain the momentum of the movement. In contrast to Occupy Wall Street, Black Lives Matter seems poised to remain a powerful presence in US culture and politics. But until the shooting ends, the question remains whether the movement will work and whether social media is in fact a viable tool for social change.

8

Social Media Toolbox

Social media can be a powerful tool for taking our ideas and our analysis to the public. It is a key dimension of public discourse. If you are not on social media, then you are not part of the conversation.

Social media is also a powerful mechanism of social inequality. All forms of social exclusion that are present offline are also present online. While inequalities of race, class, gender, sexuality, and disability are all powerful shapers of the social media experience, I argue that the greatest form of inequality that is embodied by social media is the domination of individuals by corporations. Those of us who embrace social media need to also be critical users of it.

Can tools of social exclusion be used to dismantle social inequality? I think that is still an open question. If dismantling social inequality is a matter of incremental changes, rather than broad social revolution, then we need to work with the tools that we have available and the tools that seem to have the greatest reach. To that end, I think social media needs to be an important tool for social activism and change making.

But which social media tools should we be using, and how do we use them most effectively? In this chapter I provide the tools for developing a social media strategy focused on social change and civic engagement. Although I focus significantly on Twitter, the broad philosophical principles hold true across platforms and should remain consistent as new platforms arise.

IDENTIFY YOUR GOALS

Every project in social change and civic engagement needs a statement of objectives. The same holds true as we extend our work into social media. So begin by writing a short statement of goals and purpose. The statement below can function as a starter statement for anyone who is just beginning to formulate a social media strategy:

> *Social media objective: To share, collaborate, and curate ideas about* [TOPIC] *with an audience of citizens, journalists, influencers, and policy makers.*

Over time this general statement of goals can be revised to provide a focus on specific types of ideas and activism or to broaden the types of audience.

CHOOSE YOUR IDENTITY

Your social media identity is not the online equivalent of your actual self. We all have multiple selves and multiple personae depending on the various roles that we play. So you have a lot of room to choose what your identity online will be.

Personality-Based Identities

A personality-based identity centers on the person. It includes the thoughts, aspirations, and opinions of an individual. A personality-based social media identity would usually use the individual's actual name. It could embody multiple aspects of the individual or could focus solely on an activist or professional identity. The sociologist Dalton Conley is an active Twitter user with the handle @daltonconley. His Twitter identity is largely focused on his scholarly identity. Although he acknowledges family and other aspects of his life, he does not focus on them nearly as much as he tweets about scholarship. This is a personality-based identity that is largely one dimensional.

The celebrity blogger Perez Hilton, @PerezHilton, also uses a personality-based social identity, but he prefers to be multidimensional. His professional life centers around celebrity gossip, but he tweets almost as often about his pets, fatherhood, and his own adventures in the land of celebrity (such as his season on *Big Brother UK*).

Most of us who use Facebook regularly never actively think about the kind of identity we are presenting, but we may still have developed an online profile that is at best a distorted reflection of our offline lives. To see this point, make a list of the issues that most often impact your day or interrupt your thoughts. Just list the first ten things that come to mind. For me, they would be:

- Teaching
- Cat
- Condo ownership
- Workouts at the gym
- Dating
- Young adult fantasy novels
- Healthy eating (kale, blueberries, green tea)
- Unhealthy eating (M&Ms, ice cream, cheese)
- Urban life in Philadelphia
- Social media

Reflect on what you listed. Do you post about all of them online, in roughly equal numbers? Some people post about folding laundry as often as they post about their careers. Others prefer to exclude such mundane issues from their online profiles. There is not necessarily a right answer on this issue, but you do want to keep in mind your audience and your desired audience impact. If most of your Facebook friends are actual friends, then it makes sense to be fully multidimensional on Facebook. But if you are using Facebook to promote a particular aspect of your professional life, then you likely want to reduce the scope of your online personality.

Project-Based Identities

An alternative to personality-driven social media use is to focus on social change projects (or civic engagement projects). Although a project-driven strategy could still be in the name of the individual leading that project, it is more common in this approach to use the name of the project itself.

Sociologist Tristan Bridges developed his blog *Inequality by Interior Design*[*] when he was working on a project about "man caves." The project grew in many ways, and the blog acquired a broader focus on the role of social space in generating social inequalities. His writings there are somewhat different from his writings at the multiauthor blog *Girl with Pen*,[†] which explores gender and feminism, without the spatial focus.

Inequality by Interior Design is a project-driven social media strategy that happens to have one main personality at its center. But by putting the focus on the project, and not the personality, Bridges retains the ability to bring in work by other writers who also use space to examine inequality.

Girl with Pen is a project-driven social media strategy that embodies multiple personalities. It boasts eighteen primary authors and frequently features guest authors as well.[‡] Despite all those different voices, it uses an extremely concise objective statement: "Girl w/ Pen, founded by Deborah Siegel, publicly and passionately dispels modern myths concerning gender, encouraging other feminist scholars, writers, and thinkers to do the same."

Sociologist Philip Cohen uses a project-based strategy through his blog and Twitter account. His blog is called *Family Inequality*,[§] with the following fitting goal statement: "On this site I keep a running account of the connections between families and inequality. The nature of this relationship is

---

* https://inequalitybyinteriordesign.wordpress.com/.

†http://thesocietypages.org/girlwpen/.

‡ http://thesocietypages.org/girlwpen/editors-2/.

§ https://familyinequality.wordpress.com/.

one of the central problems of inequality in modern societies."* He develops that into a much longer explanation on the "about" page for his blog, providing the backstory that led to the blog and offering us a nice model of a longer-form social media statement of goals. His Twitter account @FamilyUnequal serves as a short-form companion to his blog. The blog and Twitter feed each stand on their own, but they also generate traffic for each other.

A project-driven social media strategy can center on a social problem, a particular kind of inequality, or a desired social change. The personalities involved in a project-driven strategy are one dimensional, reduced to the focus on that central theme. However, the project itself can have multiple dimensions thanks to multiple authors, or multiple audiences, or multiple ways to engage the central questions.

Individual social media users often begin with a personality-driven account that is multidimensional. For most of us, this is a play space in which we can practice with different social media voices and practice with different audiences. It is a good way to get started in social media, because it gives us time to get comfortable with the platforms and become familiar with their capacities.

Over time many users may feel the need to run multiple accounts across several platforms, due to varied projects and interests. Some of these accounts may be strictly project based and others may center more on the user's personality. I suggest that any scholar who has been using social media platforms with a personality-driven strategy should now consider a project-driven strategy that focuses on one social problem or an opportunity for social change. Once you have chosen whether to be personality or project driven, and whether to be one dimensional or multidimensional, you are able to then make determinations about the expected audience for your social media usage.

IDENTIFY YOUR AUDIENCE(S)

Instead of gathering a seemingly random audience and then post hoc trying to figure out who they are and why they follow you, be proactive in deciding who you want your audience to be. Identifying your audience is an important

---

* https://familyinequality.wordpress.com/about/.

part of any basic social media strategy. Here are some types of people who might be in the audience for a social scientist or civic leader:

- Other activists and leaders
- Supporters or potential supporters
- Students who might be studying the topic
- Voters concerned about the topic
- Journalists who cover the topic
- Policy makers
- Anyone who is directly impacted by the topic

Most activists and leaders are likely to choose a combination of these types of people, or even all of them.

What brings these disparate audiences together? Another way to approach this is to return to the mission statement that drives your work. Who shares that mission with you or has a similar mission? Who is impacted by the issue and by the achievement of the mission? Who has something to gain or something to lose, depending on how the issue is addressed? What communities are impacted, and who is invested in those communities?

Try to write a short statement that succinctly identifies your audience in a way that explains how the various groups are united.

Your initial audience in social media is likely to be your immediate friends and colleagues. Their importance should not be underestimated. They are the ones who will follow your Twitter account before you have even posted a single tweet. But they cannot be the target audience in the long term. You want to look past those who love you (and your posts) unconditionally and focus on that much larger group of people who need more convincing about the value of your work. How do *they* decide what makes a good source to follow? Put yourself in their shoes and think about how they approach following social media outlets.

DEVELOP A TAGGING STRATEGY

Tags in social media function as an indexing system. That's good for you and great for your audience. It's good for you because it means that your posts are generating content for a searchable database of resources. Most of us have a file cabinet full of folders about various issues: taxes, birth certificate, health records, class assignments, and the like. The little tab at the top of the folder lets you tag the information so you can find it later, as long as you know what tag to look for.

In social media you can use a long list of tags, but if they are going to work, you have to have a strategy for using them consistently. I say more about creating a tagging strategy below, but first let me suggest some of the uses of tags.

Writing an Essay, Report, Manifesto, Article, or Book, One Tweet or Post at a Time

Imagine that you are a student with a sociology paper to write. While sitting in a biology class, you think of one really great insight that you want to include in the paper. You could scribble it down in your biology notes and hope to find it later, or you could tweet it as a short phrase with the hashtag #sociology. By tweeting it, you have a digital copy that you cannot lose. And your friends may start to weigh in with fresh ideas and critiques that you can use to improve your paper. But how does the hashtag factor in? If you were writing that paper for my class, the first assignment for your term paper was in week 1, but the final paper isn't due until week 15. If you have the great insight in week 2 but don't get around to incorporating it until week 13, it may have disappeared behind a river of unrelated tweets. The hashtag helps you find it. Twitter does not currently provide a way for you to search through your own tweets apart from endlessly scrolling down. But it does allow you to request an archive of your tweets. The archive arrives in a day or two, via e-mail, as an attached spreadsheet. You can use the edit>find option to find all the tweets with the tag you need. In some cases, you may not need the tag because you recall other words from the tweet. But in many cases you may not recall a particular word or phrase. You may not even recall writing the tweet itself. Searching the archive for your chosen tags, based on your tagging strategy, will remind you of these tweets so you can incorporate them into your written work.

You can do the same with tags on a blog. Those tags become an index to your entire blog. The more tags you add to a particular post, the more keywords you can use to find that post later. But if you use too many tags, the post may appear so many times that it functions more like clutter, preventing you from seeing other posts that fit those tags better. So again, you want to develop a tagging strategy that you use consistently. That way you can predict which kinds of posts appear under each keyword. You can select specific tags and create pages that link from the navigation menu, to give you quick access to all posts with that tag. So you could write a lengthy project in short segments as a series of blogs and collect them together using tags.

If you want to take your tagging even further, there are online sources for archiving your social media. My favorite is IFTTT, which stands for "if this then that."* With IFTTT, you can create "recipes" for cross-referencing your social media, communications, and online document storage platforms. For all of my major keywords, I have an IFTTT recipe that takes every tweet using that tag and drops it into a spreadsheet in Google Drive. I tweet often about comics, using the hashtag #comics. Thanks to IFTTT, I can open all of those tweets in a single spreadsheet. When I finally get around to writing my great book on comics, that spreadsheet will be my starting point.

Creating a Database of Resources

Collecting ideas about a particular topic? Perhaps for an assignment or for a project in an organization? You can tweet or blog about each item that you find, using a tag to collect them all together. Imagine you are doing a research project about gay images in comic books. As you collect information about specific artists or titles, you can tweet or post them using the hashtag #queercomics. But suppose you want to divide the project into logical subgroups of resources. You can add additional hashtags to accomplish this, such as #queercomicartists and #queercomictitles. Or simply use combinations like #queercomics #artists or #queercomics #titles. This is all in the interest of creating a database of information for yourself that you can reference later.

Teach Your Followers How to Search Your Information Across Platforms

Technically, tags are only useful in some social media formats, particularly blogs and Twitter. Facebook allows for tags, and I expect it will offer more refined uses for tags over time. But some platforms have no tagging at all. Tagging is not a part of the interface in YouTube or Pinterest. But you can create

* https://ifttt.com/.

YouTube playlists and Pinterest boards that use the same keywords as your tagging strategy. Dedicated followers will learn how to search information across your varied platforms. Moreover, it provides you with a ready-made format for organizing each new platform that you adopt. On Academia.edu I use my hashtag strategy for each post and for each paper that I upload, so that those papers and posts are likely to appear when someone searches those terms.

In addition to being a useful resource for you, the content creator, tagging is also a useful mechanism for building an audience. Many of your potential followers will find your work because they searched for a word that you use in your tags. By adding the hashtag #sociology to many of my tweets and posts, I gain new followers weekly who are sociology students or professors. The audience-centered approach to hashtagging only works if you are careful to think about how your potential audience might search for a topic. When I first started using social media to study social media, I created the hashtag #socmedia. I like it because it's a fairly short hashtag. But someone searching for thoughtful ideas about social media is more likely to find me using #socialmedia. So I have had to convert some of my hashtags as I have become more audience centered.

What does a tagging strategy actually look like? You want to start with a list of specific tags that, all combined, provide a description of your work. For example, in my work on popular culture I think a lot about different media formats, different aspects of identity, and different stages in what Wendy Griswold calls the "cultural diamond" (1994). That gives me three lists in my primary tags, as illustrated in table 8.1.

TABLE 8.1. Primary Tags for Pop Culture Freaks

Media formats	Identity	Cultural diamond
#film	#race	#production
#tv	#class	#content
#music	#gender	#audience
#fiction	#sexuality	#socialworld
#internet	#disability	
#socialmedia	#trans	
#comics	#global	

These are the tags that I use most often. If I find an article about black producers in the music industry, I tweet the link with a descriptive phrase, plus #music #race #production. That triangulation allows me to pinpoint each item within the broader framework that I use to organize my ideas.

The secondary tags that you want to incorporate into a tagging strategy are broad terms that help you connect your specific ideas to a broader audience. On Twitter, you can add these tags only when you have enough character space left over after the primary tags, or when the primary tags simply do not apply. My secondary tags are listed in table 8.2.

TABLE 8.2. Secondary Tags for Pop Culture Freaks

Discipline	Topic	Action
#sociology	#popculture	#teaching
#popculturesociology	#massmedia	#writing
#socialscience	#cultureindustries	#service
#mediastudies	#entertainment	#mentoring
#culturalstudies		
#communications		

Finally, tertiary tags are about specific information within your post. These are the tags you are least likely to use, but you can add them on whenever there is room, or whenever you want to draw an audience for that specific posting—which is a different strategy from building an audience for your whole project. I post a lot during specific pop culture moments, so those tend to produce many of my tertiary tags. Other tertiary tags relate to specific authors whom I post about or specific political issues. These tags are not central to my work, but I want to demonstrate that the topics I am studying are connected to these broader social issues. Table 8.3 provides a sampling of tertiary tags.

Table 8.3. Tertiary Tags for Pop Culture Freaks

Events	Authors	Politics
#Grammys	#RobertMerton	#NetNeutrality
#SuperBowl	#PierreBourdieu	#Ferguson
#Oscars	#LauraGrindstaff	#Globalization

BEGIN WITH TWITTER

I think that microblogging on Twitter is the most important place to start in social media. So many social activists, professionals, and leaders are missing opportunities simply by not having a Twitter account. When a colleague of mine published a book recently, I sent a tweet to encourage my followers to order copies. But this colleague was not on Twitter, which meant I couldn't include her handle in the tweet. That was a missed opportunity because potential readers lost a chance to follow her on Twitter and increase their chances of reading the book. The audience for your work may begin as the audience for your social media posts, but only if you are posting in social media.

That colleague has since joined Twitter, much to my relief. Had she not, the missed opportunities would have continued to grow. The readers for her books, eager for more of her ideas, can now follow her on Twitter and remain a loyal audience. They will know when her future articles and books appear or when she gives interviews to the press.

Students—both undergraduate and graduate—also miss opportunities by not being on Twitter. I fully sympathize with, and respect, those who avoid social media out of concerns about privacy or harassment or any of a number of issues that we confront in our increasingly digital lives. However, I also know as a sociologist that social media is now a major tool of socialization. Not being on social media today is like not having a television in the 1980s. By avoiding the technology, we practice a kind of defensive resistance, protecting ourselves from the harmful effects of technology. But the technology continues to transform the society around us just the same. Unplugging from technology means unplugging from society, which leaves us powerless to address important social problems.

So when my students tell me about the ways that they want to change the world—from fighting inequality to making positive images in the media—I say "show me the tweets!," channeling my best Jerry Maguire. Conversations about these issues are happening right now, in real time, on Twitter. You don't have to wait until you complete your degree to join the conversation. You can use Twitter to track the pulse of the issues that matter to you and build a network of like-minded change makers. That network could play an important role as students apply to graduate and professional school programs or enter the job market.

If you are interested in a career fighting racism and discrimination, you should be on Twitter actively following the Southern Poverty Law Center (@SPLC), sociologist Matthew Hughey (@ProfHughey), the Section on Racial & Ethnic Minorities of the American Sociological Association (ASA_SREM), and the Strong Black Men project (@GoodBlackMen). If you are interested in a career in professional applied social research, you need to be following professional applied social researchers on Twitter who work at places like the U.S. Census Bureau (@uscensusbureau), the Centers for Disease Control and Prevention (@CDCgov), the Equal Employment Opportunity Commission (@EEOCnews), the Urban Institute (@urbaninstitute), and the Pew Research Center (@pewresearch).

At 140 characters, Twitter should be the least intimidating social media platform to join. If you tweet once every day, you are coming up with a maximum of 140 characters, or a combination of characters and links or images. Tweeting daily should not be difficult.

If you are unsure of how to get started on Twitter, whether it is an issue of creating an account or composing a strong tweet, look at some of the multitudes of training videos on YouTube. I collect my favorites into a Pinterest board so I can reference them easily and share them with my students.*

BLOGGING COMES AFTER MICROBLOGGING

Once you have conquered Twitter, it is time to add a full-fledged blog. The most popular platforms are Tumblr, WordPress, and Blogger, but you can also create your own if you have the server space to host a website. If that server space results in a URL that is long and difficult for your audience to find, go with one of the major platforms. Tumblr is by far the most popular of the big three, but it really depends on the style that works best for you. If you use Google for everything, there is no need to stop now. You should go ahead and use Google's blogging platform, Blogger. If your work tends to attract a younger audience, you should use Tumblr. If you want your blog to be part of a larger website, you should go with WordPress. The tools that WordPress provides allow you to build a full static website around the frequently updated blog section.

As for all forms of social media, a slew of training videos is available on YouTube, and also at my Pinterest board, listed above. The individual

*https://www.pinterest.com/popculturefreak/social-media/.

platforms also provide step-by-step instructions and answers to frequently asked questions.

You can use a blog for a number of activities. Table 8.4 provides a number of items that you can include in a blog. Think of it as a place to test run your writing, promote or update your published works, expand audience engagement, and curate resources.

TABLE 8.4. Types of Posts That a Social Activist or Civic Leader Might Include in a Blog

Long-form blogs	Short-form blogs
• A selection from a work in progress • A selection from a recently published work • A selection from a past work that needs new attention • An essay about current events in your field • A review of recently published work from your field • A literature review of the major studies and findings from your field • A review of theoretical perspectives from your field	• A link to an article related to your topic • A video of you or another activist discussing work in your field • A video of a clip from television or film that illustrates a concept from your field • A video of a news story about your field • A photograph that illustrates a major concept from your field • An infographic that presents data from your field • An audio clip of an interview with a scholar or policy maker

Although it is great when blogs are updated regularly, it is perfectly fine to host a blog that is updated only once a month or even less frequently. The blog serves as a central collection point for all of your ideas and work, no matter how often you update it. Your followers will not check back regularly if you do not post regularly, but if they follow you on Twitter they should see a tweet from you every time you update the blog.

LINKEDIN, ACADEMIA.EDU, AND RESEARCHGATE

You need to have accounts in the professional spaces of your field. That means that everyone needs to have a LinkedIn account. Graduate students, undergraduates with aspirations to attend graduate school, and professors should also have accounts on Academia.edu and ResearchGate. Think of LinkedIn as your online résumé and both Academia.edu and ResearchGate as your online CV. You may have a résumé and/or CV on your personal website or your faculty profile, but that is no good to the person who reads your name in a publication and goes straight to LinkedIn to look you up. Think of LinkedIn as the world's résumé filing cabinet. Your résumé is useless if it cannot be found in the filing cabinet. You want to develop expansive networks on these sites. These are not places where you offer personal information about yourself, so worry less about protecting your privacy and more about reaching a wide audience. Every professional whom you connect with on LinkedIn, Academia.edu, and ResearchGate is embedded within their own network. Reaching these people with your message—about your new projects and positions, or about an issue that you care about—means reaching their networks as well.

LinkedIn also lets you follow major organizations and research centers and join groups that host discussions related to your field.

THE MANY FACES OF FACEBOOK

You can utilize Facebook in a number of ways. Obviously most people use Facebook as a personal space where they connect (mostly) with their actual friends, family, and colleagues. We tend to "let our hair down" on Facebook, so we prefer to use it less as a professional tool. Of course we all have those realtor friends who just don't understand those boundaries and constantly post about every house they have listed. But for the most part, Facebook profiles are not a good place to do business.

However, it is possible to have two Facebook profiles, one that is personal and another that is professional. That would allow you to use the professional account strictly for sharing about your activities and social leadership with a wide audience.

Another option is to create a page for your project on Facebook. Using the "Create Page" option allows you to make any of six types of pages: local business or place; company, organization, or institution; brand or product; artist, band, or public figure; entertainment; and cause or community. If your project has a formal organization, with offices and staff (i.e., funding), I suggest selecting "company, organization or institution." If your project centers around a cultural object like a book or documentary, I suggest choosing "entertainment." (I know social scientists do not typically think of our work as entertaining—maybe we should change that?—but in this case it is a matter of the type of product produced. *Harry Potter* may be more entertaining than the book you hold in your hand, but the point is that they are both books.) If your project is meant to generate community around social change, then I suggest selecting "cause or community." Choosing "cause or community" will also give you the option of creating a Facebook group instead of a page. That is likely to be the best option for a collaborative community.

A number of Facebook groups are already very active around a range of topics. Just a few from the field of sociology are Sociology of Gender, Teaching with a Sociological Lens, Men and Masculinities, American Sociological Association—ASA, and Shared Teaching Resources for Sociology.

Frankly, under its current formulation, I have to suggest that you not expect much from Facebook pages. They do not get a lot of traction because it is difficult to get your posts to show up on the feeds for your audience. I think it is easy enough to create a Facebook page, but I do not suggest heavy investment in Facebook pages as a tool for social activists.

Facebook groups are another matter entirely. If there is a strong sense of community, with at least a few regular posters, Facebook groups can be very productive. Facebook groups are not, however, a means of reaching a broad audience. Use them instead to collaborate with a relatively small group of leaders and activists who share a set of goals or interests.

THE POWER OF PINTEREST

Pinterest is frequently mocked as a seemingly useless scrapbooking tool. The comedian Iliza Schlesinger has a number of bits about Pinterest, including one clip from *The Tonight Show* in which she jokes about having planned three baby showers on Pinterest, even though "I don't know any babies." She calls it "porn for white women."*

It took me a while to fully understand the value of Pinterest, but now I'm hooked. It is a fantastic way to collect online tools and resources, organized around thematic issues. When racial conflicts in Ferguson, Missouri, made the national news, I felt that I needed to discuss this issue in my classes to help my students understand how social science can give us useful tools for understanding social problems. But I worried that I didn't have enough

* http://www.hulu.com/watch/648061.

information about the events at Ferguson, and about the issues leading up to those events, to thoughtfully engage my students about it. So I used the Internet to gather as many perspectives as I could. I found news clips about the events, blog posts presenting different ideological takes on the issues, and TED Talks about the history of race and racism in the United States. I collected these resources into a Pinterest board I that shared with my students.* We stepped through some of the clips and essays together and had a really difficult but smart conversation that focused on the value of empathy for understanding situations of intense conflict.

How else can you use Pinterest? Here are some examples:

- A board with information related to a social problem
- A board for each chapter of an important book
- A board focusing on a set of skills (like how to use Pinterest)
- A board with a set of resources for people confronting a particular issue
- A board with a set of teaching resources organized around various themes (for an example, check out the work of Sociological Cinema†)
- A board with information related to specific authors or specific paradigms (postmodernism, feminism, queer theory, etc.)

As students and scholars, we collect and curate information all of the time. Every student paper is a set of curated information. With Pinterest, we can share our curated information with a wider audience, using the description section to provide context and perspective.

COLLECTING AND MAKING VIDEOS

When it comes to videos, I think the best place to start is an account on YouTube. Most people use YouTube all the time without actually logging in. But creating an account lets you mark favorite videos and create playlists. I suggest creating playlists around the major themes of your social engagement. You can use the primary tags from your tagging strategy as the playlist names. You do not have to create an entire playlist in one sitting. You can simply create the playlist category and then make it a habit of adding videos to your

* https://www.pinterest.com/popculturefreak/ferguson/.

† https://www.pinterest.com/thesocycinema/.

playlists whenever you come across them. These provide useful tools for you for your blog posts or presentations, and they are useful for your audience.

Eventually you should consider making videos as well. The main tools that you need are a camera and a software tool for editing. You can use the built-in camera on your computer or the camera on your phone, but many people find that a higher end video camera produces better quality. If you purchase a camera, a tripod is a wise addition. Videos can be posted to YouTube or to Vimeo. Many professionals prefer Vimeo because it is an ad-free service. People who view your videos on Vimeo will not have to wait through an ad or have ads pop up during the video.

PLATFORMS FOR PICTURES

You may want to add a platform just for sharing images. You do not need to do this if you have a blog, because you can share your images directly through your blog. But an image service may be a valuable addition to your social media strategy if visual material is an important part of the way that you share your message. Visual material can include photographs, infographics, tables, and gifs. Many social researchers and activists neglect the visual aspect of data. If you use charts or tables to share information, then you are communicating visually. You can capture those data displays as images that you share through social media. If you work primarily through a computer, I suggest using Flickr or Picasa as your image-sharing platform. Choose Picasa if you are primarily a Google user. I prefer Flickr though, just because I think the interface is more attractive for my audience. If you capture a lot of photographs on your phone, Instagram is likely to be the better choice. A student or scholar who studies urban sociology or community anthropology can use their phone to capture images from around the community and share them with an audience to facilitate conversations about urban planning and design. The images can even be added to a map, to add a geo-social dimension.

POSTING STRATEGY

How often should you post on social media, and when are the best times to post? Marketers worry about these issues at the deepest levels because their money is on the line. I would encourage social activists and civic leaders not to get too caught up in the analytics. A bigger issue is likely to be the concern that posting on social media can consume too much time. To minimize this concern, try scheduling a limited amount of social media time. I chose Sunday mornings as my main social media posting time. But I didn't want to put out a million posts all at once and then go silent the rest of the week. So I use a platform called Hootsuite to schedule a week (or more) of posts for Twitter, Facebook, and LinkedIn. I use my Sunday mornings to write a new blog post or two and post a new image on Instagram. I save up related links most of the week and use my Sunday mornings to process them—adding some to Pinterest and others to Tumblr, or adding videos to my playlists. Putting social media on the calendar allows you to avoid spending too much time with your platforms, but it also ensures that you will not forget about them either. Tip: if you notice a lot of useful resources appearing on your Facebook feed, use the "save" option in the posts to collect them into a list that you can revisit them during your scheduled social media time.

WHO FOLLOWS A SOCIOLOGIST?

"Have we reached peak economist?" asked the *New York Times* columnist Justin Wolfers, himself an economist, on the paper's data-driven blog *The Upshot* (Wolfers 2015). Wolfers was discussing the prevalence of economic ideas and research, as compared to other social science disciplines, in public debates and media coverage. His evidence is a chart of data from the *New York Times* archive, using the Chronicle tool on the *Times* website,* which indicates that the word "economist" appeared in just under 1 percent of *New York Times* articles in 2014.† If 1 percent does not sound like much, consider the numbers for other social science disciplines: .7 percent for "historian," .3 percent for "psychologist," about .2 percent for "sociologist" and slightly less for "anthropologist," and almost no mentions of "demographer."‡ Wolfers

*http://chronicle.nytlabs.com/.

† When I tried to replicate Wolfers's chart using the Chronicle tool, I got a higher number, 1.63 percent. The tool may have been refined in the time between Wolfers's post and my own analysis, or his method may have been more specific than he indicates in his post.

‡Sociologist Philip Cohen re-ran the data on the Chronicle tool, using "professor of [discipline]" and "[discipline] professor" (i.e., "professor of sociology" and "sociology professor," and so on with the other disciplines). Cohen's narrower approach also found higher numbers than what Wolfers presented. But more important, it showed a smaller gap between sociology and economics. Cohen's discussion can be found at https://contexts.org/blog/sociology-unfound/.

explores why it is that the discipline of economics seems to have won the battle for public attention. But I want to think about this less as a battle among disciplines and more as a sign of the weakness of social science in general to capture the public imagination. It is not that social science is losing out to some other kind of expertise. I looked for other kinds of experts on the Chronicle tool—such as biologist, physicist, criminologist—and they all have very few mentions. Even journalist is only mentioned in about 2 percent of articles. But considering the wealth of research that social scientists conduct and the relevance of that research to the everyday lives of Americans, it is very disappointing that social science is not part of a richer national dialogue. Television is mentioned in over 7 percent of articles. Actors are mentioned in 2.4 percent of articles. Surely the topics that social scientists study—politics, religion, culture, media, housing, education, employment, family, and so forth—merit at least as much public discussion of our research as that received by television and actors. We may turn to television and actors for entertainment, but we turn to news sources for information.

Getting social science research, pedagogy, and community engagement into the mainstream of American public discourse will require changes in American culture generally, but it will also require changes in how social scientists operate with respect to their audiences. Many of us have very little clear idea of how our ideas and research impact the world. Our largest and most consistent audience is our students. We hope that as we share our ideas, and the ideas of our peers, with these students, they will then go out into the world and engage it in a different way. Perhaps they will vote differently, work differently, parent differently, or even go so far as to help make better public policy or better businesses. Of course, if and when they do so, they will also be acting under the influence of a wealth of ideas they received from other professors, or from their families, or friends, or colleagues, or from the culture they consume from television, film, books, music, and the Internet. So we have no real way to tell when and whether the tools learned in our classes make a specific difference.

For social scientists who are engaged in ongoing research leading to publication, another audience is the readers of those publications. This model of author/audience still depends heavily on teaching, as classes—especially small graduate seminars—are the best way to have one's ideas canonized in a field. Others will find our work, and become our audience, through citation indexes and journal databases. But let's be realistic: the audience for journal articles is small. If you publish books, you get good data on how many copies of your book are sold. Although some people will buy your book but not read it, others will read it without buying it, borrowing a copy from a library or friend. With articles, we cannot keep track of readership. Some journal subscribers will read through an issue, but most will find your work through online databases thanks to institutional subscriptions. So instead of tracking readers of your work, article authors have to track citations. Apparently some authors have all the luck. Although some authors are cited frequently, many others are not cited at all, ever. The UK-based *Times Higher Education* publishes yearly citation averages for all of the articles published in journals indexed in the Thompson Reuters Essential Science Indicators database. For all journal types, the numbers have declined sharply in the past several years. Table 8.5 presents the averages for social science journals for 2000–2010.

TABLE 8.5. Yearly Average Article Citations in Social Science Journals Indexed by the Thompson Reuters Essential Science Indicators Database

2000	2001	2002	2003	2004	2005	2006	2007	2008	2009	2010
9.25	8.63	8.37	7.67	7.21	6.19	4.82	3.49	2.02	.88	.20

Source: Times Higher Education, https://www.timeshighereducation.co.uk/news/citation-averages-2000-2010-by-fields-and-years/415643.article (retrieved July 1, 2015).

Notice the sharp decline over a decade. Most articles are not receiving any citations whatsoever. This is partly due to the rapid expansion of journal articles. More academics at more universities and colleges need more publications than ever before in order to get a job, keep a job, get tenure, get raises, and get promotions. Publishers have responded to this demand for publishing opportunities by creating a flood of new journals. But the audience for each individual article is now smaller than ever.

Let us review. Social scientists work very hard, conducting empirical research and/or crafting complex theories about real-world social issues related to housing, education, kinship, and a wide range of important topics, and then the publications that summarize their findings and theories are typically read by no one, but sit available in databases until a scholar or two cites them once, if they are lucky, typically in another article that itself will have little to no audience. The lucky few whose ideas happen to catch broader attention will then be cited in a fraction of a percent of articles published in the mainstream press. And yet the research is often about significant problems that confront real human lives and demand practical solutions. If we want these problems to actually be addressed in a way that is influenced by the careful research we are conducting, we need to create new models for building and engaging audiences. Below I outline a series of ways that we can use social media to effectively reach a range of audiences. I group them into four broad categories: peers, the general audience, journalists/influencers, and policy makers.

An Audience of Peers

If you are a social activist or civic leader, your peers are other activists and leaders, both in your organizations and in related and allied organizations. If you are an academic social scientist, your peers are any scholars who might have an interest in your work. Professionals in any field share a broad common vocabulary and use words that outsiders might rightly call jargon. But this jargon is the vernacular of their profession. An audience of peers is likely to be the easiest to gather, if you can find them on social media, but they offer the least help with influencing social policy and achieving social change.

Where do you find your peers on social media? There are four great places where I suggest that you start: Twitter and LinkedIn for social activists, and Academia.edu and ResearchGate for academics. These are the platforms where you will find the most people and the platforms that your peers are most likely to treat as professional spaces. I do connect with several peers through Facebook, but typically only ones that I actually know in the nonvirtual world. However, as discussed previously in this chapter, Facebook groups are a great way to use that platform for sharing information. Of the three platforms that I am suggesting you use to start gathering your audience, Twitter is the one to focus on the most.

How do you find your peers on Twitter? Obviously there is no master list of all the social activists that you can use, and surely it would be too long to be manageable anyway. Start by identifying the leaders in your field and search for them by name. Many of them will not be on Twitter (yet), but some of them will. Follow them, and scroll through their "following" and "followers" lists to see if you can find other peers there. Another option is to search keywords and hashtags. Try searching these words with and without the hashtag. Without the hashtag, you are more likely to catch peers who use these terms in their profile descriptions. With the hashtag, you will catch the peers who are using them in their tweets in hopes of finding audience members like you.

Make a regular practice of searching for folks on Twitter when you encounter them. Every time I meet someone at a conference or hear a great speaker, I search for that person on Twitter. Every time I read a new book or research article, I search for the author on Twitter. Every time I interact with a new research center or organization, I find it on Twitter.

Once you are established in Twitter, consider adding LinkedIn, Academia.edu, and ResearchGate to your strategy for reaching peers. Make sure your profiles are fully developed and visually striking. The strategy is similar to that for creating a good résumé or CV. In fact, I like to think of LinkedIn as an online and dynamic résumé, and of both Academia.edu and ResearchGate as spaces to post an online and dynamic CV. Follow as many people in your field, and related fields, as you can find. As a professor of sociology teaching courses on the mass media, I like to assume that any scholar I find who isn't working in my area may have a colleague who is, and that colleague may not be on social media.

There are many ways to engage with other activists, leaders, and professionals through social media. I focus on just a few here: (1) collaborating on projects, (2) sharing ideas and support, and (3) promoting your own work with the goal of increasing your audience and your participation rate.

Social media provides excellent tools for collaboration. Professionals who are writing or organizing collaboratively can share and edit documents using programs like Dropbox or Google Drive. These include text documents, spreadsheets, and presentations. You can collect media resources like articles and videos on a collaborative Pinterest board, which can then be shared with your peers and other audiences. Finally, leaders who are collaborating can bounce ideas off each other using Twitter, thus allowing others to observe the process by which ideas are formed collectively.

Using Twitter is also a great way to discuss your work with an audience of your peers. You can share ideas and ask questions through Twitter. The best way to foster a conversation on Twitter is to identify specific members of your audience using their Twitter handles (@ing them) and inviting them to share their ideas. Consider the following two sample tweets, both of which are intended to foster conversation with peers:

> "Currently reading There Goes the Gayborhood? Curious to hear how LGBT community leaders in different cities think about its findings."
>
> "Reading There Goes the Gayborhood? By @Amin_Ghaziani. Thoughts from @drcompton in #NOLA and @joshgamson in #SanFrancisco? #sociology #LGBT."

These are both fine tweets with characters to spare, but the second tweet is much better at audience engagement. Although the first tweet invites anyone who sees it to engage in the conversation, it does not actually invite anyone in particular. It is easy to read it and then simply move on to the next tweet on your feed.

The second tweet goes much further than the first in cultivating an audience. First, it adds the author of the work in question into the discussion. At a minimum, the author in question (Amin Ghaziani in this example) is likely to pay attention to any discussion that follows, and he may even choose to retweet the initial tweet, expanding the audience for the tweet by adding his network to that audience. Second, the tweet names specific peers (sociologists D'Lane Compton and Joshua Gamson) to participate in the conversation. These scholars are much more likely to engage once they have been named. As they reply, their Twitter followers get added to the audience for the tweet, and some of them may then choose to follow you. If these named peers reply, then the tweet becomes much more interesting to the larger audience, including other peers, and they are then more likely to participate as well. Adding the hashtag "sociology" is another way of inviting an audience of peers. The hashtag allows peers who don't already follow you to come across your tweet, if they happen to do a search for that hashtag.

The second tweet also invites an audience of nonpeers by including hashtags for places (New Orleans and San Francisco) and for a topic (LGBT).

There are several other spaces in social media where you can discuss your causes and activism with peers. These include Facebook groups for your field (if one does not exist, consider creating it), circles of peers on Google+, and posts on LinkedIn. LinkedIn allows for both short-form updates and longer blog-style posts. In either case, you can also tag peers and invite their responses and commentary.

General Audiences

For the general audience, we operate with a diffuse model of influence. We hope that we put our ideas out into the world, others consume them, and then they make better decisions or lead better lives as a result of our influence. Although the audience members are diffuse, they are also many. We can have higher hopes of influencing the world when we reach the general audience, as compared to simply reaching our peers. But how do we recruit this general audience?

The best platforms to use for reaching a general audience are Facebook and Twitter. Most other platforms are also good ways to recruit general audiences, but the least effective platforms for this group are LinkedIn, Academia.edu, and ResearchGate. Immediately, you can see that reaching the general audience is very different from reaching peers.

The most important way of recruiting the general public into your audience is to produce powerful content in ways that are easy to find. This can include poignant tweets, resourceful Pinterest boards, insightful blog posts, powerful videos, and helpful media links on Facebook. The more useful and interesting your content is, the more your audience will share it with their networks, helping you reach yet more audience members.

If your content is powerful, members of the general audience will keep following you over time, and then they will hopefully share your content with their larger networks. In my experience, this is the hardest audience to build and engage. It takes time. But over time, engaging this audience has the potential to really pay off.

Journalists and Influencers

Activists and leaders want to gain an audience among journalists because journalists help us to reach even bigger audiences. Journalists are content makers, and their careers depend on their ability to build and engage audiences. In the era of Web 2.0, journalists are easier to reach than ever, and they are now joined by influencers. Influencers are nonjournalists who produce content about particular themes to satisfy an interest among an audience. Perez Hilton is great example. Hilton started his blog in 2004 to share insider gossip about the entertainment industry. He was an aspiring actor with no training in journalism and no experience covering celebrities and media culture. But he knew Hollywood well and used his expertise and network of insiders to share information that most readers could not find anywhere else.

Most influencers are not as big as Perez Hilton. In evaluating an influencer, what matters is whether they have cultivated an audience that you would like to reach. In my research, one topic that I frequently examine is representations of disability in the media. Two influencers who have cultivated an audience for this topic are Maysoon Zayid and Meg Zucker. Zayid has had a long and winding career that includes acting, stand-up comedy, and commentating on *Countdown with Keith Olbermann*. Her audience soared after a TED Talk in 2014. Since then she has become an influencer for comedy, Muslim Americans, gender politics in the culture industries, and disability activism. Meg Zucker produces the blog *Don't Hide, Flaunt It*, in which she encourages people with disabilities to flaunt their differences and love their bodies. Zucker only has 237 followers (as of July 6, 2015) on Twitter, but her blog is widely read, and she has made numerous appearances on national media. Zayid has 19,000 followers. Both are great examples of influencers who have built audiences around a specific set of topics.

Journalists and influencers are network nodes. If you can reach them, you can reach many more through them. They are picky content sharers, much pickier than the general audience. But if you can get through to them, your ideas can influence not only the general public, but also discussions about policy and practice.

Start by making lists of journalists and influencers in the field that you research. It may help to divide your field into subfields and focus on them one at a time. Who are the national newspaper reporters who write about this topic? Who are the national magazine reporters who cover this topic? Who are the national television reporters who cover this topic (including cable television)? Who are the local reporters (newspapers, weeklies, magazines, TV) who cover this topic? Who are the bloggers who cover this topic? It may take some time to make these lists, but this audience is relatively easy to identify and very easy to find on social media. Once you have the list of names, find and follow them all on Twitter, see if they have pages on Facebook, and look for their blogs and any other social media platforms they use frequently. All of that information should be collected in a spreadsheet you can access easily.

Journalists and influencers are easy to find on social media, but what makes them a tricky group is that they don't like to think of themselves as audience members. Their job is to create audiences, not participate in them. On Twitter, their following lists are much shorter than their followers' list. So it will take a lot of careful work to persuade them to follow you back and to get them into your audience.

Policy Makers

Policy makers include anyone tasked with making or influencing social policy on a particular issue. A list of policy makers starts with elected officials but should also include lobbyists, agency staffers, and advocacy organizations.

In some fields, elected officials will be less important than industry leaders. For example, as someone who studies gay representations on television, I can include the Federal Communications Commission and any politicians who might be voting about media regulation on my list of important policy makers, but programming executives at the major networks are actually the professionals whose policies most impact my field. As with journalists and influencers, a strategy for reaching policy makers starts with lists of names, divided up by subfields. Once the names are listed, they can be found and followed on Twitter and other platforms (but especially Twitter).

Policy makers are accustomed to listening to concerns from a broad range of constituents. The difficult part about cultivating this audience is breaking through the clutter of voices trying to gain their attention and influence their policies. Breaking through the clutter requires good sound bites, effective presentations of data, and clear recommendations.

CAN SOCIAL MEDIA LEAD TO SOCIAL CHANGE?

Whether or not social media can trigger important social changes is still a subject of much debate. As social media users, we need to decide where we ourselves sit on the spectrum of techno-optimism and techno-pessimism. But social media is now so completely integrated into modern communications that even the techno-pessimist may need to embrace social media as a pragmatic tool that is necessary just to share information about social issues, policies, and opportunities for activism. If social media cannot actually cause change, it nevertheless seems that change cannot now happen without the support of social media.

9

Conclusion: A Social Media Revolution?

The revolution will not be tweeted, but it will be social, and there will be a lot of media involved. That is the conclusion that I have reached after reflecting on these case studies. In this chapter I make my case for this conclusion and try to demonstrate how I have arrived at a position of optimism about technology and networks but pessimism about their current corporate ownership.

The film *The Social Network* presents a fictional characterization of the real-life events that led to the creation of Facebook. The film focuses on the legal battles between the men who started Facebook, but what strikes me the most in the telling of the story is the utter centrality of privilege: class privilege, white privilege, male privilege. Women, people of color, and queer people are side characters at best. Trans folks, people with disabilities, and poor people are completely invisible. That doesn't mean that technology and social media were built solely by wealthy, cisgender, straight, white, able-bodied men. It just means that such men have controlled the narrative of social media. They also control the corporations that run the major social media platforms. Watching *The Social Network*, I was overwhelmed by the homogeneity of the characters. The stories of social media from the perspectives of women, black folks, Asian folks, Native American folks, Hispanic folks, transgender and genderqueer folks, lesbians, gays, bisexual folks, poor and working-class folks, people with disabilities, and non-American folks still need to be told and will likely prove to be the truly interesting histories of social media.

THE DANGERS OF SOCIAL MEDIA

Social media is dangerous. I love it and I hate it. I love it for the ways that it empowers me to create and share stories with a large audience and the opportunities that it gives me to listen to the stories told by other people through their tweets, videos, memes, Pinterest boards, playlists, and blogs. I hate it for the sense of privacy and anonymity that it has taken from me as a private citizen. I hate it for the way that it renders my life into a fraction of a massive database of market research and then sells my identity back to me through targeted ads that I admittedly fall prey to all too often. I hate it for the capacity of anonymous people to make scathing comments and terrifying threats with no accountability.

I am a heavy user of social media. I am on nearly every platform, and I post several times per day on some of them. I use social media in the classes that I teach, and I have run workshops and written essays urging other scholars to use social media in the promotion of their research (Kidd and Daniels 2016). But every time I share about the value of social media, I urge my audience to think very carefully before investing in social media and to be diligent about monitoring their safety and security while they use it—something I have failed at multiple times myself.

As the GamerGate case demonstrates, social media can expose users to doxxing and threats of rape, assault, and murder. In the summer of 2016 comedian Leslie Jones was subjected to a slew of racist and sexist tweets in the aftermath of a negative review of her film *Ghostbusters* by Breitbart reporter and GamerGate apologist Milo Yiannopoulos (Brown 2016). The tweets, following a review titled "Teenage Boys with Tits: Here's My Problem with Ghostbusters" (Yiannopoulos 2016), included phrases like "Your Ghostbusters ain't the first to have an ape in it"* and "big lipped coon."† Yiannopoulos whipped his followers into a frenzy by adding his own commentary with tweets like "rejected by yet another black dude" accompanied by a screen capture of Jones's Twitter account page.‡ Initially, Jones declared that she was leaving Twitter, but she agreed to remain after Twitter decided to permanently ban Yiannopoulos instead. Yiannopoulos responded with anger at Twitter but confidence in his own position:

> With the cowardly suspension of my account, Twitter has confirmed itself as a safe space for Muslim terrorists and Black Lives Matter extremists, but a no-go zone for conservatives. . . . Like all acts of the totalitarian left, this will blow up in their faces, netting me more adoring fans. We're winning the culture war, and Twitter just shot themselves in the foot. (Quoted in Richardson 2016)

He also threatened that he might find ways to get back onto Twitter. Writer and social media artist Akilah Hughes summed up the attack on Jones with a tweet that claimed these attacks are all too common: "Ask any black woman you follow on any social network. Social media companies allow plenty of racist abuse."§

---

*https://twitter.com/Lesdoggg/status/755182965060169728/photo/1?ref_src=twsrc%5Etfw.

† https://twitter.com/Lesdoggg/status/755180325840556032/photo/1?ref_src=twsrc%5Etfw.

‡ Yiannopoulos's account has since been deleted, but a screen capture of this tweet is presented in Brown 2016.

§ https://twitter.com/AkilahObviously/status/755399132441939968?ref_src=twsrc%5Etfw.

Hughes's statement holds true as well in the world of academic scholarship. In 2015 a black scholar who had recently completed her PhD and was off to start a tenure-track position at Boston University came under fire when some of her tweets related to her scholarship on race were attacked by conservative critics (Jaschik 2015b). Saida Grundy had wrapped up a dissertation on black masculinity that was driven by interviews with graduates of Morehouse College and she received a doctorate from the University of Michigan. A conservative website called SoCawlege had monitored her tweets as part of its ongoing campaign against liberalism in academia. It published a report on her tweets* that focused on statements she made critiquing whiteness and white supremacy. The report caught the attention of Fox news, and that is when Grundy experienced a national media firestorm. The tweet that was quoted the most read: "Why is white America so reluctant to identify white college males as a problem population."† The tweets were abstracted from the conversations and interactions in which they were embedded, and the source of the report was largely unscrutinized. Although Grundy retained her job at Boston University, the president of the school issued a report expressing disapproval of her tweets:

> I do not say this lightly or without a great deal of consultation and soul-searching. I understand there is a broader context to Dr. Grundy's tweets and that, as a scholar, she has the right to pursue her research, formulate her views, and challenge the rest of us to think differently about race relations. But we also must recognize that words have power and the words in her Twitter feed were powerful in the way they stereotyped and condemned other people. (Brown 2015)

For a new faculty member, a statement of reproof from the president of the university is a very daunting way to begin the tenure track. Grundy eventually made her Twitter account private and stated that she had been naïve in her social media use: "I did not account for the hunters." But she also clarified that the real problem is the relationship between the medium of Twitter and the impact of existing social inequalities on scholarship: "These issues are unavoidable for a person of color who will work on issues of race. The idea

*http://socawlege.com/boston-university-assistant-professor-saida-grundy-attacks-whites-makes-false-statements-on-twitter/.

† Ibid.

that if you shut down social media you will avoid the battles, that is a fallacy" (quoted in Jaschik 2015b). Other scholars who have come under fire for their social media posts include Steven Salaita (Cohen 2015) and Zandria Robinson (Jaschik 2015a).

THE MASTER'S TOOLS

Throughout this project, two well-known phrases have haunted me. The first is from the musician Gil Scott-Heron, who famously declared, "The revolution will not be televised" (Scott-Heron 1970). The second is from the writer-activist Audre Lorde, who stated in a panel discussion, "The master's tools will never dismantle the master's house" (Lorde 1984, 112). Reflecting on these words has helped me to better understand my pessimism about the structure of social media and its control by corporations.

"The Revolution Will Not Be Televised" is a sweeping critique of commercial mass media packed into three minutes and seven seconds. Although Scott-Heron trains his focus on television, his critiques also have some application to film, music, and print media, and they would apply today to the Internet and social media. He opens the track with these words:

> You will not be able to stay home, brother.
> You will not be able to plug in, turn on and cop out.
> You will not be able to lose yourself on skag and
> Skip out for beer during commercials,
> Because the revolution will not be televised. (Scott-Heron 1970)

What we see first is that Scott-Heron is critiquing the way that television, and media more broadly, pacify us as audience members and citizens. Our attention span shortens to the space between commercials, which means our activism diminishes and our capacity for social transformation dries up. I am struck by the way that the line "You will not be able to plug in, turn on and cop out" sounds like it could easily be a slam against the "clicktivism" of the social media era. He continues:

> The revolution will not be brought to you by the
> Schaefer Award Theatre and will not star Natalie
> Woods and Steve McQueen or Bullwinkle and Julia.
> The revolution will not give your mouth sex appeal.

The revolution will not get rid of the nubs.
The revolution will not make you look five pounds
Thinner, because the revolution will not be televised, Brother.

In this selection he is critiquing the commercial nature of television and the fact that its ultimate goal is to sell products and make a profit, the inanity of our celebrity fetish, and the ridiculous claims of advertisers and our ridiculous tendency to believe all of those commercials. In other parts of the track, he calls out the spectacle of television news and particularly the way that it diminishes the lives of black people. He closes with the line "The revolution will be live," drawing a sharp distinction between televisual life and real life that is comparable to the distinction often made today between virtual reality and offline reality.

The problem that Scott-Heron is raising is not a problem with the *medium* of television, it is a problem with the *structure* of television: a structure that dominates how we think about the medium. The television that Scott-Heron critiques is a corporate-controlled, advertiser-sponsored format in which stories are controlled by executives and ad men. The stories told about oppressed and marginalized groups are authored by those with the most social privilege. The problem is not the telling of stories through video culture; the problem is the structure that controls the storytelling process. In Scott-Heron's time, corporate television was essentially the only television. The Public Broadcasting Service (PBS) was founded the year he released "The Revolution Will Not Be Televised." Its predecessor, National Education Television (NET), was owned by the Ford Foundation. Public television cannot be equated with the people's television, as these noncommercial broadcasters have often been accused of elitism.

But today a number of artists are using the Internet as an opportunity to explore new forms of television that tell a broader set of stories without the constraints of commercial sponsors and corporate structures. A great set of examples can be found in the project Open TV.* Communications scholar Aymar Jean Christian explains the project as follows:

> Open TV is a scholarly research project in television development. Development involves organizing production and marketing completed

* http://www.weareopen.tv.

> projects. I'm experimenting with arts-based methods for understanding cultural production and distribution by queer, trans and cis-women and artists of color across media and technology. (Christian 2016)

Open TV is an experiment in creating a new type of television that just might make it possible for the revolution to be televised after all. It is stripping video-culture storytelling of its corporate structure and commercial sponsors and deliberately creating a space for storytellers whose work has been excluded from corporate television and whose identities have been marginalized by mainstream society. Can it work? This is an open question that needs serious consideration, but the project demonstrates that artists are committed to new media technologies as they search for tools that can effect social change.

This brings me to Audre Lorde's claim that "the master's tools will never dismantle the master's house." She made this statement in 1979 at The Personal and Political Panel of the Second Sex Conference held at New York University. She described the context that led to the famous statement:

> It is a particular academic arrogance to assume any discussion of feminist theory without examining our many differences, and without a significant input from poor women, Black and Third World women, and lesbians. And yet, I stand here as a Black lesbian feminist, having been invited to comment within the only panel at this conference where the input of Black feminists and lesbians is represented. What this says about the vision of this conference is sad, in a country where racism, sexism, and homophobia are inseparable. To read this program is to assume that lesbian and Black women have nothing to say about existentialism, the erotic, women's culture and silence, developing feminist theory, or heterosexuality and power. And what does it mean in personal and political terms when even the two Black women who did present here were literally found at the last hour? What does it mean when the tools of a racist patriarchy are used to examine the fruits of that same patriarchy? It means that only the most narrow parameters of change are possible and allowable. (Lorde 1984, 110–111)

To be clear about the context, Lorde was speaking to an audience of feminists, but an audience that was predominantly composed of straight, white, and middle- and upper-class women. When she said "the master's tools will never dismantle the master's house," she was speaking truth to power in a place where she had hoped not to find it.

She continued:

> Those of us who stand outside the circle of this society's definition of acceptable women; those of us who have been forged in the crucibles of difference—those of us who are poor, who are lesbians, who are Black, who are older—know that *survival is not an academic skill.* It is learning how to take our differences and make them strengths. *For the master's tools will never dismantle the master's house.* They may allow us temporarily to beat him at his own game, but they will never enable us to bring about genuine change. And this fact is only threatening to those women who still define the master's house as their only source of support. (Lorde 1984, 112; emphasis in original)

Lorde was doing the work of intersectionality long before it had become a central paradigm in academia. She also made an interesting distinction between temporarily beating oppressive forces and oppressive people at their own game, which amounts to a kind of defensive resistance, and creating actual social transformation.

"The master's tools will never dismantle the master's house" is ultimately a claim that, separated from metaphor, can be argued and perhaps even tested. But it is a claim spoken in the language of poetry and with the weight of prophecy. It could be translated into a research question like this: Can the resources that create domination also be used to undo domination? Once we isolate that question, we then need to specify exactly what it is that we think constitutes the resources that have created domination over time, or at least to specify what resources are likely holding domination in place today. Looking across history, we might name religion, capitalism, and violence, which have worked hand-in-hand in unleashing colonialism, slavery, and patriarchy. If we focus on the contemporary era, we have to examine the prison-industrial complex, the military-industrial complex, and the media, among other resources. These three examples demonstrate immediately that the tools we are discussing are extremely powerful and extremely large, much bigger than something as simple as a tweet. But a tweet sits squarely on the side of the media, like a panel on the side of a massive tank. Can a panel from a tank be used to dismantle the tank, let alone the whole army that the tank is a part of?

Is a tweet one of the tools of the masters of the matrix of domination? No, but it is a component part of one of those tools: the media industry. That industry has spent decades giving us narratives that either distract from the realities of social inequality or outright legitimize those realities. I am referring to the **controlling images*** of black, Hispanic, and Asian people in the media; the invisibility of Native Americans; the patronizing of people with disabilities; and the sexualization and objectification of women.

To push the metaphor further, what if we could dismantle the tools but find new uses for the component parts? In this case, what if we really could put social media to work in the project of social change? What would have to happen to make that possible? The key issue is not the tools, but the ownership of the tools. I argue that social media can be used as a very powerful tool for social change, but not so long as it is controlled by massive corporations helmed by a small handful of people who represent the most privileged in our society.

Given that so many activists and artists view social media as a powerful tool for both political organization and creative expression, I am searching for a possibility that could rescue this tool from being one of "the master's tools." The key is to address the issue of control.

ART, INEQUALITY, AND SOCIAL CHANGE

Before media, there was art. Media is just the institutional structure of a corporatized art. Art is the highest form of literacy, because through art we find our voice, our audience, our message, and the words to say it.† Art encompasses all of the ways that we tell stories about ourselves and about each other, about our past and about our possible futures. The path to upending social inequality may be filled with public policy and political unrest, but it is

* The concept of controlling images is from Collins (1990); it provides a useful way to think about and beyond the issue of stereotypes.

† This sentence is borrowed from a video animation that I made on the topic of digital media literacy. That animation is available on my website at http://www.dustinkidd.net. A transcript of this video appears in the appendix.

propelled forward by art—by stories that inspire us and give us a vision that makes another world possible.

But art is not without its own inequalities. Writer and literary scholar bell hooks addresses this issue well in her book *Art on My Mind* (1995):

> [C]onservative white artists and critics who control the cultural production of writing about art seem to have the greatest difficulty accepting that one can be critically aware of visual politics—the way race, gender, and class shape art practices (who makes art, how it sells, who values is, who writes about it)—without abandoning a fierce commitment to aesthetics. Black artists and critics must continually confront an art world so rooted in a politics of white-supremacist capitalist patriarchal exclusion that our relationship to art and aesthetics can be submerged by the effort to challenge and change this existing structure. (hooks 1995, XII)

While hooks is critiquing the racism, sexism, and classism of the institutional systems that control structures in the art world—from arts education and funding to awards and criticism—she is also soundly declaring a commitment to art. What is embodied in a "fierce commitment to aesthetics?" I suggest that it is both a belief in the integrity of artistic discipline *and* a passion for the power of art to transform the world. As hooks observes: "Art constitutes one of the rare locations where acts of transcendence can take place and have a wide-ranging transformative impact" (hooks 1995, 8).

One of the conditions that makes social inequality so durable is the inability of most of us to see ourselves as artists and to embrace our capacity to create new visions of the world. It is difficult to believe that you can make change happen if you do not believe that you have the capacity to create the world around you. Artists are builders who create structures, mix colors, author conversations, and choreograph movement. If more of us insisted on our right to claim the identity of an "artist," we could expand the parameters of social change.

Getting there requires more people, of all ages, to pursue artistic training of all kinds, including training in new media. We need painters and actors and choreographers, but we also need coders and developers. Existing programs like Black Girls Code are working to make this a reality.* In addition

* http://www.blackgirlscode.com.

to technical skills, we also need entrepreneurial thinking that can create new ways of organizing the cultural industries. We need to replicate the Open TV experiment across a wide range of cultural fields and to rescue art from the commercial enterprise and the scandal of the sponsor. We need to build new platforms of expression and connection that are driven by cultural needs rather than economic ones. We need alternatives to Twitter and Facebook and Google that reflect the political and expressive needs of all people and of the grassroots organizations that are working to build a transformed world.

The matrix of domination is the house that corporations live in. They inherited this house, as they gained their corporate personhood, from the paragons of privilege who built it and them. Social media is a powerful new resource and a tremendous new well of artistic possibility, but a corporate-controlled social media industry run by a cabal of the most privileged people in the world will never dismantle the matrix of domination. Transformative change demands a transformation in both *how* we make the tools we need and *who* gets to make them. To paraphrase Marx: Coders of the world, unite!

APPENDIX: DIGITAL MEDIA LITERACY

The best readers are also writers because they understand the craft.* So to be a great reader, you need to know how to write. But we teach literacy backwards. We focus on reading instead of writing.

When shifting from textual literacy to digital media literacy, the same principle holds. If you want to understand the digital media that pours into your life throughout the day, you need to know how it gets made, and the best way to do that is to make it yourself.

What is exciting about social media is that despite its many flaws, it gives citizens the tools to make media and thus to make the world around them.

So what practices lead to digital media literacy?

The first key practice is play. You have to approach the world with curiosity, and you have to tinker! Push all the buttons, design and redesign your profile, and try creating and posting all different types of content.

The second practice is voice. Everyone has a voice, and every voice is distinctive. Do you know what your voice sounds like? Reread and review all of your tweets, posts, images, memes, and videos, until you start to recognize what you sound like and when you stop sounding like yourself.

The third practice is empathy. Who is your audience? How do they hear and see the message that you are sharing? How might they take away a different meaning than you intended? How can you use your voice to listen to them?

The fourth practice is understanding. This seemingly common word actually refers to an important concept from the German sociologist Max Weber:

* This is the transcript for a video animation that I made. The animation can be found on my website at http://www.dustinkidd.net.

Verstehen. We all have a special insight, or a deep understanding, that we can share with the world.

The fifth practice is art. Making digital media is a creative act. It is a craft that involves that mix of inspiration and perspiration, creativity and productivity, that drives every artistic discipline.

Play, voice, empathy, understanding, and art. The greatest of these is art. Art is the highest form of literacy, because through art we find our voice, our audience, our message, and the words to say it.

GLOSSARY

4chan: An English-language, image-based Internet message board created by Christopher Poole and modeled on the Japanese site 2chan. Poole sold 4chan to Hiroyuki Nishimura, the founder of 2chan. 4chan.org.

8chan: An English-language, image-based Internet message board created by Fredrick Brennan and modeled on 2chan and 4chan. 8chan has fewer content restrictions than 4chan. 8ch.net.

Academia.edu: A social networking site for scholars and students, founded in 2008, that allows users to create networks based on research interests, academic disciplines, and academic subfields, and to share publications, teaching resources, and other scholarly information. Academia.edu is similar to ResearchGate.

agency: A sociological concept that refers to the capacity of social actors to act and make choices, even when the options are not of their choosing.

"All Lives Matter": A rhetorical device that has been used to silence proponents of the social movement Black Lives Matter.

Anonymous: An anonymous network of computer hackers and activists that originated from 4chan.

art: Disciplined, creative work that may be performed by both artistic professionals and outsiders or amateurs.

baiting: Posting content on the Internet and in social media that is solely intended to generate an argument.

Black Lives Matter: A grassroots social movement founded in 2013 by Alicia Garza, Patrisse Cullors, and Opal Tometi in response to the acquittal of George Zimmerman for the murder of Trayvon Martin.

black Twitter: An informal collection of primarily black Twitter users who have developed a cultural discourse around a range of issues that include race, humor, black scholarship, and many other issues. Known for its creative use of hashtags.

blacktags: A slang term for the hashtags used in black Twitter.

Blogger: A platform for publishing blogs, founded in 1999 and acquired by Google in 2003.

cisgender: A term used to connote individuals whose gender identity matches that assigned at birth, that is, individuals who are not transgender.

color-blind racism: Eduardo Bonilla-Silva's conception of a racial ideology that argues against any explicit acknowledgment of race or racial identity and results in inequality because of its incapacity to acknowledge both historical and current racism.

compulsory able-bodiedness: A social structure that creates the privileging of able-bodiedness and the oppression of people with disabilities, associated with the work of disability studies scholar Robert McRuer.

constructive failure: The characterization of Occupy Wall Street by cofounder Micah White, which takes the position that the movement failed but provided many lessons about social revolutions.

controlling images: Sociologist Patricia Hill Collins's conception of stereotypes and other images that are meant to remind individuals of social hierarchies, including racial hierarchies, gender hierarchies, and class hierarchies.

corporate interlocks: Points of connection between corporations that undermine competition and instead promote interconnectedness and a sense of shared interests.

crip theory: A paradigm of social theory that places disability and embodiment at the center of analysis.

cultural object: A material resource that is encoded with meaning or sets of meanings.

cultural practices: A social process that is encoded with meaning or sets of meanings.

cultural studies: An academic paradigm in the humanities and social sciences that emphasizes the analysis of a wide range of cultural objects and practices, often treating them as texts that mandate a level of analysis comparable to that which is traditionally applied to canonical literature.

diagonal integration: The tendency for corporations to expand their holdings into new sectors.

doxxing: An act of hostility online that involves tracking down personal documentation about an individual and publishing that information online. The documentation might include home and e-mail addresses, family members' names, or financial information.

drama: Using social media to heighten and extend an interpersonal conflict.

essentialism: Beliefs that explain human identity as inscribed on our bodies and presumed to be real or unchanging.

Facebook: A social networking service founded in 2004 by students from Harvard University, primarily attributed to Mark Zuckerberg. Facebook is a publicly traded company.

Feminist Frequency: A social media project founded by cultural critic Anita Sarkeesian that critically examines popular culture, especially video games, through a feminist lens.

Foursquare: A social media platform, founded in 2009, that originally allowed users to post check-ins with their locations and activities. In 2014 those original functions were moved to the app Swarm, and Foursquare became a competitor to Yelp by focusing on helping users find services based on geospatial information and allowing users to post and search reviews of those services.

freak: A term used in this book to describe a sociological type whose origins are internal to a society, but who is pushed to the margins of that society by hegemonic forces and who embraces this marginalized identity as a source of empowerment. Intended as a contrast to Simmel's conception of the stranger.

Friendster: A social networking service, founded in 2002, that allowed users to create social networks and share information. Friendster relaunched as an online social gaming service in 2011, but suspended service in 2015.

game jam: A short event of typically one day or one weekend in which game developers work together to generate a new game.

GamerGate: A controversy initiated in 2014 in the video game industry in which some male gamers accused female gamers, female game developers, and feminist cultural critics of undermining the industry.

Google: An Internet technology company founded in 1998, primarily as a web search tool, that now offers a range of platforms for organizing and sharing information.

Google+: A social networking service, launched in 2011, that is part of the wide array of Google platforms and services.

hashtags: An indexing tool in social media used to attach particular posts to broader conversation, indicated by use of the hash symbol (#).

hegemony: A form of domination that is based on culture and politics, as contrasted with domination based on violence and military control.

homophily: The sociological tendency to associate based on similarities, including cultural and racial similarities.

horizontal integration: The tendency for corporations to expand their share of the market within the field.

information flows: The streams of posts, replies, and reposts of specific stories on social media. Information flows are studied to determine what types of users produce the most shared information and what types of sharers have the largest audiences.

inspiration porn: Any celebration of the exceptional success of disabled bodies.

Instagram: An image-sharing social media service, launched in 2010 and acquired by Facebook in 2013.

institutional review board: A panel of experts and community members who provide oversight of research that involves human subjects.

institutional surveillance: The use of social media by organizations and businesses to monitor the activities of their members or employers.

Internet Archive: The name of both a digital library and the organization that maintains it. The Wayback Machine is one of the most used resources of the Internet Archive.

Internet of things: The sprawling network of computers, appliances, and other devices that send and receive information through the Internet, often via wireless connectivity.

interpersonal surveillance: The use of social media by an individual or group to monitor the activity of another individual or group, including stalking.

interpretive sociology: A social science paradigm that focuses on the ordering power of culture (systems of meaning).

intersectionality: A social science paradigm that examines inequality and privilege, with a focus on the connections among systems of hierarchy, particularly race, class, and gender.

legitimizing identity: The identity systems held by dominant groups that ultimately function to justify their power, as contrasted with resistance identity and project identity. From the work of Manuel Castells.

LinkedIn: A professional networking platform, founded in 2002, that allows users to post digital résumés and connect with other professionals.

market surveillance: The use of social media by corporations to monitor the shopping and purchasing patterns of consumers.

medical model of disability: A paradigm for understanding disability that focuses on bodily impairment and the capacity for the medical system to treat such impairment.

meme: A cultural object that is widely circulated, typically on the Internet. Memes can take many forms, but the most common is a square image with two lines of text, one across the top and once across the bottom.

multimodal networking: The combination of online social networks with offline organizing.

MySpace: A social networking service, founded in 2003, that allowed users to share text, music, and video posts. It relaunched as a music-sharing service in 2013.

NEET: An acronym for Not in Education, Employment, or Training. It originated in the United Kingdom, but online it is associated with the Japanese concept of Hikikomori, which describes a withdrawal from society.

network society: Manuel Castells's term for the current economic mode, marked by a shift from industrial capitalism to informational capitalism.

occupation: A social movement strategy of assembling in public space to attract attention, foster discourse, and disrupt usual activity.

Occupy Wall Street: The initial political action of the Occupy movement, called into being by Kalle Lasn and Micah White of the magazine *Adbusters*. The action began on September 17, 2011.

peer review: A process within academic publishing, for both journal articles and books, in which manuscripts are reviewed, critiqued, and either rejected or accepted for publication by a group of experts in the field. Many manuscripts initially receive a status of "revise and resubmit," but eventually the revised manuscript is either rejected or accepted.

people's assembly: A social movement strategy associated with Occupy Wall Street and earlier actions that involves a consensus-based, open discussion among movement participants.

Pinterest: A social media platform, founded in 2010, that allows users to create and curate topical "boards" by "pinning" images and videos together around a central theme and to share those boards with other users.

police surveillance: The use of social media by police or other state agencies to monitor the activities of citizens, typically in search of criminal activity but potentially in service to a political agenda.

political/relational model of disability: A paradigm for understanding disability that focuses on the connections and interactions between the body and various social institutions such as medicine and the state.

primary sources: Texts of all types that are the focus of scholarly analysis. That analysis is often supported with additional discussion of secondary sources.

project identity: A new identity system introduced by social actors who are seeking social transformation, as contrasted with legitimizing identity and resistance identity. From the work of Manuel Castells.

queer theory: A paradigm of social theory that places sexuality and queerness, broadly understood, at the center of analysis.

racial frames: Eduardo Bonilla-Silva's conception of ideological clusters that give rise to specific and widely shared systems for legitimizing racial inequality.

racial ideologies: Systems of belief about race that are used to explain racial difference and racial inequality.

racial structure: Eduardo Bonilla-Silva's conception of the complex system of social relationships and social meanings that generate racial inequalities and affirm white supremacy and privilege.

Reddit: An English-language text and image-based Internet message board created by Steve Huffman and Alexis Ohanian. Reddit.com.

redditors: All Reddit users. As a mash-up of Reddit and editor, the term describes the type of cultural work that Reddit users engage in to share, rate, and aggregate information gathered from social media and news outlets.

research ethics: The acknowledgment of, reflection on, and attempt to minimize the potential negative impact of research on the larger physical and social world and on the subjects of the research. Research ethics are embodied in the practices that scholars employ to minimize harm.

ResearchGate: A social networking site for scholars and students, founded in 2008, that allows users to create networks based on research interests, academic disciplines, and academic subfields, and to share publications, teaching resources, and other scholarly information. ResearchGate is similar to Academia.edu.

resistance identity: A counter-model of identity subscribed to by oppressed or marginalized groups, as contrasted with legitimizing identity and project identity. From the work of Manuel Castells.

rhizomes: Literally, an underground network of stems for certain types of plants, but in social theory a rhizome refers metaphorically to the spread of ideas through intertwining, nonhierarchical human networks. Associated with the philosophical writings of Gilles Deleuze and Felix Guattari.

robots exclusion standard: A protocol on websites that determines whether and how an automated system can search and index the site, published on the site as a robots.txt document.

secondary sources: Texts by scholars that are used by other scholars, often as part of an analysis of primary texts. Secondary sources usually take the form of academic journal articles or scholarly books.

sexting: A portmanteau of "sex" and "texting," it is the use of a short message service (SMS) to engage in a sexual conversation and may also include the exchange of explicit photographs or videos.

SJW: An initialism for social justice warrior, associated with and heavily used in GamerGate. It is meant as a derogatory term for cultural critics and social movement leaders who campaign against inequality.

slash fiction: A form of fan fiction that focuses on same-sex relationships between characters in existing stories. The word "slash" refers to the forward slash between the names of the two characters that constitute the relationship, such as Harry/Draco or Kirk/Spock.

social media: In general parlance, a broad category of Internet and mobile technology platforms that allow users to join broad networks with others and to share content in the form of text, images, video, and links. In this book, social media is also viewed as an artistic method through which art can be both created and shared.

social model of disability: A paradigm for understanding disability that focuses on social order and inequality and treats disability as one of many systems that create hierarchies of human bodies.

sousveillance: Surveillance from below. In social media research, it refers to the use of social media by users and groups to monitor the practices and policies of corporations, especially the corporations that run social media.

stirring the pot: Using social media to resurrect drama after it has started to simmer.

stranger: Georg Simmel's term for a sociological type who enters society from an external origin and decides to remain, providing a contrasting reference point to those whose origins are internal to the society.

symbolic interactionism: A paradigm in social science that examines the ways that groups create meaning through social interactions.

The 99%: A term used by the Occupy movement to refer to the bulk of citizens (in the United States and globally) who do not control the bulk of wealth.

thick description: A social science method, originated by anthropologist Clifford Geertz, that is used to capture and analyze layers of meaning that are hidden in deep structures and routine social practices.

TL;DR: An initialism for "Too Long; Didn't Read," used on message boards and in social media. It is usually followed by a short summary of a longer post or series of posts.

troll: In Internet and social media parlance, someone who posts content that is intended to generate an argument.

Tumblr: A blogging platform, founded in 2007 and acquired by Yahoo in 2013.

Twitter: A microblogging social media platform, founded in 2006, best known for its use of short-form text posts along with videos, images, and links.

vertical integration: The tendency for corporations to expand their share of the production and distribution process.

viral: The term used for content that is unexpectedly widely shared.

virtual ethnography: An application of ethnographic methods to the Internet, social media, and related digital technologies such as e-mail, text messaging, VOIP, and video conferencing. Other terms for this method are netnography, online ethnography, and digital ethnography.

vlogger: A portmanteau of "vlog" and "blogger" (which itself is a variation on the original term "weblog," an online journal). A vlogger is someone who regularly records journal entries in video format, often posted to YouTube or Vimeo.

VOIP: An acronym for Voice Over Internet Protocol, which refers to the method of transmitting voice communications via the Internet.

Wayback Machine: A specific application of the Internet Archive that allows users to view archived copies of websites from across time.

Wizardchan: An English-language, image-based message board created by a former 4chan user whose identity is unknown. It was briefly owned by Fredrick Brennan before he started 8chan. Wizardchan caters to male virgins over age thirty who subscribe to a NEET lifestyle.

WordPress: An open-source blogging and content management system, founded in 2003.

Yahoo: An Internet technology company founded in 1994, primarily as a web search service, that now offers news, e-mail, and other services.

Yelp: A social media platform, founded in 2004, that allows users to find services based on geospatial coordinates, as well as to post and read reviews of those services.

YouTube: A video-sharing service, founded in 2005 and acquired by Google in 2006.

REFERENCES

Aaker, Jennifer, and Andy Smith. 2010. *The Dragonfly Effect: Quick, Effective, and Powerful Ways to Use Social Media to Drive Social Change*. San Francisco, CA: Jossey-Bass.

Alberty, Erin. 2014. "Anita Sarkeesian Explains Why She Canceled USU Lecture." *Salt Lake Tribune*, October 16. Retrieved June 28, 2015, from http://www.sltrib.com/sltrib/news/58528113-78/sarkeesian-threats-threat-usu.html.csp.

Alexander, Leigh. 2014. "'Gamers' Don't Have to Be Your Audience: 'Gamers' Are Over." August 28. Retrieved June 28, 2015, from http://gamasutra.com/view/news/224400/Gamers_dont_have_to_be_your_audience_Gamers_are_over.php.

Allaway, Jennifer. 2014. "#Gamergate Trolls Aren't Ethics Crusaders; They're a Hate Group." Jezebel. Retrieved June 28, 2015, from http://jezebel.com/gamergate-trolls-arent-ethics-crusaders-theyre-a-hate-1644984010.

Allen, Kathleen P. 2014. "Tweeting, Texting, and Facebook Postings: Stirring the Pot with Social Media to Make Drama—Case Study and Participant Observation." *The Qualitative Report* 19 (4): 1–24.

Asakura, Kenta, and Shelley L. Craig. 2014. "'It Gets Better' . . . But How? Exploring Resilience Development in the Accounts of LGBTQ Adults." *Journal of Human Behavior in the Social Environment* 24 (3): 253–266.

Baker, Paul M. A., John C. Bricout, Nathan W. Moon, Barry Coughlan, and Jessica Pater. 2013. "Communities of Participation: A Comparison of Disability and Aging Identified Groups on Facebook and LinkedIn." *Telematic and Informatics* 30: 20–34.

Benjamin, Jeff. 2013. "Janelle Monae Says 'Q.U.E.E.N.' Is for the 'Ostracized & Marginalized'." Fuse. September 18. Retrieved July 11, 2016, from http://www.fuse.tv/videos/2013/09/janelle-monae-queen-interview.

Beydoun, Khaled A., and Priscilla Ocen. 2015. "Baltimore and the Emergence of a Black Spring." Al Jazeera. May 5. Retrieved November 29, 2015, from http://www.aljazeera.com/indepth/opinion/2015/05/baltimore-emergence-black-spring-150504123031263.html.

Biddle, Sam. 2013. "Twitter CEO Takes Fire Over All-Male Board of Directors." ValleyWag. October 7. Retrieved January 15, 2015, from http://valleywag.gawker.com/twitter-ceo-takes-fire-over-all-male-board-of-directors-1441983747.

Bonilla-Silva, Eduardo. 2013. *Racism Without Racists: Color-blind Racism and the Persistence of Racial Inequality in America*. 4th ed. Lanham, MD: Rowman & Littlefield.

Boursiquot, Bernice L., and Matthew W. Brault. 2013. "Disability Characteristics of Income-Based Government Assistance Recipients in the United States: 2011." In *American Community Survey Briefs*. Washington, DC: United States Census Bureau.

Bowe, Greg. 2010. "Reading Romance: The Impact Facebook Rituals Can Have on a Romantic Relationship." *Journal of Comparative Research in Anthropology and Sociology* 1 (2): 61–77.

boyd, danah. 2011a. "Dear Voyeur, Meet Flâneur . . . Sincerely, Social Media." *Surveillance & Society* 8 (4): 505–507.

boyd, danah. 2011b. "White Flight in Networked Publics? How Race and Class Shaped American Teen Engagement with MySpace and Facebook." In *Race After the Internet*, edited by Lisa Nakamura and Peter A. Chow-White, 203–222. New York: Routledge.

boyd, danah. 2014. *It's Complicated: The Social Lives of Networked Teens*. New Haven, CT: Yale University Press.

boyd, danah m., and Nicole B. Ellison. 2008. "Social Network Sites: Definition, History, and Scholarship." *Journal of Computer-Mediated Communication* 13: 210–230.

Brault, Matthew W. 2012. "Americans with Disabilities: 2010." In *Household Economic Studies*. Washington, DC: United States Census Bureau.

Brown, Kristen V. 2016. "How a Racist, Sexist Hate Mob Forced Leslie Jones Off Twitter." Fusion. July 19. Retrieved August 4, 2016, from http://fusion.net/story/327103/leslie-jones-twitter-racism/.

Brown, Laura. 2011. "Britney Spears: One Sexy Mother Interview." *Harper's Bazaar*, January 27. Retrieved September 12, 2015, from http://www.harpersbazaar.com/celebrity/latest/news/a719/britney-spears-pregnant-interview/.

Brown, Robert. 2015. "Letter from President Brown." Boston University Office of the President. May 12. Retrieved August 3, 2016 from http://www.bu.edu/president/letters-writings/letters/2015/5-12/?utm_source=social&utm_medium=facebook&utm_campaign=prbumain.

Browning, Tod. 1932. *Freaks* (film). MGM.

Byron, Paul, Kath Albury, and Clifton Evers. 2013. "'It Would Be Weird to Have That on Facebook': Young People's Use of Social Media and the Risk of Sharing Sexual Health Information." *Reproductive Health Matters* 21 (41): 35–44.

Byrum, Erica Campbell. 2013 (May 23). "Pinterest: Should It Be a Part of Your Marketing Plan?" RISMedia. Retrieved January 29, 2015, from http://rismedia.com/2013/05/23/pinterest-should-it-be-a-part-of-your-marketing-plan/.

Campbell, Colin. 2014. "How 'Game Jam,' an Indie Game Dev Reality Show, Collapsed on Its First Day of Filming." Polygon. March 31. Retrieved June 28, 2015, from http://www.polygon.com/2014/3/31/5568362/game-jam-reality-show-maker-studios.

Campbell, Mikey. 2014. "Secret App to Restrict Photo Uploads, Block Posts with Real Names in Update." AppleInsider. August 22. Retrieved February 2, 2015, from http://appleinsider.com/articles/14/08/22/secret-app-to-restrict-photo-uploads-block-posts-with-real-name-in-update.

Castells, Manuel. 1996. *The Network Society*. Vol. 1 of *The Information Age: Economy, Society, and Culture*. Oxford and Cambridge, MA: Blackwell Publishers.

Castells, Manuel. 1997. *The Power of Identity*. Vol. 2 of *The Information Age: Economy, Society, and Culture*. Oxford and Cambridge, MA: Blackwell Publishers.

Castells, Manuel. 1998. *End of Millennium*. Vol. 3 of *The Information Age: Economy, Society, and Culture*. Oxford and Cambridge, MA: Blackwell Publishers.

Castells, Manuel. 2009. *Communication Power*. Oxford: Oxford University Press.

Castells, Manuel. 2012. *Networks of Outrage and Hope: Social Movements in the Internet Age*. Cambridge, UK: Polity.

Caton, Sue, and Melissa Chapman. 2016. "The Use of Social Media and People with Intellectual Disability: A Systematic Review and Thematic Analysis." *Journal of Intellectual and Developmental Disability* 41 (2): 125–139.

Chaulk, Kasey, and Tim Jones. 2011. "Online Obsessive Relational Intrusion: Further Concerns About Facebook." *Journal of Family Violence* 26: 245–254.

Chayko, Mary. 2014. "Techno-social Life: The Internet, Digital Technology, and Social Connectedness." *Sociology Compass* 8 (7): 976–991.

Christensen, Christian. 2011. "Twitter Revolutions? Addressing Social Media and Dissent." *Communication Review* 14: 155–157.

Christian, Aymar Jean. 2016. "The State of Open TV—Development Report 1." *Televisual*. January 6. Retrieved August 6, 2016, from http://tvisual.org/2016/01/06/the-state-of-open-tv-development-report-1/.

Chu, A. 2014. "It's Dangerous to Go Alone: Why Are Gamers So Angry?" *Daily Beast*, August 28. Retrieved June 28, 2015, from http://www.thedailybeast.com/articles/2014/08/28/it-s-dangerous-to-go-alone-why-are-gamers-so-angry.html.

Cirucci, Angela M. 2013. "First Person Paparazzi: Why Social Media Should Be Studied More Like Video Games." *Telematics and Informatics* 30: 47–59.

Cohen, Jodi S. 2015. "University of Illinois OKs $875,000 Settlement to End Steven Salaita Dispute." *Chicago Tribune*, November 12. Retrieved August 3, 2016, from http://www.chicagotribune.com/news/local/breaking/ct-steven-salaita-settlement-met-20151112-story.html.

Colao, J. J. 2012. "With 60 Million Websites, WordPress Rules the Web. So Where's the Money?" *Forbes*, September 5. Retrieved January 22, 2015, from http://www.forbes.com/sites/jjcolao/2012/09/05/the-internets-mother-tongue/#574639c355fe.

Collins, Patricia Hill. 1990. *Black Feminist Thought: Knowledge, Consciousness, and the Politics of Empowerment*. New York: Routledge.

Daly, S. 2014. "The Fine Young Capitalists' Noble Goals Don't Excuse Them from Scrutiny." Gameranx. September 3. Retrieved June 28, 2015, from http://www.gameranx.com/features/id/23968/article/the-fine-young-capitalists-seemingly-noble-goals-don-t-excuse-them-from-scrutiny.

Davey, Monica, and Alan Blinder. 2014. "Ferguson Protests Take New Edge, Months After Killing." *New York Times*, October 13. Retrieved November 25, 2015, from http://www.nytimes.com/2014/10/14/us/st-louis-protests.html.

Davison, Patrick. 2012. "The Language of Internet Memes." In *The Social Media Reader*, edited by Michael Mandiberg, 120–134. New York: New York University Press.

Day, Elizabeth. 2015. "#BlackLivesMatter: The Birth of a New Civil Rights Movement." *The Guardian*, July 19. Retrieved September 23, 2015, from http://www.theguardian.com/world/2015/jul/19/blacklivesmatter-birth-civil-rights-movement.

Deleuze, Gilles, and Felix Guattari. 1987. *A Thousand Plateaus: Capitalism and Schizophrenia*. Minneapolis: University of Minnesota Press.

Demby, Gene. 2014. "The Birth of a New Civil Rights Movement: 2014 Was an Epochal Year for Social Justice; 2015 Could Be Even More Dramatic." *Politico Magazine*, December 31. Retrieved October 2, 2015, from http://www.politico.com/magazine/story/2014/12/ferguson-new-civil-rights-movement-113906.

Dickerson, Jessica. 2014. "#MyBlackLifeMattersBecause Spreads Powerful Message That Race Shouldn't Affect One's Value." *Huffington Post*, August 15. Retrieved April 1, 2014, from http://www.huffingtonpost.com/2014/08/15/michael-brown-my-black-life-matters-hashtag_n_5682816.html.

Dubs, Jamie. 2009. "Leave Britney Alone." Know Your Meme. Retrieved September 12, 2015, from http://knowyourmeme.com/memes/leave-britney-alone.

Durkheim, Emile. 2008. *The Elementary Forms of Religious Life*. Translated by Carol Cosman. Oxford: Oxford University Press.

Eligon, John. 2014. "Anger, Hurt and Moments of Hope in Ferguson." *New York Times*, August 20. Retrieved November 25, 2015, from http://www

.nytimes.com/2014/08/21/us/in-ferguson-anger-hurt-and-moments-of-hope.html?_r=0.

Ellis, Katie. 2014. "*The Voice* Australia (2012): Disability, Social Media and Collective Intelligence." *Continuum: Journal of Media & Cultural Studies* 28 (4): 482–494.

Facebook. 2013. "Annual Report." Retrieved January 20, 2015, from http://investor.fb.com/annuals.cfm.

Fernback, Jan. 2007a. "Selling Ourselves? Profitable Surveillance and Online Communities." *Critical Discourse Studies* 4 (3): 311–330.

Fernback, Jan. 2007b. "Beyond the Diluted Community Concept: A Symbolic Interactionist Perspective on Online Social Relations." *New Media & Society* 9 (1): 49–69.

Fernback, Jan. 2013. "Sousveillance: Communities of Resistance to the Surveillance Environment." *Telematics and Informatics* 30: 11–21.

Fiegerman, Seth. 2014. "Friendster Founder Tells His Side of the Story, 10 Years After Facebook." Mashable. February 3. Retrieved January 16, 2015, from http://mashable.com/2014/02/03/jonathan-abrams-friendster-facebook/#V5kjwkaGciqt.

Fincher, David. 2010. *The Social Network* (film). Columbia Pictures.

Fine Young Capitalists, The. 2014. "On Apologizing for Getting Punched in the Face." September 3. Retrieved June 28, 2014, from http://thefineyoungcapitalists.tumblr.com/post/96578864050/on-apologizing-for-getting-punched-in-the-face.

Freeland, Chrystia. 2011. "In 2011, the Revolution Was Tweeted." Reuters. December 29. Retrieved September 1, 2015, from http://blogs.reuters.com/chrystia-freeland/2011/12/29/in-2011-the-revolution-was-tweeted/.

Fuchs, Christian. 2011. "Web 2.0, Prosumption, and Surveillance." *Surveillance & Society* 8 (3): 288–309.

Futrelle, David. 2014. "Zoe Quinn's Screenshots of 4chan's Dirty Tricks Were Just the Appetizer: Here's the First Course of the Dinner, Directly from the IRC Log." We Hunted the Mammoth. September 8. Retrieved June 28, 2015, from http://wehuntedthemammoth.com/2014/09/08/zoe-quinns-screenshots-of-4chans-dirty-tricks-were-just-the-appetizer-heres-the-first-course-of-the-dinner-directly-from-the-irc-log/.

Gaines, Donna. 2003. *A Misfit's Manifesto: The Sociological Memoir of a Rock & Roll Heart*. New York: Random House.

Gaming Admiral. 2014. "4Chan Mods Shutting Down #GamerGate Discussions." Attack on Gaming. September 17. Retrieved June 28, 2015, from http://attackongaming.com/gaming-talk/4chan-mods-shutting-down-gamergate-discussions/.

Gamson, Joshua. 1998. *Freaks Talk Back: Tabloid Talk Shows and Sexual Nonconformity*. Chicago: University of Chicago Press.

Gates, Gary J. 2011. "How Many People Are Lesbian, Gay, Bisexual and Transgender?" April. The Williams Institute on Sexual Orientation and Gender Identity Law and Public Policy at UCLA School of Law. Retrieved January 28, 2015, from http://williamsinstitute.law.ucla.edu/research/census-lgbt-demographics-studies/how-many-people-are-lesbian-gay-bisexual-and-transgender/.

Geertz, Clifford. 1973. *The Interpretation of Cultures*. New York: Basic Books.

Gerbaudo, Paolo. 2012. *Tweets and the Streets: Social Media and Contemporary Activism*. New York: Pluto Press.

Gershon, Ilana. 2011. "Un-Friend My Heart: Facebook, Promiscuity, and Heartbreak in a Neoliberal Age." *Anthropological Quarterly* 84 (4): 865–894.

Gilbert, David. 2014. "Hacker, Hoaxer, Whistleblower, Spy: The Many Faces of Anonymous—Review." *International Business Times*, October 31. Retrieved February 1, 2015, from http://www.ibtimes.co.uk/hacker-hoaxer-whistleblower-spy-many-faces-anonymous-review-1472581.

Gjoni, E. 2014. "TL;DR." *The Zoe Post*, August 16. Retrieved June 28, 2015, from https://thezoepost.wordpress.com/2014/08/16/tldr/.

Gladwell, Malcolm. 2010. "Small Change: Why the Revolution Will Not Be Tweeted." *New Yorker* 86 (30): 42–49. Retrieved September 1, 2015, from http://www.newyorker.com/magazine/2010/10/04/small-change-malcolm-gladwell.

Goldstein, Devan. 2016. "Glass-Steagall Act: 1933 Law Stirs Up 2016 Presidential Race." *NerdWallet*, February 8. Retrieved June 1, 2016, from https://www.nerdwallet.com/blog/banking/glass-steagall-act-explained/.

Granovetter, Mark S. 1973. "The Strength of Weak Ties." *American Journal of Sociology* 78 (6): 1360–1380.

Granovetter, Mark S. 1974. *Getting a Job: A Study of Contacts and Careers*. Cambridge, MA: Harvard University Press.

Grayson, Nathan. 2014a. "Admission Quest: Valve Greenlights 50 more games." *Rock, Paper, Shotgun*. January 8. Retrieved June 28, 2015, from http://www.rockpapershotgun.com/2014/01/08/admission-quest-valve-greenlights-50-more-games.

Grayson, Nathan. 2014b. "The Indie Game Reality TV Show That Went to Hell." *Kotaku*, March 31. Retrieved June 28, 2015, from http://tmi.kotaku.com/the-indie-game-reality-tv-show-that-went-to-hell-1555599284.

Griswold, Wendy. 1994. *Cultures and Societies in a Changing World*. Thousand Oaks, CA: Sage.

Gudelunas, David. 2012. "There's an App for That: The Uses and Gratifications of Online Social Networks for Gay Men." *Sexuality & Culture* 16: 347–365.

Guynn, Jessica. 2015. "Meet the Woman Who Coined #BlackLivesMatter." *USA Today*, March 4. Retrieved September 23, 2015, from http://www.usatoday.com/story/tech/2015/03/04/alicia-garza-black-lives-matter/24341593/.

Hargittai, Eszter, and Eden Litt. 2011. "The Tweet Smell of Celebrity Success: Explaining Variation in Twitter Adoption Among a Diverse Group of Young Adults." *New Media & Society* 13 (5): 824–842.

Hasinoff, Amy Adele. 2012. "Sexting as Media Production: Rethinking Social Media and Sexuality." *New Media & Society* 15 (4): 449–465.

Hassanpour, Navid. 2014. "Media Disruption and Revolutionary Unrest: Evidence from Mubarak's Quasi-Experiment." *Political Communication* 31: 1–24.

Hathaway, Jay. 2014. "What Is Gamergate and Why? An Explainer for Non-geeks." Gawker. October 10. Retrieved June 28, 2015, from http://gawker.com/what-is-gamergate-and-why-an-explainer-for-non-geeks-1642909080.

Hern, Alex. 2014. "Feminist games critic cancels talk after terror threat." *The Guardian*, October 15. Retrieved June 28, 2015, from http://www.theguardian.com/technology/2014/oct/15/anita-sarkeesian-feminist-games-critic-cancels-talk.

Hine, Christine. 2000. *Virtual Ethnography*. London: Sage.

Hoffman, John. 2012. "Sharing Our Way Toward Equality: Social Media and Gay Rights." *Nonprofit Quarterly*, May 12. Retrieved September 20, 2015, from https://nonprofitquarterly.org/policysocial-context/20326-sharing-our-way-toward-equality-social-media-and-gay-rights.html.

hooks, bell. 1995. *Art on My Mind: Visual Politics*. New York: New Press.

Horwitz, Josh. 2013. "Semiocast: Pinterest Now Has 70 Million Users and Is Steadily Gaining Momentum Outside the US." TheNextWeb. July 10. Retrieved February 1, 2015, from http://thenextweb.com/socialmedia/2013/07/10/semiocast-pinterest-now-has-70-million-users-and-is-steadily-gaining-momentum-outside-the-us/.

Hounshell, Blake. 2011. "The Revolution Will Be Tweeted: Life in the Vanguard of the New Twitter Proletariat." *Foreign Policy*, June 20. Retrieved September 1, 2015, from http://foreignpolicy.com/2011/06/20/the-revolution-will-be-tweeted/.

Howard, Philip N. 2015. *Pax Technica: How the Internet of Things May Set Us Free or Lock Us Up*. New Haven, CT: Yale University Press.

Isaac, Mike. 2012. "Instagram Beats Twitter in Daily Mobile Users for the First Time, Data Says." AllThingsD. September 27. Retrieved January 23, 2015, from http://allthingsd.com/20120927/instagram-beats-twitter-in-daily-mobile-users-for-the-first-time-data-says/.

Jaschik, Scott. 2015a. "The Professor Who Wasn't Fired." *Inside Higher Ed*, July 1. Retrieved August 3, 2016, from https://www.insidehighered.com/news/2015/07/01/twitter-explodes-false-reports-u-memphis-fired-professor-why.

Jaschik, Scott. 2015b. "Saida Grundy, Moving Forward." *Inside Higher Ed*, August 24. Retrieved August 2, 2016, from https://www.insidehighered.com

/news/2015/08/24/saida-grundy-discusses-controversy-over-her-comments-twitter-her-career-race-and.

Java, Akshay, Xiaodan Song, Tim Finin, and Belle Tseng. 2007. "Why We Twitter: Understanding Microblogging Usage and Communities." In *Proceedings of the 9th WebKDD and 1st SNA-KDD 2007 Workshop on Web Mining and Social Network Analysis*, 56–65. San Jose, CA: ACM.

Johnson, Amber. 2013. "Antoine Dodson and the (Mis)Appropriation of the Homo Coon: An Intersectional Approach to the Performative Possibilities of Social Media." *Critical Studies in Media Communication* 30 (2): 152–170.

Johnston, Casey. 2014. "Chat Logs Show How 4Chan Users Created #GamerGate Controversy." *Ars Technica*, September 9. Retrieved June 28, 2015, from http://arstechnica.com/gaming/2014/09/new-chat-logs-show-how-4chan-users-pushed-gamergate-into-the-national-spotlight/.

Kafer, Alison. 2013. *Feminist Queer Crip*. Bloomington: Indiana University Press.

Kain, Erik. 2014. "#GamerGate Is Not a Hate Group, It's a Consumer Movement." *Forbes*, October 9. Retrieved June 28, 2015, from http://www.forbes.com/sites/erikkain/2014/10/09/gamergate-is-not-a-hate-group-its-a-consumer-movement/.

Kass, Dani. 2014. "U.Va. Students Protest Against Police Brutality." *Richmond Times Dispatch*, September 5. Retrieved April 16, 2016, from http://www.richmond.com/news/state-regional/u-va-students-protest-against-police-brutality/article_9dac2e68-3568-11e4-a0f1-001a4bcf6878.html.

Kidd, Dustin. 2014. *Pop Culture Freaks: Identity, Mass Media, and Society*. Boulder, CO: Westview Press.

Kidd, Dustin, and Jessie Daniels. 2016. "Building Your Audience Through Social Media: An Interview with Dustin Kidd." *Footnotes* [newsletter of the American Sociological Association] 44 (4): 15.

Kidd, Dustin, and Keith McIntosh. 2016. "Social Media and Social Movements." *Sociology Compass* 10 (9): 785–794.

Kidd, Dustin, and Amanda Turner. 2016. "The GamerGate Files: Misogyny and the Media." In *Defining Identity and the Changing Scope of Culture in the Digital Age*, edited by Alison Novak and Imaani Jamillah El-Burki, 117–139. Hershey, PA: IGI Global.

Knapp, Alex. 2012. "How George Takei Conquered Facebook." *Forbes*, March 23. Retrieved May 23, 2016, from http://www.forbes.com/sites/alexknapp/2012/03/23/how-george-takei-conquered-facebook/#5bf651ca10fc.

Kotzer, Zack. 2014. "Female Game Designers Are Being Threatened with Rape." *Vice*, January 23. Retrieved June 28, 2015, from http://www.vice.com/en_ca/read/female-game-designers-are-being-threatened-with-rape.

Kozinets, Robert V. 2010. *Netnography: Doing Ethnographic Research Online*. Los Angeles: Sage.

Lady Gaga. 2009. "Manifesto of Little Monsters" (liner notes). *The Fame Monster*. Streamline.

Lalinde, Jamie, Rebecca Sacks, Mark Guiducci, Elizabeth Nicholas, and Max Chafkin. 2012. "Revolution Number 99." *Vanity Fair*, January 10. Retrieved June 1, 2016, from http://www.vanityfair.com/news/2012/02/occupy-wall-street-201202.

Lauer, Matt. 2006. "A Defiant Britney Spears Takes on the Tabloids." *NBC News*, June 20. Retrieved September 12, 2015, from http://www.nbcnews.com/id/13347509/ns/dateline_nbc/t/defiant-britney-spears-takes-tabloids/#.V6N0TGX5wyc.

Lawler, Ryan. 2014. "That Secret App Is Becoming Silicon Valley's New Blind Item." TechCrunch. February 6. Retrieved February 3, 2015, from https://techcrunch.com/2014/02/06/that-secret-app-is-becoming-silicon-valleys-new-blind-item/.

Lee, Dave. 2014. "Zoe Quinn: GamerGate Must Be Condemned." BBC News. October 29. Retrieved June 28, 2015, from http://www.bbc.com/news/technology-29821050.

Liebelson, Dana. 2016. "Tow Truck Driver Leaves Woman with Disabilities on Side of Highway Because She Supports Bernie Sanders." *Huffington Post*, May 4. Retrieved May 12, 2016, from http://www.huffingtonpost.com/entry/tow-truck-driver-refuses-to-help-bernie-supporter_us_572a75b4e4b096e9f090403f.

Lindsay, Andrew. 2014. "Black Lives, Shadow Lives: A Response to 'All Lives Matter'." *The Amherst Student*, October 22. Retrieved April 16, 2016, from http://amherststudent.amherst.edu/?q=article/2014/10/22/black-lives-shadow-lives-response-all-lives-matter.

Lorde, Audre. 1984. "The Master's Tools Will Never Dismantle the Master's House." In *Sister Outsider*, 110–113. Berkeley, CA: Crossing Press.

Lotan, Gilad, Erhardt Graeff, Mike Ananny, Devin Gaffney, Ian Pearce, and danah boyd. 2011. "The Revolutions Were Tweeted: Information Flows During the 2011 Tunisian and Egyptian Revolutions." *International Journal of Communications* 5: 1375–1405.

Manjoo, Farhad. 2010. "How Black People Use Twitter: The Latest Research on Race and Microblogging." Salon. September 3. Retrieved October 5, 2015, from http://www.salon.com/2013/09/03/black_twitters_not_just_a_group_its_a_movement/.

Marcelo, Philip. 2014. "U.S. Cities Brace for Protests Off Ferguson Decision." Associated Press. November 15. Retrieved November 25, 2015, from http://thegrio.com/2014/11/15/cities-brace-ferguson-decision/.

McGee, Matt. 2013. "Google+ Hits 300 Million Active Monthly 'In-Stream' Users, 540 Million Across Google." MarketingLand. October 29. Retrieved

January 20, 2015, from http://marketingland.com/google-hits-300-million-active-monthly-in-stream-users-540-million-across-google-63354.

McNally, Victoria. 2014. "A Disheartening Account of the Harassment Going on in Gaming Right Now (and How Adam Baldwin Is Involved)." The Mary Sue. August 28. Retrieved June 28, 2015, from http://www.themarysue.com/video-game-harassment-zoe-quinn-anita-sarkeesian/.

McRuer, Robert. 2006. *Crip Theory: Cultural Signs of Queerness and Disability*. New York: New York University Press.

Miller, Claire Cain. 2013. "Larry Page Says Vocal Cord Paralysis Causes His Voice Problems." *Bits* (blog), *New York Times*, May 14. Retrieved January 15, 2015, from http://bits.blogs.nytimes.com/2013/05/14/larry-page-says-vocal-cord-paralysis-causes-his-voice-problems/?_r=1.

Milner, Murray. 2006. *Freaks, Geeks, and Cool Kids: American Teenagers, Schools, and the Culture of Consumption*. New York: Routledge.

Moodie, Clemmie. 2008. "Britney Condemned for Driving with Baby on Lap." *Daily Mail*, February 8. Retrieved September 12, 2015, from http://www.dailymail.co.uk/tvshowbiz/article-376502/Britney-condemned-driving-baby-lap.html.

Morley, Julie. 2014. "Autobótika's Lola Barreto Discusses The Fine Young Capitalists." Cliqist. August 26. Retrieved June 28, 2015, from http://cliqist.com/2014/08/26/autobotikas-lola-barreto-discusses-the-fine-young-capitalists/.

Morozov, Evgeny. 2011. *The Net Delusion: The Dark Side of Internet Freedom*. New York: Public Affairs.

Murthy, Dhiraj. 2013. *Twitter: Social Communication in the Twitter Age*. Cambridge, UK: Polity.

Mused. 2014. "#BlackLivesMatter Ride for Justice Proves Young Blacks Can Mobilize." *Mused Magazine Online*, September 16. Retrieved April 2, 2016, from http://www.musedmagonline.com/2014/09/blacklivesmatter-ride-justice-proves-young-blacks-can-mobilize/.

Neas, Katy. 2014. "Social Security Disability Fraud Is Rare." *The Hill: Congress Blog*, January 16. Retrieved May 24, 2016, from http://thehill.com/blogs/congress-blog/economy-budget/195559-social-secuity-disability-fraud-is-rare.

Nelson, Ted. 1987 [1974]. *Computer Lib/Dream Machines*. Digital edition. Self-published.

Nordeen, Bradford. 2014. "Private Dancers: Social Media Platforms and Contemporary New York Drag Performance." *Afterimage* 41 (4): 12–15.

Norden, Martin F. 1994. *The Cinema of Isolation: A History of Physical Disability in the Movies*. New Brunswick, NJ: Rutgers University Press.

Ogilvy Public Relations Worldwide and The Center for Social Impact Communication at Georgetown University. 2011. *Dynamics of Cause Engagement*.

Washington, DC: Georgetown University Center for Social Impact Communication.

Pearl, Mike. 2014. "This Guy's Embarrassing Relationship Drama Is Killing the 'Gamer' Identity." *Vice*, August 29. Retrieved June 28, 2015, from http://www.vice.com/read/this-guys-embarrassing-relationship-drama-is-killing-the-gamer-identity-828.

Plunkett, Luke. 2014. "We Might Be Witnessing the 'Death of an Identity'." *Kotaku*, August 28. Retrieved June 28, 2015, from http://kotaku.com/we-might-be-witnessing-the-death-of-an-identity-1628203079?utm_.

Poo, Ai-Jen, and Alicia Garza. 2014. "On Women's Equality Day, ALL Lives Matter." *Ms.*, August 26. Retrieved April 15, 2016, from http://msmagazine.com/blog/2014/08/26/on-womens-equality-day-all-lives-matter/.

Quah, Nicholas. 2015. "Here's a Timeline of Unarmed Black People Killed by Police Over Past Year." BuzzFeed. May 1. Retrieved April 2, 2016, from https://www.buzzfeed.com/nicholasquah/heres-a-timeline-of-unarmed-black-men-killed-by-police-over?utm_term=.dfMkQo4l5#.qp3OLEAnK.

Quinn, Zoë. 2014. "Unreality: My Takeaways After Being on and Subsequently Walking off a Reality Show About Game Jams." *Dispatches from the Quinnspiracy*, March 31. Retrieved June 28, 2015, from http://ohdeargodbees.tumblr.com/post/81317416962/unreality-my-takeaways-after-being-on-and.

Ralph Retort, The. 2014. "The Ralph's Exit Interview with Internet Aristocrat." November 29. Retrieved June 28, 2015, from http://theralphretort.com/theralph-s-interview-with-internet-aristocrat/.

Richardson, Bradford. 2016. "Milo Yiannopoulos Banned from Twitter." *Washington Times*, July 20. Retrieved August 4, 2016, from http://www.washingtontimes.com/news/2016/jul/20/milo-yiannopoulos-banned-twitter/.

Rogers, Kaleigh. 2014. "The FBI Is Investigating #GamerGate." Motherboard. December 18. Retrieved June 28, 2015, from http://motherboard.vice.com/read/the-fbi-is-investigating-gamergate.

Romano, Aja. 2014. "The Sexist Crusade to Destroy Game Developer Zoe Quinn." *Daily Dot*, August 20. Retrieved June 28, 2015, from http://www.dailydot.com/geek/zoe-quinn-depression-quest-gaming-sex-scandal/.

Roose, Kevin. 2015. "The Next Time Someone Says 'All Lives Matter,' Show Them These 5 Paragraphs." Fusion. July 21. Retrieved April 18, 2016, from http://fusion.net/story/170591/the-next-time-someone-says-all-lives-matter-show-them-these-5-paragraphs/.

Ross, Michael W., Rigmor C. Berg, Axel J. Schmidt, Harm J. Hospers, Michele Breveglieri, Martina Furegato, and Peter Weatherburn. 2013. "Internalised Homonegativity Predicts HIV-Associated Risk Behavior in European Men Who Have Sex with Men in a 38 Country Cross-sectional Study: Some Public Health Implications of Homophobia." *BMJ Open* 3: 1–13.

Russell, Stephen T. 2005. "Beyond Risk: Resilience in the Lives of Sexual Minority Youth." *Journal of Gay & Lesbian Issues in Education* 2 (3): 5–18.

Schreier, Jason. 2014. "The Anita Sarkeesian Hater That Everyone Hates." *Kotaku*, November 13. Retrieved June 28, 2015, from http://kotaku.com/the-anita-sarkeesian-hater-that-everyone-hates-1658494441.

Schudson, Michael. 1989. "How Culture Works: Perspectives from Media Studies on the Efficacy of Symbols." *Theory and Society* 18 (2): 153–180.

Scimeca, Dennis. 2014. "Indie Developer Mocks GamerGate, Chased from Home with Rape and Death Threats." *Daily Dot*, October 13. Retrieved June 28, 2015, from http://www.dailydot.com/geek/brianna-we-gamergate-threats/.

Scott-Heron, Gil. 1970. "The Revolution Will Not Be Televised." Track 1 on *Small Talk at 125th and Lennox*. Flying Dutchman/RCA.

Seraphita, Nicole. 2014. "Truth in Gaming: An Interview with The Fine Young Capitalists." APG Nation. September 9. Retrieved June 28, 2015, from http://apgnation.com/articles/2014/09/09/6977/truth-gaming-interview-fine-young-capitalists.

Sheets, Connor Adams. 2012. "What Does TLDR Mean? AMA? TIL? Glossary of Reddit Terms and Abbreviations." *International Business Times*, March 29. Retrieved June 28, 2015, from http://www.ibtimes.com/what-does-tldr-mean-ama-til-glossary-reddit-terms-abbreviations-431704.

Shifman, Limor. 2011. "An Anatomy of a YouTube Meme." *New Media & Society* 14 (2): 187–203.

Shirky, Clay. 2008. *Here Comes Everybody: The Power of Organizing Without Organizations*. New York: Penguin Books.

Shu, Catherine. 2013. "YouTube Confirms Renewed VEVO Deal, Takes Stake in Company." TechCrunch. July 2. Retrieved January 25, 2015, from https://techcrunch.com/2013/07/02/youtube-renewed-vevo-deal/.

Simmel, Georg. 2010. "The Stranger." In *Sociological Theory in the Classical Era: Texts and Readings, Edition 2*, edited by Laura Desfor Edles and Scott Appelrouth, 302–305. Los Angeles: Pine Forge Press.

Simon, Harvey. 2015. "Black Lives Matter Too." *Huffington Post*, October 19. Retrieved April 18, 2016, from http://www.huffingtonpost.com/harvey-simon/black-lives-matter-too_b_8316882.html.

Singer, Michelle. 2007. "Timeline: Britney's Meltdown." *CBS News*, February 20. Retrieved September 7, 2015, from http://www.cbsnews.com/news/timeline-britneys-meltdown/.

Singh, Anneliese A. 2013. "Transgender Youth of Color and Resilience: Negotiating Oppression and Finding Support." *Sex Roles* 68: 690–702.

Smith, Aaron. 2010. "Technology Trends Among People of Color." Pew Internet and American Life Project. Pew Research Center. Retrieved October 5, 2015, from http://www.pewinternet.org/2010/09/17/technology-trends-among-people-of-color/.

Smith, Aaron. 2011. "13% of Online Adults Use Twitter, and Half of Twitter Users Access the Service on a Cell Phone." Pew Internet and American Life Project. Pew Research Center. Retrieved October 5, 2015, from http://www.pewinternet.org/files/old-media/Files/Reports/2011/Twitter%20Update%202011.pdf.

Smith, Christian. 2009. *Moral, Believing Animals: Human Personhood and Culture.* Oxford: Oxford University Press.

Stokel-Walker, Chris. 2011. *The Revolution Will Be Tweeted? How Social Media Inspired—and Failed—the Middle Eastern Revolutionaries of 2011.* Raleigh, NC: Lulu Press.

Stuart, Keith. 2014. "Zoe Quinn: All Gamergate Has Done Is Ruin People's Lives." *The Guardian*, December 3. Retrieved June 28, 2015, from http://www.theguardian.com/technology/2014/dec/03/zoe-quinn-gamergate-interview.

Sullivan, Andrew. 2009. "The Revolution Will Be Twittered." *Daily Dish* (blog), *Atlantic*, June 13. Retrieved September 1, 2015, from http://www.theatlantic.com/daily-dish/archive/2009/06/the-revolution-will-be-twittered/200478/.

Terkel, Amanda. 2014. "Tennessee GOP Lawmaker Behind 'Don't Say Gay' Bill Loses Primary Election." *Huffington Post*, August 8. Retrieved May 19, 2016, from http://www.huffingtonpost.com/2014/08/08/stacey-campfield-primary-loss_n_5661813.html.

TMZ Staff. 2007. "Brit Boo-hoos After VMA Bomb." TMZ, September 10. Retrieved September 12, 2015, from http://www.tmz.com/2007/09/10/brit-boo-hoos-after-vma-bomb/.

Totilo, Stephen. 2014. "From the EIC." *Kotaku*, August 20. Retrieved June 28, 2015, from http://kotaku.com/in-recent-days-ive-been-asked-several-times-about-a-pos-1624707346.

Trottier, Daniel. 2012. *Social Media as Surveillance: Rethinking Visibility in a Converging World.* Farnham, UK: Ashgate.

Tuncalp, Deniz, and Patrick L. Le. 2014. "(Re)Locating Boundaries: A Systematic Review of Online Ethnography." *Journal of Organizational Ethnography* 3 (1): 59–79.

Turkle, Sherry. 2011. *Alone Together: Why We Expect More from Technology and Less from Each Other.* New York: Basic Books.

Underberg, Natalie M., and Elayne Zorn. 2013. *Digital Ethnography: Anthropology, Narrative, and New Media.* Austin: University of Texas Press.

Usher, William. 2014. "TFYC Discuss #GamerGate, Recovering from Hacks, 4chan Support." Cinema Blend. September 10. Retrieved June 28, 2015, from http://www.cinemablend.com/games/TFYC-Discuss-GamerGate-Recovering-From-Hacks-4chan-Support-67239.html.

Veinot, Tiffany Christine, Chrysta Cathleen Meadowbrooke, Jimena Loveluck, Andrew Hickok, and Jose Artruro Bauermeister. 2013. "How 'Community' Matters for How People Interact with Information: Mixed Methods Study of Young Men Who Have Sex with Other Men." *Journal of Medical Internet Research* 15 (2): 1–21.

Wade, Cheryl Marie. 1994. "Disability Culture Rap." In *The Ragged Edge: The Disability Experience from the Pages of the First Fifteen Years of the Disability Rag*, edited by Barrett Shaw, 15–18. Louisville, KY: The Avocado Press.

Washington, Jesse. 2011. "New Digital Divide Seen for Blacks, Hispanics: Using a Cellular Phone to Gain Access to Web Cuts Down on Options." *Washington Times*, January 9. Retrieved October 5, 2015, from http://www.washingtontimes.com/news/2011/jan/9/new-digital-divide-seen-for-blacks-hispanics/?page=all.

Weber, Max. 1978. *Economy and Society: An Outline of Interpretive Sociology*. Vols. 1 and 2. Edited by Gunther Roth and Claus Wittich. Berkeley: University of California Press.

Week, The. 2011. "Occupy Wall Street: A Protest Timeline." November 21. Retrieved May 31, 2016, from http://theweek.com/articles/481160/occupy-wall-street-protest-timeline.

Werner, Maggie. 2014. "Reaping the Bloody Harvest: 'Don't Ask, Don't Tell' and the US Imperial Project." *Feminist Formations* 26 (1): 93–114.

White, Micah. 2016. *The End of Protest: A New Playbook for Revolution*. Toronto: Knopf.

Wikipedia. 2015a. "Jewish Internet Defense Force." Retrieved June 28, 2015, from http://en.wikipedia.org/wiki/Jewish_Internet_Defense_Force.

Wikipedia. 2015b. "The Fine Young Capitalists." Retrieved June 28, 2015, from http://en.wikipedia.org/wiki/The_Fine_Young_Capitalists.

Wilchins, Riki. 2014. *Queer Theory, Gender Theory: An Instant Primer*. 2nd ed. New York City: Magnus Books.

Wilson, Devin. 2014. "A Guide to Ending 'Gamers'." Gamasutra. August 28. Retrieved June 28, 2015, from http://gamasutra.com/blogs/DevinWilson/20140828/224450/A_Guide_to_Ending_quotGamersquot.php.

Wolfers, Justin. 2015. "How Economists Came to Dominate the Conversation." *The Upshot* (blog), *New York Times*, January 23. Retrieved June 30, 2015, from http://www.nytimes.com/2015/01/24/upshot/how-economists-came-to-dominate-the-conversation.html?abt=0002&abg=0.

Wolff, Janet. 1984. *The Social Production of Art*. New York: New York University Press.

Wu, Brianna. 2015. "I'm Brianna Wu, and I'm Risking My Life Standing Up to Gamergate." Bustle. February 11. Retrieved June 28, 2015, from http://www.bustle.com/articles/63466-im-brianna-wu-and-im-risking-my-life-standing-up-to-gamergate.

Xu, Sitina. 2014. "Administration Addresses 'All Lives Matter'." *Amherst Student*, October 29. Retrieved April 16, 2016, from http://amherststudent.amherst.edu/?q=article/2014/10/29/administration-addresses-all-lives-matter.

Yiannopoulos, Milo. 2014. "Feminist Bullies Tearing the Video Game Industry Apart." Breitbart. September 1. Retrieved June 28, 2015, from http://www.breitbart.com/london/2014/09/01/lying-greedy-promiscuous-feminist-bullies-are-tearing-the-video-game-industry-apart/.

Yiannopoulos, Milo. 2016. "Teenage Boys with Tits: Here's My Problem with Ghostbusters." Breitbart. July 18. Retrieved August 4, 2016, from http://www.breitbart.com/tech/2016/07/18/milo-reviews-ghostbusters/.

Young, Sean D. 2013. "Social Media Technologies for HIV Prevention Study Retention Among Minority Men Who Have Sex with Men (MSM)." *AIDS & Behavior* 18: 1625–1629.

INDEX

Aaker, Jennifer, 22, 23
Abrams, Jonathan, 49
abstract liberalism, 188–189
Academia.edu, 205–206
  audience of, 213–214, 216
  description, 67–68
  leadership, 34, 45
  tagging, 201
acampanadas movement, 19, 157, 158
activism
  in Arab Spring, 24, 157
  audience of peers for social activists, 213–215
  disability, 110–112, 114, 117
  high-risk, 22, 23
  relationship between technology and, 23
  See also social change, tools for
activism tactics
  hashtags, 160–162
  leaderlessness, 160
  memes, 162–164
  occupation, 158
  people's assemblies, 158–160
Adam4Adam, 84
Adbusters, 147, 150–153, 157, 160
advertisements, 60, 224
After Life Empire (game), 130
agency, 14, 15, 18, 78, 86
Ahmadinejad, Mahmoud, 18
Alexander, Leigh, 141
alienation, 10–11
Al Jazeera, 190
Allaway, Jennifer, 142
Allegiance (play), 98
Allen, Kathleen, 12
"all lives matter," 172, 182–190
Alone Together (Turkle), 16
Amazon, 14, 63, 68
American Community Survey, 107–109
Americans Disabled for Accessible Public Transit (ADAPT), 110, 116
Americans with Disabilities Act (ADA), 110
Anderson, Fred, 42
Anderson, Tanisha, 172
Anderson, Tom, 49
Andreessen, Marc, 36
anonymity, 52, 141, 151, 155–157, 220
Anonymous
  anonymity, 141
  4chan and, 65, 129
  Occupy Wall Street, 150–151, 153
  police surveillance of, 13
Arab Spring, 19–20, 23–24, 157, 190–191
Archive.is, 47
Archive-It tool, 47
archive.org, 51
archives, 46–47, 200
Arment, Marco, 56
Ars Technica, 138
art
  function in the network society, 10
  humorous, 119
  inequality and, 227–228
  meaning of, 5–6
  nonart distinction, 4–5

art *(continued)*
queer social media, 73–74
social media, 4–6
Art on My Mind (hooks), 228
Asakura, Kenta, 88–90
Atlantic, 18
audience, 210–218
general, 215–214
identification of yours, 197–198
journalists and influencers, 216–217
peers, 213–215
policy makers, 217–218
tagging strategy for connecting with, 200–202
authoritarian regimes, 22–23
Autobótika, 126–127, 130
avoidance, in new racism, 189

Bader-Wechsler, Chrys, 67
baiting, 13
Baldwin, Adam, 121, 136–137, 143
Banking Act of 1933, 149
Barreto, Lola, 126
Battle, George, 44
Bernardi, Daniel, 57
Beyoncé, 161
Black Girls Code, 228
Black Lives Matter, 169–191
origin story, 170–173
overview of movement, 173–177
project identity, 95, 191
relationship with social media, 179–182
blackouts, 23
Black Spring, 190–191
blacktags, 180
black Twitter, 180–181
blindness, 118
Blogger, 2, 34, 40, 54–58, 204
blogging, 54–57, 204–205
blogs, 199–200, 204–205, 205 (table)
Blogspot, 55
Bonilla-Silva, Eduardo, 187–190
Boon Hill (game), 124
Bowe, Greg, 81, 82
boyd, danah, 14, 52, 75, 155, 168
Boys in Tech, 74
Breitbart, 137, 143, 221
Bridges, Tristan, 196
Brin, Sergey, 39
Brisbon, Rumain, 172
Brown, Michael, 171–172, 176–177
Browning, Tod, 7
B2/cafelog, 55
bullying, 12, 66, 75, 95
Butler, Judith, 76
Byttow, David, 67

Cached View, 47
Campfield, Stacey, 99
Candy Crush, 136
capitalism, 8–10, 28
Caption Meme, 119
Castells, Manuel, 8–10, 19–20, 24, 29, 95, 143
Chatterbox, 26
Chaulk, Kasey, 82
Chernin, Peter, 38
choreography of collective action, 24
Christensen, Christian, 23
Christian, Aymar Jean, 224–225
Chronicle tool, 210–211
Cirucci, Angel, 15
cisgender, 29, 33, 35–37, 39, 41–45, 220
civic engagement. *See* social change, tools for
civil rights movement, 22, 180
Clark, Jamar, 170
Clash of Clans (app), 34
class consciousness, 33
Classmates.com, 49
Clinton, Hillary, 165
Cohen, Philip, 196–197
Colbert, Stephen, 137
collaboration, 214
collective action, 21, 24, 165
Collins, Patricia Hill, 110, 173
Colon Cancer Alliance, 128–129
color-blind racism, 187–190
Common Sense (Paine), 11

Communication Power (Castells), 19
community, 14, 16–17
Compton, D'Lane, 215
compulsory able-bodiedness, 112–116
Computer Lib (Nelson), 10–11
computers, liberatory potential of, 11–12
Conley, Dalton, 195
constructive failure, 165
content management systems, 55
controlling images, 227
corporate interlocks, 32, 33, 39–40
corporations
  control by, 223–227, 229
  diagonal integration, 33
  domination of individuals by, 194
  horizontal integration, 32
  owners of social media, 32, 34–45
  vertical integration, 32
Costolo, Dick, 37–38
Craig, Shelly L., 88–90
Crawford, John, III, 172
Crawley, Dennis, 44
creativity, 5–6
crip sociology, 117–119
crip theory, 110–117
crip time, 117
Crocker, Chris, 72–73, 79, 95
Cullors, Patrisse, 171, 174
cultural diamond, 201
cultural objects, 79, 119, 206
cultural practices, 26, 79
cultural studies, 79
curation, 63–64
curative imaginary, 117
curriculum vitae, Academia.edu as online, 67, 206, 214
Currie, Peter, 38
cyber-utopians, 22
cynicism, avoiding, 178–179
Cyrus, Miley, 74, 164

Daily Dot, 131
Daly, Stephen, 127
dangers of social media, 220–223
database of resources, creating, 200
dating, online, 49
Davison, Patrick, 119
Deleuze, Gilles, 161–162
democratic nature of social media, 31–32
Depression Quest (game), 122–124, 130–131, 134, 136, 142
derogatory language, reclaiming, 7
Derrida, Jacques, 76
DeWolfe, Chris, 49
diagonal integration, 32, 33
diaries, online, 54–55
Digital Millennium Copyright Act (DMCA), 134
Dingman, Hayden, 124
disability, 97–120
  activism, 110–112, 114, 117
  crip sociology, 117–119
  crip theory, 110–117
  cultural perspective, 109–110
  defined, 107–109, 112
  drawing, 102–103
  embrace of "crip" label, 111–112
  fraud, 102–105, 114, 116, 119–120
  inspiration porn, 114–115
  intellectual, 117–118
  medical model of disability, 115
  political/relational model of disability, 115
  politics, 107, 109–111
  reclaiming derogatory language by communities, 7
  social model of disability, 115
  wheelchair image as signifier of, 101
disability/miracle meme, 97–106, 109, 113–117, 119–120, 143
disability studies, 110–111
discussion board, online, 123
diversity, 45–46, 46 (table)
Dodson, Antoine, 85–86
Doerr, L. John, 39–40
dominant groups, identity systems of, 9
Donaker, Geoff, 43

Don't Ask, Don't Tell, 91
Don't Hide, Flaunt It (blog), 217
Don't Say Gay law, 98–99
Dorsey, Jack, 37–38, 52
doxxing, 126, 128, 221
The Dragonfly Effect (Aaker and Smith), 22
drag queens, 86–87
drama, 12–13
Dream Machines (Nelson), 10–11
Droege, Drew, 95
Dude, That's So Takei! (video), 99
Durkheim, Emile, 166

Eakins, Thomas, 26
8chan, 138–139, 143
Ellis, Katie, 118
Ellison, Nicole, 52
Ello, 2
embedded codes, videos shared via, 60–61
empowerment, myth of, 14
essentialism, 102
ethics, research, 155–157
ethnography
  collecting and sharing sources through social media, 132–133
  defined, 25
  netnography, 25
  principles of, 178–179
  virtual, 25–27, 132–133, 156, 178–179, 206

Facebook
  archives, 47, 51
  assets of large companies, 28
  audience of, 216
  author's use of, 1–2, 210, 213
  blackouts, 23
  corporate interlocks, 36
  creating a page for your project on, 206–207
  design changes, 50
  disability and aging groups, participation of, 117
  drag queens, use by, 86–87
  gay individuals, use by, 84, 94
  George Takei on, 98–101
  geosocial networking, 63
  GLAAD Media Award, 93
  groups, 207, 213, 215
  Instagram ownership, 36, 59
  launch, 50
  leadership, 34, 35–37
  online personality, 195–196
  photographs, 58
  professional account, 206
  properties owned by, 36–37
  racial difference in usage, 182
  repeal of Don't Ask, Don't Tell, analysis of, 91
  romantic relationships, as force in, 81–83
  Secret as partner app to, 66
  The Social Network (film), 50, 220
  sousveillance communities, 13
  tags, 200
  tool for political upheaval, 19
  trans youth, use by, 87
  user time spent on, 51
  worth of assets, 37
The Fame Monster (Lady Gaga), 73–74
Family Inequality (blog), 196–197
fan fiction, 77–78
fantasy-theme analysis (FTA), 91
Farmville, 136
Federline, Kevin, 70
Feminist Frequency, 137
Feminist Queer Crip (Kafer), 115
feminists/feminism
  gaming and, 122, 126, 135, 137, 140–144
  Girl with Pen (blog), 196
  reclaiming derogatory language, 7
femslash, 77
Fenton, Peter, 38, 42
Ferguson, Missouri, 171–172, 175, 177, 182–183, 207–208
Fernback, Jan, 13–14, 16–17
Fiasco, Lupe, 145

Fichenscher, Horst, 45
Filming Difference (Bernardi), 56–57
The Fine Young Capitalists (TFYC), 126–139
flaneurs, 14
flattened organizational hierarchies, 20
flattened social movements, 10
Flickr, 34, 42, 57, 58, 132, 209
Ford, Ezell, 172
Foreign Policy (magazine), 28
Foucault, Michel, 76
4chan, 8, 67, 143
  Anonymous and, 65, 129
  description, 64–65, 129–130
  doxxing, 126
  The Fine Young Capitalists (TFYC) and, 128–130
  GamerGate and, 138–139
Foursquare, 34, 44, 61–63
freak, 3, 6–8, 29, 75
Freaks (film), 7
Freaks Talk Back (Gamson), 7
Friends Reunited, 49
Friendster, 48–49, 51
Futrelle, David, 138

Gadde, Vijaya, 37
Gamasutra, 141
game jam, 48–49, 51, 124–126
GAME_JAM, 124–126, 131, 134, 136
Gameranx, 127
GamerGate, 121–125, 134–144, 173, 221
gamer identity, 141, 142
gaming, online, 51, 121–144
gaming journalism, 123, 133–135, 137, 141
Gamson, Joshua, 7–8, 215
Garner, Eric, 172
Garza, Alicia, 170–171, 173–174, 182–184, 191
Gawker, 125
Gay and Lesbian Alliance Against Defamation (GLAAD), 92–93
gay people
  hookup sites, 84–85
  social media use, 84–86
  urban center association, 72
Geertz, Clifford, 105
gender
  identification, 127–128
  issues in gaming, 121–144
general public license model, 56
geosocial networking, 61–63
Gerbaudo, Pablo, 24
Gershon, Ilana, 82–83
GetGlue, 63
Ghaziani, Amin, 214–215
Ghostbusters (film), 221
Gibbs, Robert, 42
Girl with Pen (blog), 196
Gjoni, Eron, 130–134, 142
Gladwell, Malcolm, 22–23
Glass, Noah, 53
Glass-Steagall, 149–150
Glueck, Jeff, 44
Gmail, 52
goals, general statement of, 194
Goodreads, 63
Google
  assets of large companies, 28
  Blogger ownership, 40, 55, 56, 204
  corporate interlocks, 39
  leadership, 38–40
  multiple accounts, 52
  Picasa ownership, 40, 57
  social media assets, 34
  universal log-in system, 52
  Vevo ownership, 40
  worth of assets, 40
  YouTube ownership, 32, 34, 40, 59
Google+, 34, 40, 51–52, 54, 59, 215
Google Drive, 200, 214
Google Photos, 59, 132
GPS function of smartphones, 61–62
Graeber, David, 149, 159
Graham, Donald E., 36
Gramm-Leach-Bliley Act, 150
Granovetter, Mark, 23
Gray, Freddie, 173

Grayson, Nathan, 123–126, 131, 134–136
Greenlight, 122–123, 130
Grindr, 84
Griswold, Wendy, 201
Grundy, Saida, 222
Guattari, Felix, 161–162
Gurley, Akai, 172
Guy Fawkes mask, 150–151

hacktivists, 64–65, 129
Hall, Todrick, 75, 95
Hamilton, Dontre, 172
Handler, Chelsea, 2
harassment, 66, 84, 95
Harper's Bazaar (magazine), 70
Harris, Eric, 173
Harry Potter fan fiction, 77–78
hashtags
  as activism tactic, 160–162
  All Lives Matter, 182
  audience-centered approach to use, 201
  Black Lives Matter, 170–171, 177
  blacktags, 180
  conventions, 160
  GamerGate, 136–138
  memes, 147
  memification, 162–163
  Occupy, 163–164
  rhizomes, 161–162
  to track tweet to larger conversation, 18
  Tumblr, 57
  use in finding audience of peers, 213, 215
  use in tagging strategy, 199–202
  value of, 161
Hasinoff, Amy Adele, 83–84
Hassanpour, Navid, 23
Hastings, Reed, 36
hate group, 142
Hedda Lettuce (drag queen), 86
Hegel, Georg Wilhelm Friedrich, 9
hegemony, 3
Hellman, Susan Desmond, 36
Hennessy, John L., 40
Here Comes Everybody: The Power of Organizing without Organizations (Shirky), 21
Hilton, Perez, 70, 72, 195, 216
Hine, Christine, 25
history of social media, 48–68
  blogging, 54–57
  curation, 63–64
  geosocial networking, 61–63
  media-based media, 63
  microblogging, 52–54
  short-form video, 61
  social images, 57–59
  social media overworld, 67–68
  social media underworld, 64–67
  social networking, 48–52
  social video, 59–61
HIV, 90
Hoffman, John, 94
Hoffman, Reid, 43, 67
Hofmayer, Sören, 45
Hogue, Andrew, 44
homophily, 32, 33, 80, 188
homophobic language on Twitter, 92
hooks, bell, 228
hookup sites, 84–85
Hootsuite, 2, 210
horizontal integration, 32
horizontal systems, 9, 10
Housh, Gregg, 151
Howard, Philip N., 20
Huffington Post, 184
Hughes, Akilah, 221–222
Hughes, Chris, 50
Hughey, Matthew, 204

identity
  choosing your social media identity, 194–197
  dominant groups, identity systems of, 9
  gamer, 141, 142
  legitimizing, 9, 95, 143

personality-based, 195–196
project, 9, 29, 95, 143, 168, 191, 196–197
public, 35–36
resistance, 9, 95, 143
self identification, 127–128
sexual, 85
IFTTT, 200
imageboards, 123
Image collections, 132
images
apps, 119
disability/miracle meme, 97–106, 113–117, 119–120
4chan and, 64, 129
Instagram, 58–59
meaning imposed on, 102–104
platforms for sharing, 209
role in social media, 101
social, 57–59
in social media strategy, 209
as social structures, 105
I'm from Driftwood, 72
immersion, social media and, 15
Indignados movement, 158–159
industrial capitalism, 8–10
inequality
art, 228
families and, 196–197
matrix of domination, 110
Occupy movement and, 148
project-driven social media strategy, 197
racial, 179, 187–188
social, 193–194
Inequality by Interior Design (blog), 196
influencers, 216–217
information age, 6, 8, 21
The Information Age: Economy, Society and Culture (Castells), 8, 19
informational capitalism, 9
innovation, social change and, 166
inspiration porn, 114–115
Instagram
author use of, 2, 210
Brendan Jordan and, 74, 75
description, 58–59
Facebook ownership, 36, 59
geosocial networking, 63, 209
for phone images, 209
screen captures, 132
videos, 61
Institute for Sexual Minority Studies and Services (ISMSS), 91–92
institutional review board, 156
institutional surveillance, 13
integration, 32–33
intellectual disabilities, 117–118
Internet Archive, 46–47, 65
Internet Aristocrat, 122, 134–135
Internet of things, 20
InterOccupy tool, 164
interpersonal surveillance, 13
interpretive sociology, 105–106
intersectionality, 173, 177, 226
Irvine, Diane, 42
It Gets Better Project, 88–89, 94–95
It's Complicated: The Social Lives of Networked Teens (boyd), 75, 155

James, Sue, 41
Jasmine revolution, 19
Jay-Z, 164
Johnson, Amber, 85–86
Jones, Leslie, 221
Jones, Tim, 82
JonTron, 125
Jordan, Brendan, 73–75, 95
journal
audience for publications, 211–212, 212 (table)
online, 54–55
journalism, gaming, 123, 133–135, 137, 142
journalists, gaining audience of, 216–217

Kafer, Alison, 115–117
Kain, Erik, 142
Karp, David, 56–57
Kilgore, Leslie, 44

Kinsey, Alfred, 94
Kinsey Institute, 93–94
Kipnis, Anna, 130
Kitchenware revolution, 19
Klein, Zack, 60
Know Your Meme, 72
Kordestani, Omid, 39
Kotaku (gaming blog), 125, 134–136, 141
Kotzer, Zack, 123
Koum, Jan, 36
Kozinets, Robert V., 155, 157
Kramer, Maya Felix, 128
Kreiger, Mike, 58
Krolik, Rob, 43

Lady Bunny (drag queen), 86
Lady Gaga, 73–74
Lasn, Kalle, 147, 157, 160
Lauer, Matt, 70
leaderless movement, 146, 160, 167
leadership diversity profile
  Facebook, 36 (table)
  Google, 39 (table)
  LinkedIn, 43 (table)
  Twitter, 37 (table)
  Yahoo, 41 (table)
  Yelp, 42 (table)
Leahcar, Rachael, 118
Leave Britney Alone video, 71–72, 79
legitimizing identity, 9, 95, 143
Lesham, Matti, 124–125
Levchin, Max, 41, 42
Levine, Jeremy, 42
Levitin, Michael, 158
LGBTQ (lesbian, gay, bisexual, transgender, and queer)
  Don't Say Gay law, 98–99
  drag queens, 86–87
  Gay and Lesbian Alliance Against Defamation (GLAAD), 92–93
  I'm from Driftwood online story archive, 72
  It Gets Better Project, 88–89, 94–95
  queer theory, 76–78, 111, 208
  reclaiming derogatory language, 7
  representations in the media, 93
  resilience, 89–90
  slash fiction, 77
  social media art, 73–74
  social media use by gays, 84–86
  trans youth, 87–88
Liberty Square Blueprint, 154
LinkedIn
  audience of peers for social activists, 213–215
  description, 67
  disability and aging groups, participation of, 117
  leadership, 34, 43–44
  as online résumé, 67, 205–206
  worth of assets, 43
links, videos shared via, 60–61
Little, Mike, 56
Lodwick, Jake, 60
Loehmann, Timothy, 172
Lohanthony, 95
Lorde, Audre, 28, 223, 225–226
Lund, Ben, 45

Madisch, Ijad, 45
male dominance, 33
Manhunt, 84
Manjoo, Farhad, 180
Manning, Chelsea, 13
Mapplethorpe, Robert, 5
marginalized groups
  embrace of social media, 4
  reclaiming derogatory language, 7
  resistance identity, 9
market surveillance, 13
marriage, same-sex, 94
Martha Graham Cracker (drag queen), 86
Martin, Trayvon, 169–170, 174, 177
Marx, Karl, 33, 166
massive open online course (MOOC), 52
Match.com, 49
Mather, Ann, 40

matrix of domination, 110, 173, 227, 229
Mayer, Marissa, 40, 42
McCollum, Andrew, 50
McInerney, Thomas, 41
McRuer, Robert, 112, 115
media-based media, 63
media conglomerates, 33
medical model of disability, 115
Mematic, 119
meme, 85, 147, 162–165
  apps, 119
  Black Lives Matter, 180
  Brianna Wu and, 138–140
  description, 57
  disability/miracle, 97–106, 109, 113–117, 119–120, 143
  hashtags, 147
  ideal type, 119
  Occupy Wall Street, 147, 163–164
  as piece of culture, 119
Meme Generator, 119
Meme Producer, 119
men, victimization of, 129
Meresman, Stanley, 44
Metacafe, 72
microblogging, 52–54
militarization of police, 165
Milk, Harvey, 94
Miller, Terry, 88–89
Mimi Imfurst (drag queen), 86
minority groups
  embrace of social media, 4, 46
  lack of representation in leadership, 46
mockery, 98, 104, 142
Monae, Janelle, 3, 7
The Money Book for the Young, Fabulous, and Broke (Orman), 55
Moritz, Michael J., 44
Morozov, Evgeny, 22–23
Moskovitz, Dustin, 50
Mousavi, Mir-Hossein, 18
MoveOn.org, 99
MPreg, 77
Mubarak, Hosni, 24
Mulally, Alan R., 40
Mullenweg, Matthew, 56
multimodal networking, 19
MundaneMatt, 133–135
Murdoch, Rupert, 51
Murthy, Dhiraj, 23–24
music, on MySpace, 50, 51
music video, 60
MySpace
  Chris Crocker and, 72–73
  description, 49–52
  launch, 49
  Leave Britney Alone video, 72
  ownership of, 32
  racial difference in usage, 182
  uses, 50

Nachman, Joseph R., 43
Naficy, Mariam, 43
NEET (Not in Education, Employment, or Training), 123–124
negative messages, 3
Nelson, Theodor H., 10–12
neoliberalism, 82–83, 113
The Net Delusion: The Dark Side of Internet Freedom (Morozov), 22
netnography, 25, 155
Netnography (Kozinets), 155
networking
  cyberspatial, 20
  geosocial, 61–63
  multimodal, 19
  social, 48–52
networks
  leaderless, 24
  multimodal networking, 19
network society, 6, 8–10, 19–20, 78
Networks of Outrage and Hope: Social Movements in the Internet Age (Castells), 19
News Corporation, 32, 51
newsfeed, 2
New York Times (newspaper), 171–172, 210

the 99%, 149, 151, 155
the 99 Percent Declaration, 154–155
NoHomophobes Project, 91–92, 95
Nordeen, Bradford, 87
Norden, Martin, 118
Nurse, Sandra, 160

Obama, Barack, 147, 152
objective, social media, 194
occupation, 12, 152–153, 157–159, 163–164
occupied space, 19
The Occupied Wall Street Journal (newsletter), 158
Occupy Wall Street (Occupy movement), 19, 24, 145–168
  choreography of collective action, 24
  as constructive failure, 165
  flattened social movement, 10
  InterOccupy tool, 164
  as leaderless movement, 146
  meme, 163–164
  multimodal networking, 19
  project identity, 95, 168, 191
  rhizomatic structure, 162, 164
  strategies of, 157–164
  success of, 164–165
Oculus VR, 36–37
online communities, 16–17
online obsessive relational intrusion (o-ORI), 82
open carry laws, 140–141
Open TV, 224–225, 229
Orman, Suze, 55
Otellini, Paul, 40
owners of social media, 32, 34–45
  Academia.edu, 45
  Facebook, 35–37
  Foursquare, 44
  Google, 38–40
  LinkedIn, 43–44
  management, 34–35
  Pinterest, 44
  ResearchGate, 45
  Twitter, 37–38
  Yahoo, 40–42
  Yelp, 42–43
  See also specific corporations

Page, Larry, 39
Paine, Thomas, 11
Pantaleo, Daniel, 172
Papers, Please (game), 124
Parker, Dante, 172
participation
  lessening level of motivation required for, 23
  privacy minimization by, 14
pax technica, 20–21
peer review, 79–80
peers, audience of, 213–215
people's assembly, 153, 158–160
personality-based identity, 195–196
pets, on Instagram, 59
photographs. *See* images; *specific social media platforms*
Picasa, 40, 57, 209
Pinterest, 32, 52, 216
  author's use, 2, 26, 204, 207–208, 210
  collaboration, 214
  description, 63–64
  keyword boards, 201
  leadership, 34, 44
  power of, 207–208
  use for, 208
  as virtual ethnography resource, 133
platforms, 34–68
play, social media as space for, 78
playlists, YouTube, 133, 201, 208–209
poking people, 82
police interactions with black Americans, 170, 172, 180, 182–184, 187, 191
police surveillance, 13
policing, 113
policy makers, gaining audience of, 217–218
political/relational model of disability, 115

politics
 all lives matter, 182–183
 of corruption by financial industry, 149
 disability, 107, 109–111
 queer theory and, 76
Poo, Ai-Jen, 182
Poole, Christopher, 64, 129
Pop Culture Freaks (Kidd), 3, 26–27
Pope, Lucas, 124
porn, inspiration, 114–115
posting strategy, 209–210
postmodernism, 76, 113
posts
 tagging, 199–200
 types to include in a blog, 205 (table)
PostSecret, 66
The Power of Identity (Castells), 9
Prezi, 133
Price, Richard, 45
primary sources, 79
privacy, 14–15, 155–157
privacy policies, 14
project identity, 9, 29, 95, 143, 168, 191, 196–197
projection, in new racism, 189–190
pseudonyms, 157
publications, audience for, 211–212, 212 (table)
public displays of affection (PDA), 81–82
Pulse Nightclub mass shooting, 166

Queen Latifah Show, 73
queer play, 78
queer readings, 77–78
queer social media makers, 73
queer theory, 76–78, 111, 208
Queer Theory, Gender Theory: An Instant Primer (Wilchins), 76
Quinn, Zoë, 122–136, 138, 141

racial frames, 188
racial ideologies, 188
racial structure, 188
racism, 221, 228
 Black Lives Matter, 183
 color-blind, 187–190
 cultural, 188
 reverse, 187, 189
 styles of expression, 189–190
Racism Without Racists (Bonilla-Silva), 187, 190
Rappard, Matthew, 126–128, 135
Reddit, 131, 135
 Black Lives Matter movement, 185–187
 controversial subreddits, 65–66
 description, 65
 doxxing, 126
 GamerGate, 6, 142–143
redditors, 65, 185–186
Reid, Jerame, 172
religion, role in social change, 166
research ethics, 155–157
ResearchGate
 audience of, 213–214, 216
 description, 68, 206
 leadership, 34, 45
resilience, 89–90
resistance identity, 9, 95, 143
résumé, LinkedIn as, 67, 205–206
rhizomes, 161–162, 164
Rice, Tamir, 172
Ritter, Matthew, 124
Robin Hood rule, 149
Robinson, Tony, 172
Robinson, Zandria, 223
robotics, 16
Robots Exclusion Standard, 47
Rock, Paper, Shotgun, 123–124, 134–135
romantic relationships, 81–83
Rosenblatt, David, 38
Rowling, J. K., 78
RuPaul, 74, 86
Russell, Stephen T., 89

Sachs, Jeffrey, 147
safety and security in social media use, 220

Salaita, Steven, 223
Sandberg, Sheryl, 35–36
Sanders, Bernie, 145, 164–165
Sargon of Akkad, 135–136
Sarkeesian, Anita, 135, 137, 140–141, 143–144
Savage, Dan, 88–89
Saverin, Eduardo, 50
Scardino, Marjorie, 38
Schlesinger, Iliza, 207
Schmalz, Bill, 147
Schmidt, Eric E., 39
Schudson, Michael, 27
Schwab, Charles, 41
Sciarra, Paul, 64
Scott, H. Lee, 41
Scott, Walter, 173
Scott-Heron, Gil, 28, 223–224
screen captures, 132
secondary sources, 79
Secret, 52, 66–67
seeding information, 20
self identification, 127–128
selfie, 59
sexting, 83–84
sexual capital, 85
sexuality, 69–95
  hookup sites, 84–85
  queer theory, 76–78, 111, 208
  research on social media, 91–95
  romantic relationships, 81–83
  sexual health, 90–91
  study with social media, 88–91
Shangela (drag queen), 86
Sharon Needles (drag queen), 86
Sharp, Evan, 44, 64
Shaw, Jane E., 41
Shirky, Clay, 21
Shriram, K. Ram, 40
Siegel, Deborah, 196
Silbermann, Ben, 44, 64
SillySlader, 135
Silverman, Sarah, 71
Simmel, Georg, 6–8
Simmons, Russel, 62
Simon, Harvey, 184
Singh, Anneliese, 87
SIPP (Survey of Income and Program Participation), 108–109
sit-ins, 158
SJW (social justice warrior), 129, 133–136, 138
slash fiction, 77–78
Smith, Andy, 22, 23
Smith, Christian, 166
SMS (short message service), 52
Snapchat, 38, 40, 180
Snowden, Edward, 13
SoCawlege (website), 222
social change
  new models for, 165–167
  project-driven social media strategy, 197
social change, tools for, 194–218
  Academia.edu, 206
  blogging, 204–205
  choosing your identity, 194–197
  Facebook, 206–207
  goal identification, 194
  identification of audience(s), 197–198
  LinkedIn, 205–206
  Pinterest, 207–208
  platforms for pictures, 209
  posting strategy, 209–210
  ResearchGate, 206
  tagging strategy, 198–203
  Twitter, 203–204
  YouTube, 208–209
social construction, race as, 187–188
social contract, disability definitions as, 109
social exclusion, 193–194
social images, 57–59
social inequality, 193–194
social justice warrior (SJW), 129, 133–136, 138
social media
  as art, 4–6
  dangers of, 220–223

disability perspectives, 97–120
embraced by marginalized and minority groups, 4
gender perspectives, 121–144
history of, 48–68
leadership of, 45–46
negative aspects, 3–4
not being on, 203
political use of, 21, 23–24
promises or pitfalls, 12–17
sexuality perspectives, 69–95
social movements and, 17–19
social structure of, 31–68
as tool, 3–4
as video game, 15
social media overworld, 67–68
social media underworld, 64–67
social model of disability, 115
social movements, social media and, 17–19
social networking, 48–52
social networking sites (SNSs), 52
The Social Network (film), 50, 220
social power, continuum of positions on, 18
social structure of social media, 31–68
social video, 59–61
social web, 16
sociology, crip, 117–119
sock puppets, 128
Socrates, 59
sources
authoritative, 79
collecting and sharing through social media, 132–133
evaluating, 78–81
peer review, 79
primary, 79
secondary, 79
tips for evaluating online, 80
sousveillance, 13
Spanish Indignados movement, 19, 24, 150
Spears, Britney, 69–72
spirituality, role in social change, 166
Spotify, 2
stalking, 82
Steam, 122, 130
Steinback, John, 44
stereotypes, representational, 15
stirring the pot, 13
Stokel-Walker, Chris, 28
Stone, Biz, 53
Stoppelman, Jeremy, 43, 62
stranger, 6–8
structuralism, 166
suicide, 89, 90
Sullivan, Andrew, 18
Super Bowl advertisements, 60
surveillance, 13–15
by citizens, 13
institutional, 13
the internet of things, 20
interpersonal, 13
market, 13
police, 13
protecting ourselves from, 14
sousveillance, 13
Survey of Income and Program Participation (SIPP), 108–109
Swarm, 44, 61–63
symbolic interactionism, 17
Systrom, Kevin, 58
Sze, David, 44

tagging strategy, 198–203
connecting to your audience, 200–202
creating a database of resources, 200
as help in your written work, 199
primary tags, 201 (table), 202
secondary tags, 202, 202 (table)
tag as indexing system, 198–199
tertiary tags, 202, 202 (table)
Tahrir Square protests, 19, 147–149, 152, 158
Takei, George, 98–101, 119
talk show, daytime TV, 7–8
techno-ambivalence, 18, 23–24

technology
  alienation from, 11
  relationship between activism and, 23
  unplugging from, 203
techno-optimism, 18, 19–22
techno-pessimism, 18, 22–23
television, 223–225, 229
thick description, 105–106
Thiel, Peter A., 36
Tilghman, Shirley, 40
Timberlake, Justin, 51
timehop, 2
Tinder, 85
tipping point, 17
TL;DR (Too Long; Didn't Read), 130–131, 134
Tometi, Opal, 171, 174
Totilo, Stephen, 135, 136
trans youth, 87–88
troll, 178–179
Trottier, Daniel, 13
Tsou, Rose, 40
tumblelog, 56
Tumblr
  author use of, 2, 26, 210
  Black Lives Matter, 171, 175
  description, 56–57
  The Fine Young Capitalists (TFYC) on, 126
  gay men, use by, 84
  hashtags, 57
  Yahoo ownership of, 34, 42, 56
  young audience of, 204
Turkle, Sherry, 16
TVTag, 63
TV talk shows, 7–8
tweets
  archive of your, 199
  searching, 161
  size of, 53
  tagging, 199–200
Tweets and the Streets: Social Media and Contemporary Activism (Gerbaudo), 24
Twine, 123
Twitter
  Adam Baldwin on, 137
  archives, 47, 199
  assets of large companies, 28
  audience of, 213–216
  Black Lives Matter, 171
  blackouts, 23
  black Twitter, 180–181
  Brendan Jordan and, 74, 75
  categories of users, 15
  corporate interlocks, 38
  description, 52–54
  drag queens, use by, 87
  gay men, use by, 84
  handles, 214
  hashtag search, 161
  homophobic language on, 92
  identity, 195–197
  importance of being on, 203–204
  information flows on, 20
  leadership, 34, 37–38
  racial divide in usage, 181
  repeal of Don't Ask, Don't Tell, analysis of, 91
  research use, 27
  rhizomatic conversations, 162
  role in Arab Spring, 23–24
  sock puppets, 128
  tags, 199–200
  tool for political upheaval, 19
  trans youth, use by, 87
  user time spent on, 54
  videos, 61
  Vine ownership, 38, 61
  worth of assets, 38
  Yiannopoulos ban from, 221
  YouTube training videos, 204
Twitter: Social Communication in the Digital Age (Murthy), 23–24
Tyra Sanchez (drag queen), 86

underworld, social media, 64–67

Vanity Fair (magazine), 149
vertical integration, 32

Vevo, 40, 60
V for Vendetta (film), 151
Vice (magazine), 122–123, 132
video game, social media as, 15
videos
  collecting and making, 208–209
  Instagram, 61
  Its Gets Better project, 89–90
  Leave Britney Alone, 71–72, 79
  music, 60
  short-form, 61
  social, 59–61
  Vevo, 60
  Vimeo, 60–61, 209
  Vine, 61
  See also YouTube
Vietnam War protests, 158
Vimeo, 60–61, 209
Vine, 38, 61, 74, 75
viral, 20, 21, 72–74, 85–86, 147
virtual ethnography
  description, 25, 27
  institutional review board, 156
  interpretive sociology and thick description, 106
  principles of, 178–179
  sources, 132–133
visibility, 113, 115
vlogger, 73, 125
voice, 100
The Voice (TV show), 118
VOIP (Voice Over Internet Protocol), 157
voluntarism, 166
vote-brigading, 142
voyeurs, 14

Wade, Cheryl Marie, 111–112
Warhol, Andy, 5
Wavey, Davey, 75, 95
Wayback Machine, 47, 51–52, 55
Webb, Maynard, Jr., 41
Weber, Max, 105
weblog, 54–55
Weiner, Jeff, 44
Weiss, Noah, 44
Werner, Maggie, 91
"We Will Ride" Denver bus protests, 110, 116
WhatsApp, 36, 180
wheelchair, image as signifier of disability, 101
Whisper, 66
White, Micah, 147, 157–158, 160, 165–167
White, Phillip, 173
white dominance, 33
white flight, digital, 182
white supremacy, 170, 174, 184, 190, 222, 228
Wikipedia, 27
Wilchins, Riki, 76
Williams, Evan, 38, 52–53
Wilson, Darren, 170, 175–176
Wilson, Devin, 141
Wizardchan, 123–124, 143–144
Wolfers, Justin, 210–211
Wolff, Janet, 5
women in gaming, 122–144
WordPress, 55–57, 204
Wu, Brianna, 138–140

Yahoo
  corporate interlocks, 41
  Flickr ownership, 34, 42, 58
  leadership, 40–42
  social media assets, 34
  Tumblr ownership, 34, 42, 56
  worth of assets, 42
Yelp
  corporate interlocks, 42–43
  description, 61–63
  leadership, 34, 42–43
  worth of assets, 43
Yiannopoulos, Milo, 221
Yik Yak, 52
YouTube, 71–75, 124–127
  advertisements, 60
  Anonymous, 150–151
  Antoine Dodson and, 85–86

YouTube *(continued)*
  author's use, 26
  Brendan Jordan and, 74–75
  creation, 59
  description, 59–60
  The Fine Young Capitalists (TFYC) page, 126, 130
  GamerGate, 142–143
  George Takei and, 99
  Google ownership, 32, 34, 40, 57, 59
  Internet Aristocrat videos, 134–135
  It Gets Better, 89
  Leave Britney Alone video, 71
  Mundane Matt video, 133–134
  playlists, 133, 201, 208–209
  queer readings, 77
  sharing videos by links or embedded codes, 60–61
  training videos for social media, 204
  trans youth, use by, 87
Yu, Corrinne, 130

Zayid, Maysoon, 216–217
ZeroDivide, 94
Zimmerman, George, 169–171, 174
The Zoë Post, 131, 133–134
Zuccotti, John, 146
Zucker, Meg, 216–217
Zuckerberg, Mark, 35–36, 50

CPSIA information can be obtained
at www.ICGtesting.com
Printed in the USA
LVOW10s1009060217
523331LV00002B/2/P